D0411127

THE CONCEPT OF EDUCATION

Contributors

R. S. PETERS

D. W. HAMLYN

PAUL H. HIRST

G. VESEY

R. F. DEARDEN

MAX BLACK

GILBERT RYLE

ISRAEL SCHEFFLER

MICHAEL OAKESHOTT

J. P. WHITE

JOHN PASSMORE

THE CONCEPT OF
EDUCATION

Edited by

R. S. PETERS

LONDON

ROUTLEDGE & KEGAN PAUL

NEW YORK: THE HUMANITIES PRESS

First published March 1967
by Routledge & Kegan Paul Ltd
Broadway House, 68–74 Carter Lane
London, E.C.4

Printed in Great Britain
by Western Printing Services Ltd., Bristol

Second impression September 1967

SBN 7100 1947 5

CONTENTS

PREFACE

This collection of articles originated in a series of Public Lectures given in the early part of 1965 at the University of London Institute of Education. This provided a nucleus (Chs. 1, 2, 7, and 10) around which the collection was gathered.

The objection to many collections of articles is often made that they are a rather haphazard agglomeration of heterogeneous items lacking any unifying theme. It was felt that merely providing a general title such as 'The Concept of Education' was insufficient to provide such a unifying theme; for the philosophy of education is in such an undeveloped state that being asked to write an article under a rubric as general as that would approximate to a Rorschach test. The editor therefore wrote the first article attempting to map the main contours of the concept, circulated it, and invited lecturers and contributors to sketch in one of the important areas in more detail. Inevitably some areas have been neglected. There is, for instance, nothing in any detail about the crucial processes of imitation and identification. But it is hoped that the collection will at least do something to indicate the main areas where work has to be done.

The authors of the articles are either 'pure' philosophers who are interested in education as an area in need of philosophical investigation, or people professionally employed as philosophers of education. Perhaps this difference is reflected in the degree of concreteness with which the discussion is related to educational issues. If there is such a difference in emphasis it is hoped that it will make the collection of interest to students both of philosophy and of education alike.

Thanks are due to the Harvard Educational Review for permission to print Professor Scheffler's article on 'Philosophical Models of Teaching' and to the University of London Institute of Education for permission to base this collection on their Public Lecture series.

R. S. PETERS

January 1966

NOTES ON CONTRIBUTORS

MAX BLACK, Professor of Philosophy, Cornell University. Author of *Language and Philosophy, Problems of Analysis*, etc., and editor of *Philosophy in America*.

ROBERT F. DEARDEN, Lecturer in the Philosophy of Education, University of London Institute of Education.

DAVID W. HAMLYN, Professor of Philosophy, Birkbeck College, University of London. Author of *Sensation and Perception; The Psychology of Perception*.

PAUL H. HIRST, Professor of Education, King's College, University of London.

MICHAEL OAKESHOTT, Professor of Politics, London School of Economics and Political Science. Author of *Experience and its Modes, Rationalism in Politics*.

JOHN PASSMORE, Professor of Philosophy, Australian National University. Author of *Hume's Intentions, A Hundred Years of Philosophy, Philosophical Reasoning*.

RICHARD S. PETERS, Professor of the Philosophy of Education, University of London Institute of Education. Author of *Hobbes, The Concept of Motivation, Ethics and Education*, etc.

GILBERT RYLE, Waynflete Professor of Metaphysical Philosophy, University of Oxford. Author of *The Concept of Mind, Dilemmas, Plato's Progress*.

ISRAEL SCHEFFLER, Victor S. Thomas Professor of Education and Philosophy, Harvard Graduate School of Education. Author of *The Language of Education, The Anatomy of Enquiry, Conditions of Knowledge*.

GEOFFREY VESEY, Reader in Philosophy, King's College, University of London. Author of *The Embodied Mind* and editor of *Body and Mind*.

JOHN P. WHITE, Lecturer in the Philosophy of Education, University of London Institute of Education.

WHAT IS AN EDUCATIONAL PROCESS?

R. S. Peters

INTRODUCTION

In exploring the concept of education a territory is being entered where there are few signposts. To use Ryle's phrase, the 'logical geography' of concepts in the area of education has not yet been mapped. This feature of the field of education was vividly brought home to me in the autumn of 1963 when I was working on my Inaugural Lecture on *Education as Initiation*, and was unable to unearth any previous explicit attempt to demarcate the concept of 'education'. It is not surprising, therefore, that in presenting at the start what amounts to a bird's eye view of the contours of this territory, I have to rely mainly on my own previous attempt to map it.

I. THE TASK-ACHIEVEMENT ANALYSIS OF 'EDUCATION'

Any such survey must start with the observation that 'education' is a concept which is not very close to the ground. By this I mean that it is not a concept like 'red' which picks out a simple quality, like 'horse' which picks out an object, or like 'running' or 'smiling' which pick out observable occurrences. We do not ask 'Are you instructing him in algebra or are you educating him in algebra?' as if these were two alternative processes. But we might ask 'Are you educating him by instructing him in algebra?' 'Education', in other words, refers to no particular process; rather it encapsulates criteria to which any one of a family of processes must conform. In this respect it is rather like 'reform'. 'Reform' picks out no particular process. People can be reformed, perhaps, by preventive detention, by reading the Bible, or by the devotion of a loving wife. In a similar way people can be educated by reading books, by exploring their environment, by travel and conversation—even by talk and chalk in a classroom. The concepts of 'reform' and 'education' have proper application if these processes satisfy certain criteria. 'Education' and 'reform' are not part of the furniture of the earth or mind; they are more like stamps of approval issued by 'Good Housekeeping' proclaiming that furniture has come up to certain standards.

How then are we to conceive of processes by means of which such standards are to be achieved? In my Inaugural Lecture I attacked misleading models which provide pictures of what goes on in terms of shaping material according to a specification, or of allowing children to 'grow'. I mentioned in a footnote, which I did not have time to develop, that a much more adequate way of conceiving of what goes on, which provides a rationale for my notion of education as initiation, is to regard processes of education as tasks relative to achievements. This accounts for the feature of education, which I rather laboured, that its standards are intrinsic not extrinsic to it. This task-achievement analysis I now propose to explain.

Aristotle made the point long ago in relation to performances such as 'learning' and 'inferring', that the end is built into the concepts. Ryle has made it more recently in relation to activities such as 'looking' and 'running'. When a man finds something that he has lost or wins a race, he does not indulge in something different from looking or running, neither does he produce something or reach an end which is extrinsic to the activity in which he is engaged. He merely succeeds in it. He achieves the standard or attains the end which is internal to the activity and which gives it point. In a similar way a man who is educated is a man who has succeeded in relation to certain tasks on which he and his teacher have been engaged for a considerable period of time. Just as 'finding' is the achievement relative to 'looking', so 'being educated' is the achievement relative to a family of tasks which we call processes of education.

'Education' is, of course, different in certain respects from the examples of achievements that Ryle gives. To start with 'education' like 'teaching' can be used as both a task and an achievement verb.[1] Teachers can work away at teaching without success, and still be teaching; but there is a sense, also, in which teaching someone something implies success. 'I taught the boy the ablative absolute construction' implies that I was successful in my task. But I can also say 'I taught him Latin for years, but he learnt nothing.' Similarly I can work away at educating people, without the implication that I or they achieve success in the various tasks which are engaged in; but if I talk of them as 'educated' there is an implication of success.

2

What is an Educational Process?

But whose success are we talking about? That of the teacher or of the learner? This is tantamount to asking to whose tasks the achievements which constitute 'being educated' are relative, those of the teacher or those of the learner. Obviously both are usually involved, but it is important to realize that the tasks of the teacher could not be characterized unless we had a notion of the tasks of the learner. For whereas 'learning' could be characterized without introducing the notion of 'teaching', 'teaching' could not be characterized without the notion of 'learning'. The tasks of the teacher consist in the employment of various methods to get learning processes going. These processes of learning in their turn cannot be characterized without reference to the achievements in which they culminate. For to learn something *is* to come up to some standard, to succeed in some respect. So the achievement must be that of the learner in the end. The teacher's success, in other words, can only be defined in terms of that of the learner. This presumably is the logical truth dormant in the saying that all education is self-education. This is what makes the notion of 'initiation' an appropriate one to characterize an educational situation; for a learner is 'initiated' by another into something which he has to master, know, or remember. 'Education' picks out processes by means of which people get started on the road to such achievements.

2. THE MORAL REQUIREMENTS OF 'EDUCATION'

The second way in which 'education' is different from ordinary cases of tasks and achievements is that it is inseparable from judgements of value. It is, as I have pointed out, a logical truth that any method of education employed by a teacher must put the pupil in a situation where he is learning, where some sort of task is presented to him. But a teacher might try to condition children to 'pick up' certain things without their realizing that they were picking anything up. In saying that this is not a process of education we would be implying that this was morally bad, because conditions of wittingness and voluntariness on the part of the pupil were missing; for we regard it as morally unjustifiable to treat others in this way. To say that we are educating people commits us, in other words, to morally legitimate procedures. Often such minimal moral demands, which are connected with respect for persons, are further extended to exclude procedures such as giving children orders, which is

3

thought by some to involve some sort of moral indignity. Discouragement of individual choice would be another procedure which many might condemn as being morally reprehensible. They might express their disapproval by saying that this was not 'education'.

The way in which moral considerations enter into the achievement aspects of education is clearer than the way in which they enter into the task aspect. For it is obvious enough that the achievements or states of mind that give content to the notion of an educated man must be regarded as valuable. Finding a thimble that has been hidden is a Rylean type of achievement: but it is a trivial one. The achievements involved in education cannot be of this type. For if something is to count as 'education', what is learnt must be regarded as worth-while just as the manner in which it is learnt must be regarded as morally unobjectionable; for not all learning is 'educational' in relation to the content of what is learnt. If it were we might have periods on the time-table devoted to astrology and to Bingo and homilies by headmasters on the art of torture.

In this respect, also, 'education' is like 'reform'; for it would be as much of a contradiction to say 'My son has been educated but has learnt nothing of value' as it would be to say 'My son has been reformed but has changed in no way for the better.' This, by the way, is a purely conceptual point. The connexion between 'education' and what is valuable can be made explicit without commitment to content. It is a *further question* what the particular standards are in virtue of which achievements are thought to be of value and what grounds there might be for claiming that these are the correct ones. It may well be that arguments can be produced to show why rational men should value some standards rather than others; but at the moment there is no such established harmony. So when people speak of 'education' it is essential to know what their standards of valuation are in order to ascertain the aspect under which some process or state of mind is being commended.

This connexion with commendation does not, of course, prevent us from speaking of 'poor' education when a worth-while job has been botched or of 'bad education' when we think that much of what people are working at is not worth-while, though it is a nice question to determine at what point we pass from saying that something is 'bad education' to saying that it is not education at all. Neither does it prevent us from using the word in a purely external descriptive way when we speak of an 'educational system' just as we can use the

4

term 'moral' of someone else's code without committing ourselves to the judgements of value of those whose code it is. Anthropologists can talk of the moral system of a tribe; so also can we talk as sociologists or economists of the educational system of a community. In employing the concept in this derivative sense we need not think that what is going on is worth-while, but members of the society, whose system it is, must think it is.

Talk of 'education', then, from the inside of a form of life, is inseparable from talk of what is worth-while, but with the additional notion written into it that what is worth-while has been or is being transmitted in a morally unobjectionable manner. But under this general ægis of desirability 'education' picks out no one type of task or achievement. People differ in their estimates of desirability. They therefore differ in the emphasis which they place on achievement and states of mind that can be thought of as desirable. This diversity is what makes talk of 'aims of education' apposite; for people who talk in this way are not suggesting aims extrinsic to education: They are enunciating their priorities in giving content to the notion of an 'educated man'.

To take a parallel : it might be said that the aim of reform was to make men better. This is harmless enough provided that it is realized that 'making men better' is built into the concept of 'reform' But something more specific might be said such as the aim of reform is to encourage a sense of responsibility. This might be countered by saying that the aim of reform is to get people to have respect for persons. Such a dispute would be an attempt to give precise content to the general notion of 'making a man better'. Similarly discussions about the aims of education are attempts to give more precise content to the notion of the 'educated man' or of a man who has achieved some desirable state of mind. Is moral education more important, for instance, than the development of scientific understanding? This might have particular point when talking about some of the children referred to in the Newsom Report. Or perhaps we talk about 'wholeness' in order to emphasize all-round excellence and sensitivity. Or we may want to stress the importance of cutting the coat of what is worth-while according to the cloth of individual aptitude. Talk of developing the potentialities of the individual is then appropriate. Such 'aims' point out specific achievements and states of mind which give content to the formal notion of 'the educated man' which is a short-hand for summarizing our notion of a form of life which is worth-while enough to deserve being handed on from generation to generation.[2]

So much, then, for the moral aspect of 'education' as a family of tasks and achievements which make it rather different from the simpler cases used by Ryle to illustrate this way of conceiving of certain classes of intentional activities. I want now to consider other criteria of 'being educated' as an achievement which have to do with knowledge and understanding. I shall then deal with the tasks which lead up to achievements falling under these criteria.

3. THE ACHIEVEMENT ASPECT OF 'EDUCATION'

We do not call a person educated who has simply mastered a skill even though the skill may be very worth-while, like that of moulding clay. For a man to be educated it is insufficient that he should possess a 'know-how' or knack. He must also know that certain things are the case. He must have developed some sort of conceptual scheme at least in the area in which he is skilled and must have organized a fair amount of information by means of it.

But even this is not enough; for we would be disinclined to call a man who was merely well-informed an educated man. To be educated requires also some understanding of principles, of the 'reason why' of things. The Spartans, for instance, were military and morally trained. They knew how to fight; they knew what was right and wrong; they were possessed of a certain kind of lore, which stood them in good stead in stock situations. They were thus able to comb their hair with aplomb when the Persians were approaching at Thermopylæ. But we could not say that they had received a military or moral education; for they had never been encouraged to understand the principles underlying their code. They had mastered the content of forms of thought and behaviour without ever grasping or being able to operate with the principles that could enable them to manage on their own. They were notorious for falling victims to potentates, priests, and profligates on leaving their natural habitat where their code was part of the order of things. Failure to grasp underlying principles leads to unintelligent rule of thumb application of rules, to the inability to make exceptions on relevant grounds and to bewilderment when confronted with novel situations.

Given, then, that being educated implies the possession of knowledge, but rules out *mere* knowledge, in that it also requires understanding of principles, could a man be educated whose knowledge and understanding is confined to one sphere—mathematics, for instance? There is a strong inclination to deny that we could call a man 'educated' who had only developed his awareness and understanding in such a limited way; for our notion of an educated man suggests a more all-round type of development. When we say that people go to a university to become educated and not just to become scientists, from what does this antithesis derive? Does it derive from the concept of 'education' or from our underlying valuations about the constituents of the good life which ought to be passed on which includes e.g. aesthetic and moral awareness as well as scientific understanding? Certainly 'training' always suggests confinement. People are trained *for* jobs, *as* mechanics, and *in* science. No one can be trained in a general sort of way. But this lack of specificity is just what is suggested by 'education'. It is not clear to me whether this is due to the concept of 'education' itself or to our refusal to grant that what is worth-while could be confined to one form of awareness. To pose the problem succinctly : Is the saying 'Education is of the whole man' a conceptual truth in that 'education' rules out one-sided development? Or is it an expression of our moral valuations about what is worth-while?

There is no necessity, for the purposes of this article, to decide between these two alternatives, as it has no particular implications for what is to count as an educational process. There is, however, another aspect of the knowledge requirement built into 'education' which has implications. This is its attitudinal aspect. By this I mean that the knowledge which a man must possess to qualify as being educated must be built into his way of looking at things. It cannot be merely inert. It is possible for a man to know a lot of history, in the sense that he can give correct answers to questions in classrooms and in examinations, without ever developing a historical sense. For instance he might fail to connect his knowledge of the Industrial Revolution with what he sees when visiting Manchester or the Welsh Valleys. We might describe such a man as 'knowledgeable' but we would never describe him as 'educated'; for 'education' implies that a man's outlook is transformed by what he knows.

It is this requirement built into 'education' that makes the usual contrast between 'education' and 'life' rather ridiculous. Those who make it usually have in mind a contrast between the activities that go on in classrooms and studies and those that go on in industry, politics, agriculture, and rearing a family. The curriculum of schools and universities is then criticized because, as the knowledge passed on is not instrumental in any obvious sense to 'living', it is assumed that is is 'academic' or relevant only to the classroom, cloister, study, and library. What is forgotten is that activities like history, literary appreciation, and philosophy, unlike Bingo and billiards, involve forms of thought and awareness that can and should spill over into things that go on outside and transform them. For they are concerned with the explanation, evaluation and imaginative exploration of forms of life. As a result of them what is called 'life' develops different dimensions. In schools and universities there is concentration on the development of this determinant of our form of life. The problem of the educator is to pass on this knowledge and understanding in such a way that they develop a life of their own in the minds of others and transform how they see the world, and hence how they feel about it.

There is another element in what I have called the 'attitudinal aspect' of the sort of knowledge which is built into the concept of 'being educated' which was first stressed by Socrates and Plato in their doctrine that 'virtue is knowledge'. Such knowledge must not be 'inert' in another sense; it must involve the kind of commitment which comes through being on the inside of a form of thought and awareness. A man cannot really understand what it is to think scientifically unless he not only knows that evidence must be found for assumptions, but cares that it should be found; in forms of thought where proof is possible, cogency, simplicity, and elegance must be felt to matter. And what would historical or philosophical thought amount to if there was no concern about relevance or coherence? All forms of thought and awareness have their own internal standards of appraisal. To be on the inside of them is both to understand this and to care. Indeed the understanding is difficult to distinguish from the caring; for without such care the activities lose their point. I do not think that we would call a person 'educated' whose knowledge of such forms of thought and awareness was purely external and 'inert' in this way. There can be no End of the Affair where The Heart of the Matter is lacking. And, of course, there never *is* an End of the Affair. For to be educated is not to have arrived; it is to travel with a different view.

The achievement aspect of 'education' connected with knowledge has now been sketched. Before passing to the task aspect, under

8

which educational processes have to be considered, it will be as well to pause and summarize the main criteria of 'education' under this aspect which are to be satisfied by an 'educated' man.

(i) An educated man is one whose form of life, as exhibited in his conduct, the activities to which he is committed, his judgements, and feelings, is thought to be desirable.

(ii) Whatever he is trained to do he must have knowledge, not just knack, and an understanding of principles. His form of life must also exhibit some mastery of forms of thought and awareness, which are not harnessed purely to utilitarian or vocational purposes or completely confined to one mode.

(iii) His knowledge and understanding must not be inert either in the sense that they make no difference to his general view of the world, his actions within it and reactions to it *or* in the sense that they involve no concern for the standards immanent in forms of thought and awareness, as well as the ability to attain them.

4. CRITERIA INVOLVED IN THE TASK ASPECT OF 'EDUCATION'

Educational processes are related to these various activities and modes of thought and conduct characterizing an 'educated man' as task is related to achievement. They are those in which people are initiated into or got going on activities and forms of thought and conduct which they eventually come to master. I have argued already that, apart from the requirement that processes belonging to this family be morally unobjectionable, they must also be considered from the point of view of the learner whose achievements give content to the concept of an 'educated man'. They must therefore approximate to tasks in which the learner knows what he is doing and gradually develops towards those standards of excellence which constitute the relevant achievement. In this family obviously are included processes such as training, instruction, learning by experience, teaching, and so on.

If we look at such processes from the teacher's point of view he is intentionally trying to get learning processes going by exhibiting, drawing attention to, emphasizing, or explicating some feature of what has to be learnt and putting the learner in a position where his experience is likely to become structured along desirable lines. From the learner's point of view such processes must be ones in which he knows what he is doing. Things may happen to him while asleep or under hypnosis which bring about modifications of his consciousness; but we would not call them processes of education. The learner must know what he is doing, must be conscious of something that he is trying to master, understand, or remember. Such processes, therefore, must involve attention on his part and some type of action, activity, or performance by means of which he begins to structure his movements and consciousness according to the public standards immanent in what has to be learnt.

It is necessary, however, to distinguish educational processes proper from other processes bordering on them which do not satisfy one or other of these criteria. There are first of all what I will call extrinsic aids and secondly what I will call rather loosely processes of 'picking things up'. Let us consider them briefly in this order.

(a) Extrinsic aids

There are all sorts of things done by teachers in classrooms which help children to learn things which are really aids to education rather than processes of education. I mean conditions such as praise and reward which help children to learn things. These are not processes of education; for their connexion with what is learnt is purely extrinsic. They may facilitate the learning of anything; but what is involved in learning anything can be explicated without reference to them. To take a parallel; it is an empirical fact that children learn things better if they are nice and warm rather than shivering with cold. So a sensible teacher will make sure that the radiators in the classroom are turned on. It may also be the case that children learn things better if the teacher smiles approvingly when the child gets things right. This is, perhaps, another empirical fact which is relevant to education. But neither turning on the radiators nor smiling at children are educational processes, whatever their status as aids to education.

The appeal to children's interests occupies a more twilight sort of status because of ambiguities in the notion of 'interests'. Such interests can be intrinsic or extrinsic to what has to be learnt. Children are naturally curious at certain ages and have a desire to master things and get them right. They may also be interested in finding out about and mastering the specific things that have to be learnt. As an interest in such worth-while things is part of what is meant by 'an educated man' the job in this case is that of fostering such intrinsic interests and superimposing on them the precision and standards of achievement which are necessary. Having such intrinsic interests is not part of what is meant by an educational process; it is built into the achievement, and this aspect of the achievement can be present at the start.

Unfortunately few children are motivated in this way all the time and many children scarcely at all. Therefore extrinsic interests have to be used, as well as other forms of pressure. For children do not have to be interested in something in order to learn it; it is often sufficient that they attend to it, for whatever reason. If they attend long enough, and if the teacher is skilled and imaginative, they may become interested. The ability to *stimulate* interest is one of the greatest gifts of a teacher. The danger of too much reliance on extrinsic interests is that a child may pick up something that the teacher does not intend, namely to become a thorough instrumentalist, the prisoner of an attitude which always looks to what things lead to rather than what they are in themselves. A child may be interested in outstripping his fellows and may be willing to learn almost anything that is geared to this end. This may be educationally very bad if what is 'picked up' is the conviction that effort should only be made if gain results. Using these sorts of interests may not be in the interests of the child. So we pass to processes of 'picking things up'.

(b) Picking things up

I used the word 'picked up' rather than 'learnt' advisedly to characterize a way of acquiring an attitude that borders on education, without being a process of education in a strict sense.[3] Obviously enough this attitude is implicit in the practice of the teacher who employs such a method and is passed on partly by identification. All sorts of things are picked up in this way—desirable things such as a passion for poetry, nuances of style and argument, objectivity towards facts, respect for persons; undesirable things such as partisan allegiances, contempt for people of different persuasions, bad manners, and class-consciousness; and trivial things such as mannerisms, a tone of voice, gestures.

My reluctance to call such goings-on processes of education is not just due to the fact that what is passed on may be trivial or undesirable, but to the difficulty of conceiving of them as tasks either on the part of the teacher or of the learner. From the teacher's point of view he is explicitly trying to get children on the inside of a form of thought or awareness; to do this he uses certain methods. Yet the fact is that so much is caught rather than explicitly taught. The best teachers are not necessarily those who are au fait with all the latest methods or very knowledgeable about their subject. They are those whose genuine concern for what they are passing on is manifest in the manner in which they do it. Education, like most meetings between human beings, is a very chancy business. The wind of the spirit bloweth where it listeth. Some catch on; others don't. It depends so much whether the learners are drawn to the teacher or not. And what is more chancy than human attractions? If the learners are so drawn, then identification, suggestion, and other such indeterminate transactions may occur. These are not 'learning' processes in a full sense; for they are different from explicit imitation or copying, where something is explicitly attended to for assimilation. They happen to people; they are not achievements. Nevertheless this kind of contagion only actually spreads if both teacher and learner are actively engaged on something. It does not happen if the teacher is just fiddling about or the children are staring out of the window. The attention of both has to be focussed on some task; then these subsidiary processes may get going. If the teacher gets too self-conscious about them, the business gets blurred. He has to have his mind on what Lawrence called 'the holy ground' between teacher and taught. His dedication to it may then become incorporated in the consciousness of his pupils, and many other nuances may be imparted.

(c) Conditioning

Cases where children pick up things without being aware of them are not confined to processes such as identification and suggestion; there are also those falling under the concept of 'conditioning'. Classical conditioning is, of course, completely irrelevant as it was concerned only with involuntary behaviour such as salivation and eye-blinks which could never be thought of as achievements. In operant conditioning what has to be learnt is not grasped by the learner to start with, if ever, as being instrumentally related to what counts as a reinforcement. Some movement is made, often of a random sort, which brings about acute pain or something attractive like food or a mate. This is not like rewarding children or punishing them when we do at least explain to them what will happen if they do something, and when what has to be learnt is presented as a means to the reward and can come to be thought of as such. Nothing like this happens in strict conditioning. Secondly there is no consciousness in conditioning of what has to be learnt as a *task*. A movement or series of movements is made and miraculously something like a pellet of food appears. It is really something of an anthropomorphism to say that the animal learns to press the lever. All that has happened is that some movement has been stamped in which we regard as an achievement. But it is more an achievement on the part of the experimenter than on the part of the animal.

It is very questionable, as a matter of fact, how much of animal learning, outside the narrow confines of laboratories, takes place according to principles of conditioning. For how often are animals in a position where their random responses are systematically reinforced? How often, too, are the situations in which they learn things such that there is no discernible relationship between obtaining something like food and movements which have to be learnt as means to this? Looked at objectively animals are 'conditioned' to do such incredibly trivial and non-functional things—pressing bars, running mazes, leaping grids, begging for biscuits, and balancing balls on their noses. The situations in which they 'learn' things by 'conditioning' are those in which opportunities for the use of intelligence are cut down to a minimum. So even at the animal level a certain amount of scepticism is necessary about the applicability of 'conditioning', in any strict sense, to the learning of animals. This perhaps should be extended to some of the things allegedly learnt in this way in laboratories.

At the human level, a fortiori, the applicability of conditioning is even more questionable. Presumably certain positive and negative reactions are picked up in this way and simple sequences of movements are stamped in before the consciousness of a child has been sufficiently differentiated to pick out objects in a public world which he wants and means that can be taken to get them. But once he can distinguish himself from others and can copy others and understand instructions, once he begins to develop a grasp of causal and means-end connexions, it is very difficult to conceive of what could be learnt by strict conditioning. For how can we be sure that what is to be learnt presents itself in no way as an intelligible means to a desired end or as something to be mastered or copied? How do we know that it is not picked up by imitation or suggestion? Certainly it is difficult to call such forms of 'learning' educational processes on the account here given of 'education'. For, apart from the moral objections to treating other human beings in this way, which do not derive solely from what is learnt, these goings-on cannot possibly be regarded as tasks culminating in achievements. When things happen to us, which occasion the development of phobias or of stereotyped patterns of reaction, is seems odd to call such goings-on processes of 'education'. For 'education' does suggest some kind of intentionality on the part of the learner, however embryonic.

5. EDUCATIONAL PROCESSES

I have now, as it were, got out of the way what I called aids to education and processes of picking things up, both of which border on being processes of education. I want now to pass on to processes of education proper which can be viewed as a family of tasks leading up to the achievement of being educated. The achievement of being 'educated', as I have set it out, is complex. It involves mastery of some skills, knowledge, and understanding of principles. For such an ideal to be realized many different sorts of things have to be learnt. In view of this it is improbable that there can be just one educational process. Too many educational theories are extrapolations from one type of learning situation which is taken as a paradigm for all. I propose therefore to isolate the different aspects of 'being educated' and consider briefly which educational processes are of particular relevance to each of them.

(a) Training

Consider, first of all, the learning of skills. This presents itself pre-eminently as a task to the learner. He is usually presented with a paradigm of a skilled performance and, by a mixture of constant practice and imitation, he may eventually come to master it. A skill is not by its very nature something that could be learnt for all time in a flash of insight. Neither can it be learnt by reading books or by instruction alone. This helps of course, but only because it provides a guide for practice. Constant practice is absolutely essential, especially under the eye of a skilled performer who both corrects and provides a paradigm of the performance. Skills are difficult to master; so extrinsic forms of motivation usually have to supplement the intrinsic motivation provided by the desire to achieve or get something right.

To a teacher 'skills' usually denote reading, writing, and computation which have to be mastered before education can proceed very far. Because of the difficulties they present to a child, all kinds of attempts are made to harness the learning of these skills to other things that the child wants to do. But this is merely an intelligent way of providing an incentive to learning; it is nothing to do with the type of learning process required to master the skill. A child may be brought to the task of reading by the incentive of advertisements or by the necessity of reading instructions if he wants to cook. But when the actual reading begins there is no escape from practice, instruction, correction and example.

The general name we have for this type of learning process is 'training'. The concept of 'training' has application when (i) there is some specifiable type of performance that has to be mastered, (ii) practice is required for the mastery of it, (iii) little emphasis is placed on the underlying rationale. Example and instruction by another are a great help in the realm of skill, but they are not absolutely essential. A person might learn to type, for instance, without either, though it would be a lengthy business. But he could never learn to do this without practice. 'Training' has application, however, in a wider realm than that of skill; for roughly speaking the concept of 'training' also has application whenever anything coming up to a clear-cut specification has to be learnt. Military training includes not only arms drill and training skills such as shooting; it also includes the inculcation of habits such as punctuality and tidiness. Such habits cannot be learnt by practice and imitations alone as might a skill like swimming or swinging a golf club, because of the lack of close connexion with bodily movements. It is conceivable that something like swimming could be just picked up or 'caught' by practice and imitation without a word being said. But a habit like that of honesty, which is not just a kind of 'know-how' or knack, could never be picked up just like this.

Consider, for instance, what a child has got to know before he can develop a habit like that of stealing. He must be able to distinguish between himself and others and must have developed the notion of property; he must also grasp that people have a right to things and that these things must not be appropriated without permission. A child, strictly speaking, cannot 'steal' who has not a range of concepts such as these. He cannot learn what 'stealing' is just by watching others. For he cannot tell what an action is just from the outside; he has also to know how the agent conceives what he is

15

doing. To realize that something is a case of theft he must, therefore, have developed the conceptual scheme without which 'theft' is an unintelligible notion. The notion of theft cannot be tied down, either, to any specifiable range of bodily movements. For all sorts of things can count as property and there are infinite number of ways of appropriating them. A child cannot therefore learn to steal or not to steal without instruction and correction as well as practice and imitation. The notion of 'moral training' as distinct from that of 'moral education' suggests the learning of a moral code which is tied down to specifiable rules such as 'Thou shalt not steal'. Moral education suggests, in addition, the passing on of the underlying rationale, the understanding of principles. But even training in this sphere, as well as in many others, involves much more than the mere mastery of a 'know-how' or 'knack'. The child has also to know that certain classes of action are wrong. Such knowledge could never just be 'caught'. The learning of skills is thus only one particular case of 'training'.

(b) Instruction and learning by experience

Knowing what things are and that certain things are the case is a matter of developing a conceptual scheme that has to be fitted to phenomena. This can only be learnt by a process which involves the meaningful use of language by a teacher to structure relevant experience by the learner. In acquiring a body of knowledge of this sort instruction and explanation are as essential as first-hand experience. There is prevalent at the moment a widespread horror of instruction because this is associated with sitting children down in rows and telling them things which may be beyond their ken and which they may not be interested in learning about anyway. It is argued in reaction to this that children have at certain ages spontaneous curiosity in what things are and why they happen; they also have a natural desire to master things, provided they are not too difficult. A wise teacher will therefore be thoroughly cognizant of the stage of conceptual development which each child has reached. She will often take the children out of the classroom where the children can be confronted with the relevant experiences and will fill the classroom itself with things which are carefully related to these stages of conceptual development. She will be at hand always when the child's natural curiosity impels him to ask questions which are almost inevitable, given the confrontation between intriguing objects and a conceptual scheme which is ripe for the next increment. In this way there can be no danger of knowledge being inert. For what is learnt is always what the child is ready to absorb and eager to discover. In this way information from adults and from books can be built firmly into the developing cognitive structure of the child in relation to first-hand experience.

This is admirable provided that the teachers attempting to practise such a method are intelligent enough to understand what they are meant to be doing and skilful enough to make provision for children to whom they cannot be attending,[4] and provided that classroom conditions and the teacher-pupil ratio do not make it a pipe-dream. But it should be realized that it is really just a more intelligent method of instruction. Rather a lot of nonsense is talked in this context about children 'discovering' things which is rather reminiscent of Socrates' demonstration in *The Meno* that even a slave can make a geometrical 'discovery' if he is given the chance. The point is that a child may find out what others know, but he does not, if he is not asked the right sort of questions at the appropriate time, and if his experience is not guided in certain directions. A certain amount of practice is required for the child to learn to use the necessary concepts; but nothing like the same amount as in the case of skills. For once the rule has been grasped governing the use of the concept further instances are easily recognized. Of course knowledge acquired in this or any other way must be used fairly often or else it may be forgotten. But the supposition is that if it is required spontaneously in relation to first-hand experience forgetting is less likely.

(c) Teaching and the learning of principles

If the knowledge of the human race had ended with Aristotle this account of knowledge and of the methods necessary to acquire it might be sufficient. It is indeed significant that those who advocate educational methods which stress the importance of first-hand experience have in mind mainly children of 7–12 who are at what Piaget calls the stage of concrete operational thought when the world of things presented through the senses is being ordered and structured. What is required at this stage is plenty of experience together with classificatory schemes to structure it. The classroom thus becomes a Lyceum in miniature.

But what of the grasp of principles necessary for understanding rather than low-level knowledge? What of the 'rape of the senses' necessary for principles like the law of inertia to emerge? What of the reliance on one typical and crucial instance so central to the hypothetico-deductive method of Galileo which Piaget postulates as developing almost naturally from the previous stage? Of what importance at this stage is all this dashing around and first-hand experience? As Hobbes put it, under the spell of Galileo: 'For when we calculate the magnitude and motions of heaven or earth, we do not ascend into heaven that we may divide it into parts, or measure the motions thereof, but we do it sitting still in our closets, or in the dark.'[5] Understanding of principles does not depend upon the accumulation of extra items of knowledge. Rather it requires reflection on what we already know, so that a principle can be found to illuminate the facts. This often involves the postulation of what is unobservable to explain what is observed. So it could never be lighted upon by 'experience'.

What then is there to be said about the learning of principles? The basic requisite is that people should first acquire in some way or other the low-level rules or assumptions which the principles illuminate. It is both logically absurd and educationally unsound to suppose that people could attain the necessary understanding of principles without first having acquired quite a lot of knowledge; for principles provide backing to rules or assumptions at a lower level of generality. In science, for instance, there could be no appeal to principles unless there were a mass of empirical generalizations which could be seen to fall under them; in morals there could be no appeal to principles without rules to justify by means of them. The grasp of principles, therefore, is inseparable from the acquisition of knowledge of a more mundane sort. This logical truth is often neglected by rationalistic educators who think that people can grasp scientific concepts, or pass them on to children, without knowing any science, or who believe that moral principles can be grasped by children who have not had a basic training in moral rules.

There is, of course, nothing absolute about what constitutes a principle. It is merely a higher-level assumption or rule that can be appealed to in order to substantiate and give unity to lower order ones. The one is thus immanent in the many. Evidence that the principles has been grasped is provided if a person knows how to go on and deal with new situations in the light of it. People are brought to a grasp of principles by a mixture of explanation and a selective survey of the many. Words like 'insight' are used in connexion with the grasp of principles. It is difficult to state precisely what is meant by such words, but once people have it very little in the way of further practice is necessary as in the case of skills. Neither are principles quickly forgotten like the lower-level information which they unify. The typical term for the educational process by means of which people are brought to understand principles is 'teaching'; for 'teach' unlike 'train' or 'instruct', suggests that a rationale is to be grasped behind the skill or body of knowledge.

(d) The transmission of critical thought

Societies can persist in which bodies of knowledge with principles immanent in them can be handed on without any systematic attempt to explain and justify them or to deal honestly with phenomena that do not fit. Fixed beliefs are thus perpetuated. When this is done we are presumably confronted with what is called indoctrination rather than teaching; for indoctrination is incompatible with the development of critical thought. Critical thought, however, is a rationalistic abstraction without a body of knowledge to be critical about. The problem of the teacher is to pass on a body of knowledge in such a way that a critical attitude towards it can also develop. If too much emphasis is placed on critical thought the danger is that all processes of education will be conceived too much in terms of what is necessary for a critical attitude to emerge. This is one of the dangers immanent in Dewey's system in which the concept of being 'educated' is more or less co-extensive with that of being critical.

There is no innate tendency to think critically, neither is it easy to acquire. Indeed as Bacon argued, it goes against the inveterate tendency of the human race which is to believe what we want to believe and to accept things that we are told on trust. The clue to how such an inveterate tendency can be overcome was provided by Plato when he described thought as the soul's dialogue with itself. It is a pity that this clue was not followed up. For the notion might not then have developed that reason is a sort of mental gadget that can be used by the individual if it is not too clogged up with passion or, as Hume described it, 'a wonderful and unintelligible instinct in our souls'. Given that critical thought about the assumptions in which we are nurtured rather goes against the grain, it will only develop if we keep critical company so that a critic is incorporated within our own consciousness. The dialogue within is a reflection of the dialogue without. This is a paradigm of an educational situation; for educational processes are those by means of which public modes of thought and awareness, which are mainly enshrined in language, take root in the consciousness of the individual and provide avenues of access to a public world.

The best way of making sure of such a living organic structure of thought is probably to employ the *ad hominem* method of question and answer used by Socrates. This brings the learner very quickly to probe into his presuppositions and to make explicit principles which were previously only dimly apprehended. If the learner is constantly prodded into doing this he gradually begins to think in a more clear, coherent, and structured way; for there is a sense in which we do not really know what we think about anything until we have had to state it explicitly and defend it. If this process continues for quite a time the learner gradually takes the questioner into his own mind and begins to develop the form of thought himself. He can come to formulate objections to his assumptions himself and keep on reformulating what he thinks or proposes to do until he hits on something to which he can find no objections.

It is important to realize that such a critical clarification of principles is a very different exercise from applying them in concrete circumstances. This seems to be the burden of Oakeshott's attack on rationalism and the starting point of his conception of political education.[6] He is not much interested in the discussion and justification of principles. What fascinates him is the judgement required to apply them in particular circumstances. He sees clearly that such judgement cannot be acquired in salons, studies, or seminars. It comes through practical experience in the presence of those who already have it.

It does not follow either that a person who has mastered a form of thought such as history, or one of the sciences, is skilled in testing the hypothesis that may emerge from reflection or discussion. He must, of course, be familiar from the inside with how experiments can be designed, or how records and manuscripts are interpreted. But many of the great theoretical scientists have been poor experimentalists just as some of the great historians have arranged the facts in a new pattern rather than discovered a lot of new ones by ingenious techniques of research. From the point of view of education what is essential is the grasp of a conceptual scheme for ordering facts rather than skill in research.[7] The various forms of thought—historical, moral, scientific, aesthetic—all have their own such schemes and thus provide different perspectives for the interpretation of experience. They can, however, only have such a transforming effect on a person's outlook if they are passed on in the right way at the right time and if they are informed by that passion for truth which lies at the heart of all of them. Without this critical discussion can degenerate into verbal leger-de-main and a parade of principles can be equivalent to name-dropping. Whether such a passion is due to fostering the natural curiosity of the child, whether it is caught from those who are already possessed by it, or whether it develops because an individual is confronted by conflicting opinions, is difficult to determine.

(e) Conversation and 'the whole man'

What then of the processes which lead to the development of an educated man in the full sense of a man whose knowledge and understanding is not confined to one form of thought or awareness? Nowadays all sorts of educational experiments are being contrived to 'liberalize' vocational training and to ensure that premature specialization does not distort a man's view of the world. No doubt formalized correctives to specialization are necessary, though it is arguable that the proper place for them is at school rather than at university. But the question is whether explicit learning situations are sufficient to bring about this integrated outlook. The classical way of ensuring this, surely, has been not courses but conversation.

Conversation is not structured like a discussion group in terms of one form of thought, or towards the solution of a problem. In a conversation lecturing to others is bad form; so is using the remarks of others as springboards for self-display. The point is to create a common world to which all bring their distinctive contributions. By participating in such a shared experience much is learnt, though no one sets out to teach anyone anything. And one of the things that is learnt is to see the world from the viewpoint of another whose perspective is very different. To be able to take an active part in a real conversation is, of course, an achievement. It is not possible without knowledge, understanding, objectivity, and sensitivity to others. But it is also a learning situation of an informal sort. A vast amount of learning all through life takes place in such informal situations. Are we losing faith in the likelihood of anything emerging if it is not carefully contrived? Or are we just the victims of shortage of space, pressure of numbers, and the bureaucratization of our educational system?

This is the point of mentioning conversation at the culmination of a lecture on educational processes which has been concerned mainly with what goes on in formal situations. For just as educational processes are not confined to classrooms, so also for an educated man the distinction between formal and informal situations of learning is only one of degree. His experience is not only transformed by all that he has mastered, learnt, and understood, but is always exemplifying the processes by means of which such mastery, knowledge, and understanding has been acquired. The achievements constantly generate new tasks. Even in his middle age he can really listen to what people say irrespective of the use he can make of it or them. This is a considerable achievement. But then as Spinoza said of the state of human blessedness: 'all excellent things are as difficult as they are rare'.

NOTES

1. See Scheffler, I., *The Language of Education* (Thomas, Springfield, 1960), Ch. IV.
2. It should be stressed that what has been said relates only to thinking of something as a form of *education*. It is only under this aspect that we are implying that there is something worth-while immanent in scientific activity, for instance, and that there is no discontinuity between the tasks and the achievements. But we can train people to do 'science' for purely utilitarian or vocational purposes if we wish. The same applies to carpentry or cooking. We *can* look at such activities in a purely instrumental way. Whether we should do so or not is a further question. In discussing this we are not engaged in a debate about the aims of education, but in a debate about whether we ought to educate people rather than train them, or whether something like science or carpentry has the intrinsic value which many would ascribe to it. It may well be too that there are many tasks and achievements engaged in at school, such as reading and computation, which, like boarding a bus or doing five-finger exercises, have a value which is almost entirely instrumental in relation to our educational aims. This may well be so. It does not contradict my thesis; rather it draws attention to the necessity of looking at what goes on in schools in a wider context. Schools are obviously concerned with things other than education—with health, for instance, with selection, and with vocational training.
3. The concept of education, could, perhaps, be extended to include such borderline processes. What exactly one calls 'education' in this

twilight area does not much matter provided that the similarities and differences are recognised.

4. See Sarason, S. B., Davidson, K. S., and Blatt, B., *The Preparation of Teachers* (John Wiley, N.Y., 1962).

5. Hobbes, T., *De Corpore* (Molesworth Ed., 1839), English Works 1, Ch. 7.

6. See Oakeshott, M., *Rationalism in Politics* (Methuen, London, 1962).

7. It is important to make this point at a time when there is a growing demand that universities should fulfil two functions which are not altogether compatible—develop research not so much for its own sake but in order to solve the practical problems of the nation, and provide a 'liberal' education for a larger percentage of the population than heretofore.

THE LOGICAL AND PSYCHOLOGICAL
ASPECTS OF LEARNING

D. W. Hamlyn

It is, I suppose, obvious enough that some children learn better when there is a smile on the face of the teacher, just as it is conceivable that others may learn better when it is all done in time to music. Some learn better when they are happy, others perhaps when the conditions are austere or comfortable enough not to be distracting. The study of such individual differences is clearly a matter for psychology, since it will be a study of the psychological processes which bear on the facility with which individuals learn. It is even possible in principle to produce generalizations in this field, statements which may apply to people in general, although it may be doubted whether these will in fact amount to more than platitudes—that people learn better in general when encouraged or rewarded, when they are given opportunities for practice, when they are given material in digestible amounts, and so on. Nevertheless, these would certainly be *psychological* generalizations if not very exciting ones. But there are questions about learning which are not psychological questions—questions such as what learning is and what is implied when it is said that someone has learnt something. To answer such questions we have to clarify the concepts which we employ in this sphere, something that requires both reflection and some familiarity with the subject-matter to which those concepts apply. Investigations of this kind are not so much a matter for the psychologist as for the philosopher.

What, then, is it to learn something? In fact, this is a question which I shall, in effect, shelve for the time being, and it may be that I shall have nothing very illuminating to say about it directly. But I shelve it quite deliberately. One might of course say that to learn something is to acquire knowledge of it through experience; but this, although correct as far as it goes, is not likely to be enlightening because, apart from other vaguenesses in the formulation, much depends on the 'something' in question. To learn a list of words or a set of formulæ, to learn to play the piano or to ride a bicycle, to learn a language or a technique, and to learn a subject or a discipline are all very different things. Although they all involve the acquisition of knowledge, that knowledge is of quite different forms. To learn a list of words, simple rote-learning, as it is called, is nothing more than to memorize that list, and the knowledge involved is merely the knowledge of the words in their appropriate order. In skills such as that involved in riding a bicycle 'knowing how' comes to play a role, and the acquisition of such skills may involve practice as much as does rote-learning, even if in a different way. But here too other things begin to emerge; for few skills could be acquired by practice alone in the most rudimentary sense of that word, and few are in any way independent of some understanding of the issues involved. You could not play the piano without some such understanding, and practice in this case, if it deserves the name, must be intelligent practice. The existence of such understanding may indeed be implied whenever we speak of knowing how to do something, and this, among other things, distinguishes knowing how to do something from merely being able to do it. When we come to learning a language or a technique, and even more so with learning a subject, the appreciation and understanding of the subject and its principles comes to the fore. With the understanding of principles goes the ability to use certain concepts. If there is a distinction to be made between my two last categories, it is that learning a language or a technique is inevitably a practical matter in a way that learning a subject is not so obviously so. But this is a matter of emphasis only; technique and intellectual understanding, theory and practice cannot be completely divorced from each other.

What I have said so far is meant to show the complexities involved in any general discussion of learning. Fortunately, for educational purposes, it is surely unnecessary to go into all this. Rote-learning and simple practice may or may not be adequate tools for educational purposes, but they cannot in any way constitute anything in the way of the essence of education. This last, I suggest, is nothing unless it brings with it understanding and appreciation of principles, their relevance and their interconnections. Understanding, moreover, involves and presupposes the acquisition and use of concepts. One can understand nothing of a subject unless one has the concepts in which that understanding is to be expressed. Hence, the process of learning a subject goes hand in hand with the process of acquiring the relevant concepts, the concepts in terms of which the subject-matter and its principles are to be formulated. I shall try to say something by way of elucidation of this in the following. But my main concern will be with two points, both of which seem to me comparatively simple. They are as follows.

(1) The subjects into which knowledge is conveniently divided are not block-entities laid out, as it were, in a Platonic realm. There is an inclination, I believe, to think that there exists objectively something called, to take one example, mathematics, and that it is the aim of education to bring the learner to a confrontation with it. Subjects are, on this account, ideal entities available for contemplation. Given this, one can then argue about the best way of bringing about this contemplation, since the subjects are too complicated to grasp all at once. Is it better to concentrate on those parts of a subject which are somehow logically prior to others or on those which are psychologically easiest to grasp? The snag about this is that it is not immediately clear what the question means, what the distinctions amounts to. Certainly, I think, the question what is easy to grasp is not a matter for psychology. On the other hand, the notion of logical priority is perhaps obscure and it has different implications according to the ways in which it is interpreted. I shall enlarge on these points directly.

(2) No one could be said to have come to understand a subject, to have learned it, without some appreciation of general principles, some idea of what it is all about. But knowing and understanding general principles is not just a matter of being able to recite the relevant general propositions. Nothing is contributed by way of understanding when people are made to recite general propositions, even if these are fundamental to a subject. Thus, to present a very young child with, say, the general principles of number theory or algebra would be a futile business; for, he must be capable of cashing such general principles in terms which mean something to *him*, if understanding is to follow. There is in the growth of understanding of any subject an intimate connection between principles and their applications or instances. Principles must always be seen cashed in there instances, but instances must themselves be seen as cases to

26

which principles are relevant. Thus an appreciation of general principles implies in the full sense an appreciation of how they are to be applied. My point is analogous to one which could equally well be made about concepts; it may be expressed in Kant's famous or notorious slogan that 'thoughts without content are empty, intuitions without concepts are blind' (where by 'intuitions' Kant means something like the reference to instances). To present a child with little bits of information without reference to general principles at all is a sure way of preventing the development of understanding; such a child would be intellectually blind. But to go to the other extreme and concentrate on principles alone is another way of producing an equally unsatisfactory end-product; the child's thought, if this could be brought about, would be empty—without reference to any particular cases through which the general principles could mean something to him. There must always be a delicate balance between principles and cases; but since there are degrees of generality it is clear that the attainment of full understanding at one level of generality must presuppose something of a balance attained at a lower level of generality, a balance between an understanding of principles in general terms and an understanding of their relevance to particular cases. Otherwise, there is little hope of the relevance of the more general principles being seen. What is the point of presenting to children the principles of set-theory if they are not capable of understanding what it is for something to be a set? This has an obvious relevance to any discussion of Piaget's 'stages', especially to the distinction between concrete and abstract operations. Indeed, I suspect that Piaget is an essentially Kantian thinker in many respects.

I shall discuss my two points in turn. They are not of course unconnected. I have said that it is a superstition to think that subjects exist as block-entities, the contemplation of which should be the goal of the learner. I do not mean by this that there are no differences between, for example, history and physics. The historian may be distinguished from the physicist by, among other things, his interests, his methodology and the concepts which he brings to his subject-matter and in terms of which he thinks about it. There are also differences between the modes of explanation which the two employ—between historical and scientific theories. All these differences—and no doubt there are others—are important. But to suppose that the real difference is that there is one body of knowledge, expressible as a set of facts, called 'history' and another called 'physics', which the two are out to discover betrays a quite erroneous conception of learning. It is to suppose that learning consists merely in the acquisition of knowledge of a set of facts, the contemplation of a set of propositions. At its lowest, it reduces learning to simple rote-learning. But it cannot be anything like that in fact. Even at the simplest level the acquisition of knowledge of facts goes hand in hand with understanding. Even in rote-learning it is essential to understand what is going on, and in higher forms of learning understanding is much more important still. Thus words like 'history', 'physics' and 'mathematics' are not just the names of bodies of knowledge, in the sense of sets of true propositions; they are, if anything, the names of approaches to facts of generally different kinds. At a certain level, perhaps, we cannot even say that; distinctions between subjects tend to break down, they become an administrative matter only, or a question merely of the differences in the background of interests on the part of those who are concerned with them.

I may be thought to be labouring the obvious. Surely, it may be said, no one really thinks that subjects exist in *that* sense. Perhaps so, but I detect suggestions of this sort in certain discussions which imply that learning should start from what is logically prior in a subject, and even perhaps in those who deny this and insist that psychological priorities are everything. Let me explain what I mean —and the best way to do this is to indicate and explain one sense of the words 'logically prior', a sense which I shall directly come to repudiate in this context.

Explanatory theories, e.g. scientific theories, have a logical structure in the sense that the propositions of which the theory is constituted can be arranged in a certain order, so that certain propositions can be derived from others. It is indeed the fact that from general laws and statements of initial conditions it is possible to derive conclusions—the facts to be explained—that provides the basis of scientific, and no doubt other kinds of, explanation. We thus expect that with the help of reference to the general we shall be able to deduce the particular. It is because of logical relationships of this kind—relationships of entailment—that we can speak of the theory having a structure, and we may say, as Aristotle said, that the general is logically prior to the particular. The same sort of thing applies in mathematics. Insofar as it is true to say that set-theory provides the basis of arithmetic it is because arithmetic can be explained in terms of set-theory. Set-theory furnishes the more general point of view under which arithmetic can be subsumed. Hence, we might say that the notion of a set is logically prior to that of, say, a number, because the latter can be explained in terms of the former, but not vice versa. The direction in which explanation must proceed, and the logical relationships which go with it, thus determine what is logically prior within a discipline.

This, however, only applies where the discipline in question constitutes a theory—to parts of science, the foundations of mathematics and so on. Where questions of explanation do not arise and do not have a place, then this sort of consideration has no place either. It is difficult to see how large parts of history or literature could be said to have a structure in this sense. But even where it could be said that this is so—where a subject admits of the formulation of a theory of it—this could have few implications for education. Even if there is *a* sense in which someone could not be said *fully* to understand arithmetic without understanding set-theory, this is only in the sense in which it might be said that someone could not fully understand, say, the movements of billiard balls without understanding the principles of sub-atomic physics. And no one, I take it, would suggest that children should be introduced to physics *by that route*. The most fundamental concepts of a subject, from the point of view of explanation, are not likely to be the most familiar. To concentrate on such concepts may hinder the understanding of how the more familiar concepts are to be applied—a matter which is just as important for complete understanding. But, to repeat the remark which I made earlier, there are subjects for which none of this makes sense, since questions of explanation do not arise within them, or do so only to a minor extent.

If this is accepted, it may be suggested that the only remaining position is that, as far as learning is concerned, the only priorities are psychological priorities. For, from the point of view of learning, the priorities that the structure of explanation provides are not relevant. That is to say that the only possible procedure for an educationalist is to find out empirically what parts of a subject are the easiest to learn and to insist that learning should start from there. For there is now no question, it might be thought, of having to start from those elements which are logically necessary if anything else in the subject-matter is to be seen as it is. There is no question of having to see the subject arranged in its proper logical order. There are no logical conditions for a proper understanding of a subject; there are only psychological conditions, e.g. that no one could grasp the difficult parts before grasping the easy ones. So it might be said. To come to this conclusion would, I think, be far too quick a deduction from what has already been established, but there is in any case something very odd about the suggestion that the easiness or difficulty of a subject or a part of a subject is a matter for psychology. It is clearly enough a matter for psychology that something is easier for one person to learn than another; for, the question why this is so could be answered only by an investigation into the people concerned. The conditions under which individuals learn something more easily is also clearly enough a matter for psychology, as I indicated at the beginning of this lecture. It is not so clear that the same thing holds good of the question why one subject or part of a subject is easier than others.

In what ways might one subject be more difficult than another? It might demand knowledge of more facts (so I have heard it said about psychology in comparison with philosophy). It might be more abstract (so I have heard it said about philosophy in comparison with psychology). It might demand knowledge of skills, procedures or ways of thinking not demanded by the other, and it might even presuppose the other in one way or another. Factors like abstractness and complexity loom large here, although these factors may arise in many more ways than one, and I would not claim that these are the only factors at stake. However, abstractness and complexity are obviously very important and I shall concentrate on them in what follows. It may be thought that these factors are relevant because of the truth of psychological generalizations such as that people generally find the abstract and the complicated more difficult to understand or grasp than the specific and the simple. But is this just a psychological generalization? *Could* a man find the abstract easier to grasp than the specific, and the complicated easier to grasp than the simple? Would this indeed make any sense? If not, then we are confronted here, not just with empirical psychological generalizations, but with some sort of *a priori* or necessary truth. That is to say that in that event abstractness and complexity will be *criteria* of difficulty; if one subject is more abstract and complex than another then it will follow necessarily that the one is more difficult than the other. I do not claim that it is always obvious whether some branch of a subject *is* more abstract or complicated than another, and to discover the truth on the matter may require investigation of a kind. The way in which this might be done is by turning what I have said on its head. Given that people *normally* find X more difficult than Y, this will be a reason for saying that X may be more complicated or abstract than Y (depending on the exact nature of the difficulties reported). The idea of what is normal is very important here, and I shall return to it later in an analogous context. The point is that if a subject is difficult people may be expected normally to find it so—just as, if something is red it is to be expected that people will normally see it so. When I say 'normally', I do not mean 'generally'; I mean 'in normal conditions'. It is this notion of what is normal which provides the link between what something is and how it appears to people or how they find it. Thus, if abstractness and complexity are criteria of difficulty we may expect that people will normally find the abstract and complicated difficult; and conversely, if people normally find something difficult, this will be an indication of its abstractness or complexity.

We need, however, to look further at the idea that there is some kind of necessary connection between the notion of difficulty and those of complexity and abstractness. Can we even conceive of a man finding the complicated or abstract easier than the simple or specific? There are of course people who feel more at home with the complicated than the simple—people of whom we say that they cannot see the wood for the trees; and there may be people who are similarly more at home with the abstract than the specific, people who fail to bring issues down to earth. But this indicates something about their habits or qualities of mind; it indicates nothing directly about the comparative easiness of the subject-matter. The man who cannot see the wood for the trees may indeed find the simple too easy for his taste. It may come to be that the simplicity of a thing constitutes an obstacle to his understanding, just because of his cast of mind; we might perhaps say that for some reason he shuts his eyes to the simple. But his case provides no grounds for denying that the complicated is normally more difficult for people than the simple. Indeed, the special explanation that is required indicates that the case is not normal. The indications, then, are that we should expect people normally to find the complex difficult. Indeed, the connection between complexity and difficulty seems to turn on certain things about the concept of understanding. The complicated may, in fact, be described as that which puts a certain kind of demand on the understanding. To grasp a complicated whole is to grasp the simpler components in their relationship with each other; hence this kind of understanding presupposes the understanding of the simpler; and where a man appears not to find it easy to take in the simple by itself, we need a special explanation of the fact. The same is true of the relation between the abstract and the concrete or specific, although this raises considerations to which I have already referred under my second heading and to which I shall return later. I conclude, however, that factors like complexity and abstractness are in fact criteria of difficulty, and that it is thus not just a psychological truth that people find the complicated and abstract difficult.

These considerations, however, open up once again the question whether there are any priorities in a learner's approach to a subject which are more than psychological. (And that there *are* psychological considerations I have no wish to deny, since, for example, personality differences between people may make one way of putting over a subject more rewarding in one man's case than in another's. Factors relative to the learning of something on specific occasions and by specific individuals are always psychologically relevant.) Now, I think that there *are* priorities in learning which are more than psychological, and they might be described as epistemological, or logical in another sense from the one already discussed. In the growth of knowledge, certain things must be done before others. Not only is it the case that certain facts must sometimes be known if one is going on to make sense of others, but it is also the case that sometimes certain things must be understood, certain concepts grasped, before progress can be made at all. For example, in arithmetic it is essential that one should understand the notion of an ordinary integer if one is to understand that of a fraction. This is quite apart from such general considerations as the priority of the simple to the complicated, to which reference has already been made. The appreciation of certain subjects demands a certain order for knowledge. That this must be so is indicated by the existence of general principles for the establishment of curricula, and if it were not so any suggestion that programmes could be laid down for teaching machines would be impossible. What I am now saying is that such programmes, such principles of order, could be established only by decisions on what is the appropriate order for the development of the knowledge and understanding of a subject. To reach such decisions demands that very knowledge and understanding of the subject itself, plus an ability and willingness to reflect upon the exact relationships between the concepts presupposed within it. This is not a matter for psychology. I would emphasize this point.

Let us consider in some detail an example which brings out the kind of consideration which I have in mind. As is perhaps well enough known, Piaget and his associates have carried out a number of studies, which have become known as 'conservation studies', concerned with the child's appreciation of such general principles as the conservation of matter, size and weight. It has been brought out that children at a certain age do not always appreciate such principles and even appear to apply them inconsistently. Moreover, they do not come to accept them all at the same time. There appears to be a general assumption in Piaget's approach that they perhaps *should* do so, and that it is surprising that they do not. There is also perhaps a sense of surprise that children should fail at all to accept the principles, despite the fact that in the actual history of thought some of these principles were not formally established until comparatively recently, at any rate during the last three or four hundred years. These studies might be represented as concerned with the understanding of concepts which fall within the general field of physics, and may thus be described as studies in the child's understanding of elementary physics. The question that arises is what could be discovered about the situations under investigation merely by reflecting about them. Let us take a specific and simple case of a Piagetian type : we have, let us suppose, a definite quantity of liquid of a specific colour, which can be poured from a wide transparent container into a similar narrow one. When the liquid is poured from the wide container into the narrow one, a child at a certain stage of intellectual development might well say, because of the comparative depth of the liquid in the containers, that there is more liquid in the narrow one. This may be so even though he sees the liquid being poured from the one container into the other. What are we to suppose has gone on here—what concepts employed and how?

Many sorts of consideration are relevant. We, who know the right answers, know that change of place and container does not affect the identity of the liquid or its volume, and that volume is not a simple function of depth. But these are not factors which we can take for granted in a child, and it does not take a great deal of reflection to see that we cannot. Moreover, the notion of the identity of a liquid (or of any other object) is not necessarily an obvious one. After all, we allow some changes in things without thereby denying that

33

they retain their identity. Liquids expand when heated without becoming thereby different liquids. If we were to maintain that the identity of a liquid has something to do with its mass, this is obviously by no means a simple notion, and is not one that could at all be taken for granted in a child. What *does* identity depend on for a child? I am anxious here only to raise such questions for consideration, and to bring out the complicated relationships that may exist between the concepts which we use even in situations which may seem obvious to us. *We* tend to take notions like that of identity for granted (even when we cannot give an account of them); but there is no saying that a child does. Nor should we expect insight into these relationships to emerge all at one time; for, some of them are more complicated than others. The notion of volume, for example, is a more complicated notion than that of depth—it introduces another dimension. The volume of a liquid is therefore necessarily more difficult to estimate than its depth. Hence, the apparent relationship between the identity of an object and its depth or height may well seem more obvious than that between the identity of an object and its volume. All this should be evident to one who is prepared merely to reflect about the situation, provided that he has the requisite concepts.

Furthermore, it is not surprising that at a certain stage of development a child may be pulled in different directions : it is the same object for him to the extent that nothing has apparently been done to it which could cause it to change its volume or indeed change at all; yet it is different because its apparent depth and therefore apparent volume have changed. In the development of the 'right' view of things social influences obviously play a large part—a point very much under-emphasized by Piaget. Similar considerations apply to the part played by the acquisition of linguistic tools. In other words, the facility with which a child may come to see the proper relationships between such factors as volume, depth and the identity of the object will depend on the extent to which he is subject to social influences of a certain sort and on his ability to formulate the relationships in words.

I have no wish to draw any other general moral than the one which I have already mentioned, i.e. the need for reflection on such situations. I certainly do not believe that it is possible to lay down any general law of development which the child must follow in acquiring concepts and coming to see the relationships between them. I would, however, point to the fact that concepts vary in complexity and abstractness, and that this determines certain general priorities. In considering how education should proceed one has to start from a knowledge of the concepts which a child possesses and the goal to be attained, and work out the intervening steps in the light of such general considerations as I have mentioned. This, I would emphasize again, can be done only by one who knows the subject and is prepared to reflect about it. There is no short cut, but that certain things must come before others in any process of this sort is a matter of logical necessity of a kind. How exactly, how precisely the priorities could be worked out is a matter for speculation, and the steps to be followed in the teaching of any given child will obviously depend on where that child is already, on what concepts he already has and on what relationships he already appreciates. For this reason, any generalized programme for teaching children of roughly the same stage of development must inevitably be a matter for compromise; but that *some* general principles can be laid down for the development of knowledge within any given sphere is of course a presupposition of any educational programme. In some disciplines the steps to be taken by the learner are comparatively easy to establish; hence their amenability to instruction by teaching machines. In other disciplines, any programme of teaching must inevitably be a hit and miss affair. It is all a question of the complexity of the relationships which exist between the concepts in terms of which the subject-matter is to be understood. An assessment of these relationships can come only from one who knows the subject. It is not a matter for one who has specialist psychological knowledge alone.

I may have given the impression that while subjects are not block entities, in the sense explained earlier, they nevertheless have a fixed order of development, and that learning consists in finding out what this is and following it up. I do not think that this would be the correct account of the situation. This is not just because it is unrealistic, not just because finding one's way may involve going down many blind alleys. Wittgenstein once described coming to understand the nature of mathematics as trying to find one's way round a strange town, and this is not a bad description of any attempt to learn a subject. Moreover, it may be that in the end one of the best ways of coming to understand the geography of a town is to get thoroughly lost and have to find one's way home despite this. The

35

apparently blind alleys may turn out not to be blind after all. Sometimes too the best first step may be to acquire a habit of going in a certain direction; habits can always be adapted later, as long as they do not become ossified. All this is true, but it does not get to the root of the problem. The analogy may or may not work even at the most abstract level of a subject, although the idea of a settled geography to be discovered may be one to be retained at any rate as an ideal. But the child in a school is not so much learning the geography of an area as acquiring the tools and techniques by which he may eventually come to make a map of it. A tool is of little use until it is decided what purposes it may be used for. Maps also may be constructed for different purposes and with different projections.

The point of this analogy is that concepts too can be thought of as tools of this kind. In making a map one has to know not only the features of the terrain to be represented on it, but also what counts as a feature of a specific kind. Similarly, concepts may be thought of as instruments for the task of attaining a familiarity in thought with some range of facts and also for attaining an understanding of what counts as a fact of a given kind. And just as the map has a purpose, so too concepts may be regarded as devices for thinking of the facts in a way which may be useful for some further end. That is why I said earlier that in considering how education should proceed one should start not only from a knowledge of the concepts which a child already has but also from a knowledge of the goal to be attained. What is the goal to be attained in teaching a young child elementary arithmetic, the salient facts of an historical period or the rudiments of English grammar? Until questions of this sort are answered it is impossible to say how we should proceed or in what order concepts should be invoked. It has, in sum, to be decided what is the goal of any given inquiry. The problem is a well-known one in connection with the learning of Classics. Until the goal to be attained in studying Classics has been decided it is pointless to argue about how to go about studying it—whether, for example, the doing of Latin proses or the study of Ciceronian cadences has any utility. Concepts are, to change the analogy, like keys too; they open doors, but if they are to be of any use one must know what door each opens, whether the door leads anywhere and whether there is any point in opening it.

I have spoken of concepts long enough without really explaining the term. I must now say something of what it is to have and acquire a concept, and this will bring me to my second main topic, about which I have in effect said something already. It must now be made explicit. The connection is this: I said earlier, in presenting my second main point, that it turned on what was involved in understanding principles. The notions of a concept and a principle are interconnected; to have a concept of something is to know the principle in accordance with which things are said to be of the relevant kind. To have a concept of, say, man is to know the principle whereby certain things may be collected together—those things, namely, which we call men. It is thus to know what it is to be a man. This entails not only being able to give an account of what sorts of things men are, but also thereby to recognise men as such. To acquire a concept thus involves acquiring this knowledge and this ability. Of course, someone may have a *certain* understanding of a concept without being able to recognise the things which fall under it. There is a sense in which a blind man may be said to have some understanding of the concept of redness. He may be able to tell you that it is a colour, and he may be able to give a formal account of what a colour is, e.g. that it is a property of the surfaces of objects that is accessible only to vision. He may indeed be able to give some account of the structure of colours and of the relation of red to the other colours. All this is possible without sight, and therefore without the experience necessary to a full understanding of what it is for an object to be red. Such a full understanding requires both the ability to give a formal account of redness and the ability to recognize instances. A concept thus gives one a principle of organization for a subject matter. If one has a given concept one has knowledge of that principle. That is why I have already talked of the understanding of a subject as a matter of appreciating certain concepts and their interrelationships.

It is a dogma of empiricism that one acquires a concept by reviewing a number of particular things and seeing what is common to them. This cannot be the correct view of the situation if only because in order to do this one must be in the position to regard those particular things *as instances*. It is necessary to know what things it is relevant to collect together for this purpose. Thus it might seem more pertinent to speak of applying concepts to things rather than abstracting them from things. The truth is what I have already said—that we have the concept in question only when we are both able to see a range of things as falling under the concept and also in the position to know what it is for them so to fall, what it is that makes them instances. For this reason, there is inevitably in the process of acquiring concepts a delicate balance between a kind of abstract understanding of what it is to be an X and a knowledge of what things conform to this criterion. In learning—that is to say, in the growth of knowledge and understanding of a subject-matter— there must at every stage be achieved a balance of this sort if progress is to be maintained. Habits of mind, habitual ways of thinking, how- ever useful when considered merely as stages in a transition to greater understanding, become intellectually dangerous if allowed to ossify. But there are other dangers also, those which I referred to earlier. There is the danger of becoming too concerned with particu- lar things to the extent that it becomes just one damned fact after another. There is also at the other extreme the danger of spinning out connections between concepts without stopping to ask for their cash value.[1]

These points which I have made are, as I indicated earlier, essen- tially Kantian. They are to be found also in a sense in Piaget, although in his case they receive a strange biological dress. A strictly philosophical point is tricked out under the guise of a rather vague and certainly misleading psychological or biological theory. I refer here to Piaget's notions of accommodation and assimilation and the balance to be achieved between these processes. What Piaget has in mind is the idea that our knowledge of objects is partly determined by what these objects are in themselves, partly by how we regard them. This comes down to the point which I have already set out, concerning the relationship between concepts and instances. But to use the notions of accommodation and assimilation to express the point is harmful in two ways at least.

(1) The idea that perception and the acquisition of knowledge gene- rally involve accommodation and assimilation amounts to the idea that in this context there is a mutual modification of subject and object. (A parallel for this idea can again be found in Aristotle, in his view that perception consists in an actualization of the corres- ponding potentialities of sense-organ and sense-object.) But this sort of view depends on analogies which are supposed to exist between perception and other situations in which there is a reciprocal causal relationship. Such reciprocal causal relationships exist often enough in biological situations, where the attainment of a balance is the

function of an organism. Thus the proper working of the body depends on the existence of physiological balances of one kind or another. The stimuli which affect certain bodily organs are themselves affected and modified by a process of feed-back when the balance is disturbed. But the relationship which comes to exist between concept and object in perception is not a causal relationship at all. A concept is not the sort of thing which can have a causal relation with an object; it makes no sense to suppose so. For, concepts are not things of this kind, as should be clear when it is remembered that, as I have already said, to have a concept of X is to know what it is for something to be an X. Correspondingly, the growth of knowledge is not itself a causal matter (however much it may depend on causal factors of a physiological kind, i.e. on bodily conditions).

(2) If the employment of a biological model is misleading in giving us an incorrect understanding of what the acquisition of knowledge consists in, it also has misleading implications of a more directly philosophical kind. It suggests that the balance to be attained is one between something about the individual which is essentially subjective, i.e. the concept, and something about the world around us which is clearly objective, i.e. the object. Knowledge is thus a blend of the subjective and the objective. But the relationship to which I have pointed as existing between concept and instance is not one between the subjective and the objective. It is not up to an individual to organize in thought what he is confronted with in any way he pleases—or if anyone shows signs of so doing we think of him as mad. I have already said more than once that to have a concept of X is to know what it is for something to be an X; hence, to see something as an instance of X is to see it as something to which this knowledge is appropriate. There is nothing subjective about this. In fitting something to a concept we are not imposing on it a subjective point of view; for, given what I have said, to have a concept can be as much an objective matter as anything else. The objectivity of a concept is bound up with the idea that it must be inter-subjective, inter-personal, just as knowledge is. Hence, it is impossible to look on the growth of knowledge as some kind of transaction between an individual and his environment, as if social, inter-personal, factors had no part to play. I have commented already on the serious under-estimation of the social in Piaget's thought. This is borne out by his adoption of this curious biological model, which effectively rules out the social

factor, and thereby undermines the objectivity of knowledge. It is most important to note the extent to which notions like that of knowledge and concepts are social ideas, and the extent to which objectivity depends on this point. For the same reason it is impossible to think of education and learning at all except from a social point of view.

An important truth nevertheless remains in all this—that a balance must be attained between the formal understanding of the principles of a subject and an appreciation of what counts as instances to which those principles are to be applied. Unless this balance is attained, one cannot be said to have a proper understanding of the concepts involved. Hence, being aware of the general principles of a subject, which itself presupposes having the concepts, the particular forms of knowledge, in which the subject-matter is to be formulated, implies also attention to instances. Of course, this is of itself to take an over-simple view of the situation, since concepts do not come by themselves, and any subject will involve connections between concepts of one degree or another of abstractness. To be made to learn these connections without any prior understanding of their relevance to instances would be to be given knowledge which was formal only, and therefore empty; the lack of understanding would make the learning equivalent to rote-learning. It would be the learning by rote of empty phrases. It is perhaps arguable that in certain spheres of knowledge progress might be better made by instilling the formal knowledge and then cashing it in instances than by building up from instances in the first place. But this is merely to make the point which I have laboured all along—that at every stage in the development of knowledge a balance is required between formal knowledge of principles and appreciation of what counts as instances, and that it is of less importance which one invokes first than that a balance should be attained. Nevertheless, it is clearly futile to expect a child to move from one extreme to the other, and the concrete and particular is clearly more obvious than the abstract and general. Is it, therefore, any surprise that what Piaget calls the stage of concrete operations must in general precede that of abstract operations? As Aristotle said, while in knowledge the general is prior in itself, the particular is prior relative to us. This is what Piaget's point comes down to.

What do I mean when I say that the concrete and particular is more obvious than the abstract and general? I do not present this as a mere fact of human psychology. It seems to me a consequence of the situation in which human-beings find themselves, of the nature of human experience. The possibility of creatures who come to knowledge of, say, the principles of physics before knowledge of their immediate surroundings is a science-fiction conception, but it corresponds to nothing human. In so far as our concept of knowledge is really a concept of *human* knowledge, it is doubtful whether the possibility which I have mentioned is even one which is intelligible to us. The development of human knowledge may be represented as an enlargement of experience, an enlargement of the individual's intellectual environment. (The part played in this by social factors is obvious.) The things which are the individual's immediate and original concern are particular and concrete. As experience is widened and enlarged, as too it becomes more inter-personal, so it must inevitably become more general and abstract.

Given all this, what seems at first sight to be merely a natural transition from the concrete to the abstract in the development of human thinking emerges as some sort of necessary principle. It is necessary because this transition is just what, as we conceive it, the development of human experience must consist in. That development can of course fail to take place, but it can have no other order; otherwise it would not be *development*. But, it may be said, has not Piaget shown by empirical investigations that the concrete comes before the abstract as a matter of fact? How can something which is supposed to be a necessary truth be discovered by empirical investigations? We must be careful here. Let us consider what Piaget's response might be to hypothetical counter-examples to his thesis. Presumably, if children did not develop from the concrete to the abstract at all, he would have to say that they were not normal children—and we would agree. If the development occurred in the reverse order, would he not have to say, as I have already indicated, that they were not human? The presumption in his investigations is that he is concerned with normal human children. One thing that he may be said to have discovered is that the subjects who at one stage employ concrete operations and only later abstract operations are indeed normal human children. What else should we expect to happen in such circumstances? The situation is similar to the one which I mentioned earlier in stressing the connection between abstractness and complexity on the one hand and difficulty on the other. If there is a way of establishing the abstractness and complex-

41

ity of a subject, this is *eo ipso* a way of establishing that people normally find it difficult, and vice versa. Similarly, if there is a way of establishing that children are normal human children, that their experience is what is normal, then this will *eo ipso* establish that their intellectual development will be along certain general lines, and vice versa.

It seems to me that Piaget's discoveries here are like discovering that circles when presented to people in a frontal plane look round to them. To insist that they generally do would be to labour the obvious. The point is that this is the normal case, and it is by reference to it that the application of concepts like 'roundness' is established; it is the norm for what counts as round. If circles presented in a frontal plane did not normally look round our understanding of notions like that of a circle and roundness would be completely different; indeed, we should not know what to think. Hence, given that the people and the situation are normal, it could not be otherwise. It needs no empirical investigation to discover that circles seen in the frontal plane look round in normal conditions. Analogously, I do not claim that the stages found in Piaget's subjects are not there as a matter of fact; I do claim that *if his subjects are normal human children*, we could not conceive it otherwise. Hence, the priority of the concrete to the abstract is something that all normal human-beings could discover by reflection on what they know about the nature of human development, of human learning; it needs no further empirical investigation. On the other hand, of course, it does need empirical investigation to discover *when* John or Mary pass from one general stage of development to another, and whether they do so at roughly the same age. But such findings of course presuppose our present educational and cultural set-up; there is no reason to suppose that the norms are unalterable. Hence, what needs even further investigation is whether what is true of John and Mary is also true of Fritz, Ali and Kwame, i.e. we need to know the effects of different cultural and perhaps genetic backgrounds on the general development of children.

Finally, let me say again that if it is thought desirable that the process of intellectual development be accelerated (something that is perhaps arguable, considering that *intellectual* development is not the only thing), then the best people to provide the answers how this is to be done are those who have reflected most deeply on what is involved conceptually in their own subject, what is best understood first, and so on. That is to say that the best person to say how the teaching of, say, mathematics should proceed is the mathematician who has reflected adequately, and perhaps philosophically, on what is involved in his own subject (especially, in the first place, in its application to experience). Of course, here again the difficulties in the way of coming up with any firm answers may be insurmountable; in which case, the only hope is to find out empirically what courses of learning children do as a matter of fact normally find most easy. For, as I have said, easiness goes with concreteness and simplicity of subject-matter, and this provides a clue to what should come first and what second in learning.

My intention in what I have had to say has been above all perhaps to delimit the roles to be performed by philosophy and psychology in this field, and to emphasize the differences between empirical and conceptual inquiries here. Psychology has much to tell us about learning—about, for example, particular cases and individual differences. It can also tell us about the effect on learning of all those factors in people which we can call psychological—personality traits, intelligence, and so on. What I have been urging is, amongst other things, that there is also required proper reflection on what learning and education are, and what they involve in consequence. For, only in this way can we be rid of misleading models which may inhibit our understanding of intellectual development and education.

NOTES

1. I ignore here the possibility of *a priori* concepts, but these would be intelligible only in some sort of connection with concepts which do have the application discussed above.

3

THE LOGICAL AND PSYCHOLOGICAL
ASPECTS OF TEACHING A SUBJECT

Paul H. Hirst

Most teachers of a form of knowledge or understanding at some time ask themselves the fundamental questions: In what ways and to what extent is the effective teaching of a subject determined by the nature of the subject itself and in what ways and to what extent is the teaching dependent on factors studied in the psychology of learning and teaching? Or putting these questions another way, how are syllabuses and methods determined by the characteristics of what is to be taught and how are they to be determined by our empirical knowledge of teaching methods? Indeed, what sort of questions are questions about how best to teach a subject? This paper is an attempt to make clear something of what is involved in answering these questions. It will, however, be concerned almost entirely with the teaching of those subjects which are indisputably logically cohesive disciplines. I have argued elsewhere[1] that although the domain of human knowledge can be regarded as composed of a number of logically distinct forms of knowledge, we do in fact for many purposes, deliberately and self-consciously organize knowledge into a large variety of fields which often form the units employed in teaching. The problems that arise in teaching such complex fields as, say, geography and educational theory, are much more difficult to analyse than those arising in such forms as, say, mathematics, physics and history. And if the teaching of such fields necessarily involves the teaching of certain areas of more fundamental forms of knowledge, then it is only when questions about the latter have been settled that we can hope to answer questions about the former.

What sort of questions then, are questions about how best to teach a subject? Manifestly these are not questions that belong to the subject itself. How to teach history is not itself a historical question, nor is how to teach chemistry a chemical question. Maybe these questions will never be satisfactorily answered without a knowledge of history or chemistry, but such knowledge is at best a necessary condition for answering the questions, certainly it is not sufficient. Questions about the teaching of history are surely quite different logically from the questions of historical scholarship and where is the evidence that there is any correlation of abilities in these two domains?

If questions about teaching are manifestly not questions within the subject domain itself, are they then simply empirical questions? If so we could hope to discover directly by experiment and observation which activities do in fact lead to pupils learning history or chemistry, and thus which activities are successful as teaching methods. Certainly unless it is the case that activities result in pupils learning history or chemistry, they are useless as teaching methods, whatever the intentions of the teacher may be, and whether or not pupils learn successfully is a matter for empirical test. This answer is, however, too simple. For before any empirical investigation of teaching methods, that has any value, can be carried out, we have to decide what will count as pupils having learnt history. And once we start looking closely at what the learning of history involves, important logical features appear which must necessarily characterize what goes on if the activities we are interested in are even to count as the teaching of history. Here then will be features which on logical grounds must determine the teaching of the subject.

What then are we after in teaching a subject? What does learning it involve? In all subjects surely, we do not just want the learning of a string of propositions. If that were all, we could quickly set out what has to be learnt and find by empirical investigation how best to teach it. But even when handing on information, we want pupils not to become like parrots but to *understand* the information, and, as soon as we say that, difficulties arise as to what exactly we mean by this term and how we would know pupils had understood what was presented to them. Generally speaking we want yet more from our teaching than this, however. What we want is that pupils shall begin, however embryonically, to think historically, scientifically or mathematically; to think in the way distinctive of the particular subject involved and even to achieve some style and imagination in doing so. Thus before we can carry out any empirical investigation of teaching methods we are faced with the difficult task of getting clear what is involved in, say, thinking historically, and thus in learning to think in this way.

45

At first sight it might be thought that to discover what historical thinking is, we must somehow carry out psychological investigations of the thought processes of historians when doing their job. Certainly these thought sequences could be investigated, but to do that means that we must be able to pick out from all their thinking when they are thinking historically and not just say day-dreaming, plotting a family holiday or perhaps thinking mathematically. In fact we are back again on the same kind of question, how can you empirically investigate until you know the criteria of what you are looking for? And it follows from this that the criteria of what constitutes historical thinking must be found independently of such investigation. The only way in which we can successfully distinguish different forms of thought is in fact by reference to the particular set of terms and relations which each of the distinct forms of thought employs. These terms and relations are fully public, and if, therefore, we wish to characterize, say, scientific or historical thought, we must do this in the first place by examining the distinctive features of scientific theories and laws or historical explanations. In science, such an analysis will at the most general level make plain, for example, the particular use of terms in expressing empirical truths, the importance of general laws and the criteria for verifying these. In history, it will involve making plain the features of historical explanation of particular events by colligation, the use of general laws and evidence from sources. Granted an analysis of these public characteristics, it is not impossible to investigate empirically the thought sequences of particular historians. But just what such investigations of historical thought could provide by way of general psychological truths cannot be laid down a priori, nor can we know beforehand what bearing they might have on problems of teaching and learning. In general, however, it is surely true to say that when as teachers we seek to develop historical thought, say, we are not aiming at any particular pattern or sequence of thought episodes. Indeed many would wish to rule out of 'coming to think historically' any suggestions that thought sequences are being stereotyped, even if this were practically possible. It would be argued that thinking historically is thinking which, irrespective of the private thought sequence involved, results in propositions which constitute valid historical accounts and explanations. Historical thought necessarily involves the recognition of the rules that govern the meaningful use of concepts and the validity of propositions, but this involves no necessary temporal order to thought. Just as playing chess involves making moves in accordance with the rules of chess, though it involves no one particular order of moves, so thinking historically involves thinking in accordance with historical criteria, though it involves no particular sequences of thought.

Certainly, on this view of historical thinking, what we want pupils to acquire, both in structure and content, can be totally characterized without recourse to any psychological investigation of thought sequences. This does not, however, preclude the possibility that such investigation would enable us to find more effective means of teaching historical thinking, and it might ultimately lead to a reformulation of what we wish to achieve in history teaching. An empirical investigation, not only of the private thought sequences of historians, but also of their more public methods of procedure, for instance in marshalling sources, working from analogy and so on, might be of great value here. Yet whatever possibilities such empirical investigation might open up, it remains true that there must first be clear logical analysis of what criteria distinguish historical thought. This is in fact to say that the effective teaching of a subject necessarily depends on knowing certain features which characterize it, which can be disclosed only by logical analysis of the meaning of 'historical thinking', though once the criteria for this are plain, empirical evidence about thinking based on the use of these criteria becomes important too.

But granted this very rough indication of the boundaries between the logical and the psychological or empirical characterization of 'historical thinking', we now wish to know further how far the logical analysis of historical thinking determines the teaching of historical thinking. For having got to this point it might be argued that, given a grasp of the criteria of historical thinking, a philosophically self-conscious historian can in fact set out clearly all that is to be aimed at, and that it is then a matter of empirical investigation how far various teaching methods are successful in achieving these aims. Certainly such a historian could set out in detail what had to be mastered, the concepts, the forms of explanation and their criteria, the content, the methods of investigation and so on. But to make all other factors in determining teaching methods an empirical matter, is to take too simple a view of the contribution of logical analysis to determining the teaching of a subject. For though it is quite possible, granted a clear statement of what is to be taught, to investigate different teaching methods, yet a great deal of investigation approached in this way might well turn out to be quite unnecessary. The reason is simply that experiment and observation cannot but confirm matters of logical truth, and all that is necessarily implied by learning to think historically has not yet been made clear. Maybe there are truths about teaching and learning which are rather like that hoary truth beloved of philosophers that all bachelors are unmarried. To prevent irrelevant complications let us take the proposition that all bachelors resident in the London postal area are unmarried. Faced with the question of the truth of this proposition someone might wish to answer the matter by conducting an empirical survey. This would, however, be impossible without clear criteria by which to distinguish bachelors and unmarried people. In the same way it has been maintained that empirical investigation into the teaching of historical thinking is impossible without criteria for distinguishing historical thinking. But granted such criteria, it is a further question whether or not the truth of the proposition depends on empirical investigation. In fact it is immediately clear that empirical investigation cannot but confirm the truth of the proposition as it happens to be logically true. Granted an understanding of the meaning of the terms, it is necessarily the case that the bachelors must be discovered to be unmarried and the empirical investigation is therefore redundant—it cannot but confirm what is logically true. In a similar way there might well be truths about the teaching and learning of historical thinking for which empirical evidence is quite beside the point. We must therefore take a closer look at what is implied logically, not simply in, say, historical thinking, but in coming to think historically.

In the first place such learning involves coming to understand historical propositions, and this in turn involves learning the use of a network of related concepts. It is necessarily the case that any area of knowledge can only be mastered in so far as the use of concepts according to the complex rules that relate them to each other is acquired. Granted this, even the briefest examination of these rules then seems to indicate that it is logically impossible to acquire certain concepts without previously acquiring others; for until the rule-governed use of some terms is achieved, the rule-governed use of others is beyond achievement. In this way the concept of being a bachelor presupposes the concept of marriage, the concept of acceleration presupposes the concept of velocity, the concept of revolution presupposes that of authority. Because of these relations it would seem to be a logical truth that one cannot learn, for instance, about acceleration without first learning about velocity and that therefore any teaching of this area of knowledge must recognize this order of priority in the concepts.

Further it would seem to be a necessary truth about any form of knowledge that there is some ordered sequence to the truths concerned, for the validity of some propositions presupposes the validity of others. If, therefore, the grounds of validity for propositions are to be understood by pupils, the teaching of the area of knowledge must reflect these logical priorities in the order of justification.

But what precisely can we say along these lines about teaching and learning? In the past extravagant claims have often been made to the effect that the problems of teaching a subject are simply problems of logical ordering and that for this, common-sense is all that is necessary beyond a knowledge of the subject itself. Recently there has been a tendency to swing to the opposite extreme with far too much ill-considered appeal to empirical investigation. What is needed is a much more careful examination of what the logically necessary features of areas of knowledge are and, in particular, the extent to which learning a subject involves adherence to what can loosely be called rules of logical order. Once these questions are answered, we can hope to see more useful empirical investigation in this area.

Although there is a strict limit to what can be said in general terms about the logical characteristics of knowledge, it is important to pursue further what is meant by such phrases as logical order, logical method and logical organization, as these play an important part in the now rapidly growing literature on these questions. John Dewey was the first philosopher to use such terms in an educational context. In a celebrated chapter in *Democracy and Education* he distinguishes two methods of teaching. In one, which is referred to as the logical method :

> Pupils began their study of science with texts in which the subject is organized into topics according to the order of the specialist. Technical concepts, with their definitions, are introduced at the outset. Laws are introduced at a very early stage, with at best a few indications of the way in which they were arrived at. The pupils learn a 'science' instead of learning the scientific way of treating the familiar material of ordinary experience.[2]

Of the logical order which such teaching follows he writes :

> Logical order is not a form imposed on what is known; it is the proper form of knowledge as perfected. For it means that the statement of subject matter is of a nature to exhibit to one who understands it the premises from which it follows and the conclusions to which it points. . . . To the non-expert however this perfected form is a stumbling block. . . . From the standpoint of the learner scientific form is an ideal to be achieved, not a starting point from which to set out.[3]

The other method of teaching which is contrasted with the logical, Dewey refers to as the 'psychological' or chronological method. In this the pupil

> by following in connection with problems selected from the material of ordinary acquaintance, the methods by which scientific men have reached their perfected knowledge, (he) gains independent power to deal with material within his range and avoids the mental confusion and intellectual dictates attendant upon studying matter whose meaning is only symbolic.[4]

Dewey of course made no sharp distinctions between different forms of knowledge, regarding all knowledge as ultimately scientific in character. What he said about the two methods of teaching he therefore thought of very wide application, but so as to avoid complications arising from possible differences between science and other forms of knowledge, I shall here consider these remarks solely in relation to undisputably scientific content. Granted this, there is certainly no doubt which of the two methods of teaching Dewey thought more desirable, and these passages are in fact part of a sustained attack on traditional teaching methods. There have been more extreme attacks which question the existence of a logical order to knowledge at all, but the argument here certainly accepts a logical order of some kind in science. It denies, however, that this is of any significance for the temporal order of events in teaching. Logical order is the end product in scientific understanding. It is a pattern which in teaching is pieced together as one puts together the pattern of a jig-saw. The logical order does not prescribe a series of steps which must be taken. There is a great variety of ways in which the jig-saw can be made up and the same is true in teaching science. The logical order emerges as you go along. The order is not an order of learning or of teaching—it is strictly a logical order not a temporal one. From this it would seem at first sight that the temporal order in teaching, in piecing together the pattern of relations, is for Dewey a matter of the empirical investigation of ways for achieving the pattern. Just what non-logical determination of methods he advocated we will return to later.

The question to be asked first, however, is whether or not the logical features of some form of understanding can simply be regarded as an end product. Is logical order the ideal that Dewey implies? For was it not being suggested earlier that without adherence to the logical characteristics of some form of knowledge even the concepts which that subject uses cannot be grasped? Must not every element of historical knowledge that is taught, necessarily be true to the conceptual structure of that domain? Is it not false therefore to suggest that in developing understanding one can start *anywhere*? And even if logical order is an ideal in some sense, does it not exercise a perpetual control over the method by which it is approached? In a jig-saw the pieces will only fit together one way so as to make up the picture, and the picture has one and only one pattern in the end. Is not knowledge like that?

Obviously if we are to get any further with the problem we must get clearer what is meant by logical order. In doing this, it would seem to be important to recognize that, within any form of knowledge, in, say, a science like physics or in history, at least two separable levels of logical relations can be distinguished, at both of which elements of logical order can arise. There is first the network of relations between particular concepts, relationships by virtue of which meaningful propositions can be formed. In physics the term electron has a certain use. It is only meaningful to say certain things of it, it has to conform to a pattern of relations, and the rules for its use do not permit us to speak of its temperature, its aesthetic qualities or moral value. In religious discourse you cannot use the term God in any old way. He is not an object or being in space and time, he has no extension or colour. He does not act as a human being acts. We must, therefore, stick strictly to the rules for the use of the terms or we do not have meaning. At this level, a domain of knowledge can be said to have a logical grammar, which consists of the rules for the meaningful use of the terms it employs.

Secondly, there is the network of relations between propositions in terms of which valid historical or scientific explanations are formed. The logical analysis of historical or scientific explanations seeks to make plain the criteria for valid explanations in this area. But using these formal criteria in any given case does, of course, presuppose the validity of the propositions in terms of which the explanations are given. Thus the valid explanations in any subject area would seem to depend on the progressive establishment of what I shall call a logical sequence of validated propositions. Any explanation of the repeal of the corn laws in 1846, for instance, must rest on valid propositions about the economic effects of the laws, the famine in Ireland, the political policy of Peel and so on. Similarly, the explanation of the truth that the lengths of the sides of a right-angled triangle satisfy the equation $a^2 = b^2 + c^2$ rests on the truth of a sequence of earlier propositions which, in turn, depends on the axioms of Euclidean geometry.

If then there are two levels at which elements of logical order within a subject can occur, what are the implications of this for teaching? According to the first, any statement to be meaningful must necessarily be true to the logical grammar of the forms of knowledge. Thus the teaching of this form of understanding must always, in all respects, conform to the logical grammar if it is to be intelligible. This logical grammar is therefore no ideal, that might not be attained in some area of understanding. It is implicit in any meaningful statement that belongs to the domain at all, though no one statement will involve more than a very limited number of the rules of such a grammar. Coming to have a new concept involves mastering its often complex logical grammar, and this may involve a long period in which its relation with other concepts and its precise application are being learnt. The concept of a dog is relatively easy to acquire compared with, say, the concept of a matrix or the Christian concept of God. What elements of the logical grammar of a term a person comes to appreciate first may not be important, and many of our very hazy concepts become more refined in time as we acquire the appropriate grammar more thoroughly. In this process of acquiring new concepts a person is heavily dependent on the concepts he has already, but as extremely complex networks of relationships have to be built up in any area of knowledge, it is surely a mistake to think that there is only one order in which all our concepts can be acquired. Certain concepts do undoubtedly depend for their meaning on their relation to certain logically prior concepts. How can one know what a bachelor is unless one can distinguish between men and women, between the married and the unmarried? But how many of our concepts are so clearly and precisely related to others in logical order? In mathematics and the sciences there is frequently such an order, and new concepts are often explicitly composed in this tight way by defining them from other concepts. In many other areas of discourse, in moral and historical matters for instance, such conceptual relations are far from common, the relations are not hierarchical in this way. But in so far as there are elements of conceptual order in any subject the teaching of it must of course fully respect these.

Yet three things must be noted. First, in so far as a child has begun to make the distinctions between men and women and the married and the unmarried, he is, to that extent, able to begin to form the concept of a bachelor. In one sense, learning a concept is not an all or nothing business; for one can know some of the criteria for a concept without knowing them all, and one can begin to build other higher order concepts on this partial knowledge. Secondly, even if this order of conceptual development cannot be intelligibly ignored, yet the teacher does not have to approach the concept of a bachelor by verbal definition. Even if the order of acquisition is logically determined, the means or manner of acquisition is not. Thirdly developments in those subjects which do involve detailed conceptual order, can at times result in conceptual re-organization. New mathematical relations or physical properties can lead to a restructuring of a theory, or system, in which the order in which certain concepts enter is changed.

What emerges from this discussion is that it is necessary in teaching a subject that the logical grammar of its key concepts be understood by the teacher; for otherwise vital elements in what he is teaching are not fully clear to him and not adequately under his control. The logical grammar is something given for him; it is not something he can dispense with and yet continue to teach the subject. In so far as the logical grammar reveals elements of logical order, then the teaching must equally respect these too. What they are in any given subject is a matter for the detailed analysis of the concepts of that subject.

When Dewey objected to teaching methods that conformed to a logical order, if he was referring to order in the logical grammar of the subject, he was surely misdirecting his attack. All teaching must be true to this, if it is to be the teaching of the subject. In part he was certainly objecting to the presentation of science as an ordered body of statements developed from definitions, complaining that the

53

pupils then failed to understand. In this case his criticisms were no doubt warranted, but they must be construed as criticisms of the means and manner in which pupils were expected to acquire new concepts, not of the need for adherence to logical order in the learning of new concepts. To learn a new concept is to learn how to use the concept in relation to others and how to apply it. It is not to learn a series of truths about its relations with other concepts. Learning a concept is like learning to play tennis, not like learning to state the rules and principles that govern play. Equally learning to think scientifically is not learning the formal definitions of terms and a series of true propositions. Indeed such formal learning would seem to be not even a necessary, let alone a sufficient, condition for learning to think scientifically. As far as logical grammar is concerned then, Dewey's criticisms, to be valid, must be regarded as an attack on the manner of adherence to it rather than the necessity for such adherence.

But what of the question of the logical sequence of a subject? If, to be meaningful, the teaching must be true to the logical grammar, must it not, if the validity of the explanations and theories is to be communicated, follow a logical sequence in establishing the appropriate propositions? In so far as it is a body of knowledge one is teaching, and not just a body of beliefs, is there not an order in which its true propositions must be presented?

That there is *one* such logical sequence of the truths in any domain of knowledge must surely be rejected immediately. Even in mathematics the existence of alternative sets of axioms for any given system is now common knowledge. In the sciences equally, alternative ways of demonstrating scientific laws are a common phenomenon, and the discovery of whole new orders of demonstration is not unheard of. There is, therefore, no one logical sequence in which the truths of a subject must be communicated, even in those subjects which seem most strictly sequential. Maybe a great deal of the trouble here has sprung from a confusion between the two forms of logical order that are being distinguished, those elements of order in the logical grammar and those in what is here being called logical sequence. Once a strict distinction is drawn between them it can be seen that, though adherence to any elements of order within the logical grammar is necessary for intelligibility in teaching, no such adherence to any one logical sequence is demanded in the same way.

But if the idea of a domain of knowledge having *one* implicit logical sequence of truths must be rejected, this is not to say that a subject can be taught without attention to *some* appropriate logical sequence. In any teaching of a form of knowledge the question of the justification of the propositions, explanations and theories is vital, and pupils need to appreciate, not only why these particular elements are true, but the kind of justification there is in general within this form of knowledge. Without this one cannot be said to have taught this subject in any significant sense. The teaching must therefore involve the development of some logical sequence appropriate to the subject, that is it must involve the development of an ordered body of truths according to the criteria for validating historical explanations or mathematical theorems.

From this it is tempting to conclude that the subject must be taught so as to build up the truths in strict order, following in temporal sequence some particular logical sequence. In reply to this, it must first be remembered that logical sequence is not an order necessary to the intelligibility of the propositions, as elements of order within logical grammar are. It is only when one is concerned with questions of validity and justification that this matter of logical sequence ever arises. Further, it is surely a mistake to think that explanations are seen to be valid only when the elements are pieced together by a temporal following of a logical sequence. To grasp a valid proof or explanation is to recognize, in the end, an overall pattern of logical relations between propositions that satisfy certain criteria. To insist that this sequence of truths can only be grasped as truths, by temporally building on previously adequately established truths, is to take the characteristics of what is to be achieved as an end for the characteristics of the process by which the end is achieved. Maybe the analogy with a jig-saw puzzle is valuable here. In a valid explanation the elements must fit together as if to establish the pattern of the puzzle; but there is no one temporal order in which the pieces must be fitted together to produce the pattern.

A perpetual problem in teaching formal geometry illustrates this point; for pupils often find it difficult to grasp that the temporal sequence of the steps by which a geometrical problem is solved is rarely the logical sequence of steps laid out in the formal proof. To solve the problem one must somehow complete the vital logical sequence; the proof simply sets out the established sequence for all to see. To do a jig-saw puzzle is to somehow complete the picture which is then clear for all to see; but one does not have to start piecing together from the bottom left-hand corner or even the edges. Thus though the significant teaching of a subject must establish at least some logical sequence distinctive of that subject, this is not a demand that the order of teaching temporally follow along logically prescribed lines. The question of temporal sequence is a matter to be decided on empirical grounds, once the logical sequence to be established is clearly determined by the teacher.

Having said this, however, it must not be forgotten that because questions of logical grammar and intelligibility can to some extent be separated from questions of logical sequence and justification, a great deal of so called teaching can, of course, be conducted without much concern for any logical sequence. It is possible to have a great deal of scientific information and little idea of even the kind of justification on which it rests. How far teaching of this kind is defensible is a debatable and a non-philosophical question. To many, such teaching is not in any sense describable as teaching the subject; for the distinctive forms of justification and the criteria for truth in the domain are elements that are necessarily part of the form of knowledge, even if these prescribe no one logical sequence and no one teaching order. But that a great deal of such instruction goes on at present in schools cannot be denied.

In so far, then, as Dewey was objecting to teaching methods conforming to a logical sequence his criticisms are valid; for logical sequence must not be confused with a temporal learning sequence. His comments are, however, misleading in so far as they imply that there is in science, or any other form of knowledge, any one logical sequence. There are, in fact, many such sequences, similar in kind and exemplifying the distinctive logical characteristics of valid explanations in the domain. Further, in so far as his comments suggest that science can be taught without necessarily aiming at any logical sequence, and his views have sometimes been interpreted as implying that the logical 'ideal' of science is only important for would-be professional scientists, they would seem to be dangerously mistaken. Both the method he advocates and the method he rejects must, to be the teaching of science, be true to all the logical features of science, and thus involve the development of some logical sequence.

Some of Dewey's disciples certainly took him to be saying that the outcome of learning can be a personal or 'psychological' organization of knowledge rather than a logical organization appropriate for research specialists. Why cannot knowledge be organized round an interest in some practical activity for instance, rather than as a theoretical pursuit? Bode took this distinction between logical and psychological organizations to be worth the argument that the latter are of more limited value than the former.[5] But what is this a distinction between exactly? If what has been argued earlier is correct there is no non-logical organization of knowledge; the logical features are those which necessarily characterize knowledge. The contrast cannot, therefore, be between logical organization and non-logical organization. What is more, if someone acquires knowledge of any kind, this is necessarily a personal psychological matter. A person cannot have non-psychologically organized knowledge. The contrast can, therefore, only be one between the different organizations of knowledge which we present to children, organizations respecting both the logical features of the knowledge concerned and the necessity for the pupils to individually come to acquire this knowledge. In the end the distinction would seem to come down to whether or not we should teach as school subjects such distinct, logically cohesive disciplines as mathematics, physics and history, or rather teach second-order organizations of knowledge which we compose of elements from these primary divisions, such units as 'the neighbourhood', 'power' or 'the seventeenth-century mind'. Maybe the interest of pupils is more easily aroused when we organize what we teach in such second-order fields and they therefore learn more effectively. But there is here no different *logical* organization of knowledge as such. The pupils' grasp of the meaning and validity of all the elements in such a second-order organization depends on their appreciating these elements as logically related to other elements within the primary divisions of knowledge.[6] The distinction here then is a concern about what is taught but not one that turns on logical questions. Whether or not we should teach according to the primary divisions of knowledge or according to second-order units is a matter that cannot be settled on philosophical grounds.

It might be expected that Dewey's rejection of what he calls the logical teaching method would be complemented by his advocating the empirical investigation of teaching and that his 'psychological' approach would be based squarely on the results of this. In fact this is not what he does; for the method he advocates, though justified to some extent by practical experience with children, rests primarily on assumptions as theoretical and doctrinaire as those behind the method he rejects. Instead of following some logical sequence Dewey suggests that teaching methods should follow the method that lies behind scientific investigation and discovery. This method he elaborates in a series of stages in which from a 'genuine situation of experience', a problem develops 'as a stimulus to thought' about which information and observations are collected, a solution is formulated and tests for validity are carried out.[7]

Dewey advocated this method for reasons connected with his own distinctive views of logic and his pragmatic theory of truth. He considered the methods of enquiry found in science to be the foundation of all knowledge and thus wanted above all that pupils should master, not a subject, but the fundamentals of scientific method as he saw these. This meant that they must learn what is involved in enquiry by conducting enquiries themselves. Certainly *if* we want to teach skill in a methodology, we shall wish pupils to practise such methods; for a skill is necessarily something learnt in this way. This is but to say that the teaching methods employed must be activities designed to produce the relevant learning. But if we take a wider view of what is to be learnt, even within science, we may well question whether the methodology of scientific discovery, assuming there is such a thing, should provide the basis of a general teaching method. Certainly discovery is one way of learning, but it is not the only way, and whether or not it is in general the best way, is an open question that Dewey never seems to consider. Whether or not there is a methodology of scientific discovery and, if there is, whether Dewey is right in his characterizations of it, are also large questions on which there is room for a great divergence of opinion. If, however, we consider other areas of knowledge than science, there would seem little reason to think that scientific methodology can solve our problems of teaching method. And to take in each area the methodology of the subject as a paradigm for the methodology of teaching the subject, is either to confuse methods which are in many ways concerned with achieving different ends, or to prejudge matters which can only be determined on the basis of much empirical evidence. It is, to say the least, ironical that Dewey, in his desire that pupils should acquire a problem-solving outlook, was himself as guilty of pre-judging some of the very empirical questions of teaching method as the advocates of the logical method he so condemned.

In this paper I have tried to maintain that :

(*a*) A subject like physics or history has a logical grammar which governs the meaningful use of the terms of the subject. All teaching of the subject must necessarily conform to the rules of this grammar or it will not be the teaching of the subject at all.

(*b*) In some cases this logical grammar involves an order of terms such that the meaning of certain terms presupposes the meaning of others. In this case the teaching of the subject must of course respect these elements of logical order.

(*c*) An understanding of the meaning of terms is not to be thought of as necessarily built up in strict order as a wall is built with bricks. Concepts are acquired by learning the complex use of terms in relation to other terms and their application in particular cases. A subject's logical grammar and the order within it must be respected in all teaching methods, but this leaves a vast area in which experimental investigations about the effectiveness of different methods can and must be carried out.

(*d*) Any subject like history or physics or mathematics is based on the use of certain logical principles in terms of which the explanation and theories distinctive of the subject are validated. I refer here to the logic of historical explanations, of scientific explanations, mathematical proofs and so on. These principles, however, do not determine any *one* particular logical sequence for the propositions. Any teaching method for the subject must therefore respect the fundamental logical principles without which no understanding of the distinctive form of validity peculiar to this subject is possible. This means that *some* logical sequence of propositions using these logical principles must emerge in the teaching of the subject. There are alternative logical sequences which may be taken and advances in knowledge often suggest new sequences.

(*e*) To say that some logical sequence must emerge in the teaching of the subject is not to say that the teaching must follow that sequence in temporal order. It is an order that is understood to hold together in the end. It does not have to be built up in any one way.

(*f*) The logical grammar involved and the various possibilities for the logical sequence to be used, are matters for determination by an analysis of the subject to be taught, not for empirical investigation. How far these logical features do determine the teaching of a subject, and areas within the subject, can be worked out in detail only in terms of the specific content that is to be taught.

(*g*) It is only when the fullest logical analysis of what is involved in teaching a subject has been carried out, that the profitable empirical investigation of methods can be conducted. How much further we can get by general philosophical discussion of the kind in this paper is not clear. What is clear, however, is that, if our teaching methods are not to remain the hit and miss business they are at the moment, the careful, detailed analysis of the logical features of exactly what we wish to teach must be pursued far more thoroughly than it has been thus far. More philosophical clarity can, of its own, certainly help us to produce more effective and more rationally defensible teaching methods.

NOTES

1. Hirst, P. H., 'Liberal Education and the Nature of Knowledge', in Archambault, R. D. (ed.), *Philosophical Analysis and Education* (Routledge and Kegan Paul, 1965).
2. Dewey, J., *Democracy and Education* (Macmillan, N.Y., 1916), p. 257.
3. Dewey, J., pp. 256–7.
4. Dewey, J., p. 258.
5. Bode, B. H., *Modern Educational Theories* (Vintage Books), Ch. 3.
6. See Hirst, P. H., op. cit.
7. Dewey, J., p. 192.

CONDITIONING AND LEARNING

Godfrey Vesey

(I) Is being conditioned to do something learning to do it? (II) If not, could we have been conditioned to do the sort of things we have in fact learnt to do?

[I]

The first of these questions must be answered affirmatively if the criterion of learning having taken place is that someone has acquired, otherwise than simply by maturation, an ability to respond to a situation in a new way. Most modern psychologists do, in fact, accept this as the criterion of learning having taken place. They may talk, not of 'response', but of 'behaviour', but they mean by this neither what is ordinarily meant ('behave' being opposed to 'misbehave'), nor even what one might reasonably suppose them to mean ('behaviour' referring to a person's actions, like kicking a football, as opposed to mere responses, like the knee-jerk reflex). If there is any opposition at all implied in psychologists' use of the term 'behaviour' it would seem to depend on views about the proper manner of psychological investigation (not by introspection) and the proper level of psychological explanation (not the level of physiological explanation). Thus, behaviour is publicly observable, and is 'molar'.

I shall not beg the first question by adopting the psychologists' use of the word 'learn'. Instead I shall try to answer both questions in terms of what we ordinarily mean by 'learning' and by 'doing things'. Furthermore I shall not, in my answer, go beyond what can be said on the basis of these ordinary meanings. I shall consider only whether it makes sense to talk of our abilities being acquired by a process of being conditioned, not whether they could in fact be so acquired. In other words, my investigation is a purely conceptual one, as befits a philosopher.

What, then, do we ordinarily mean when we say that someone has learnt to do something?

We are less likely to fall into dogmatism if we develop our conceptual distinctions against the background of some fairly life-like situations. Let us consider three such situations. One of them might occur in a primary school, another in a technical school, and the third in a University psychological laboratory.

A. A little girl acquires the ability to skip with a skipping rope to music. At first she sees the teacher doing it, and tries to do the same, but with no success; she cannot even skip, never mind skip in time with the music. The teacher holds her by the hands, facing her, and does the jump and rebound movements in time with the music. The little girl picks it up and can soon do the jump and rebound movements by herself. Then come the arm and wrist movements. Perhaps it takes a little time for these to become co-ordinated with the jump and rebound movements. Finally, the skipping rope. The teacher holds her breath : has the little girl acquired the knack or not? Yes, she has, thanks to her natural muscular sense and the right sort of coaching. With some children, even though they may be brighter than the others when it comes to the theory of movement, it is always an uphill battle. But to this little girl it came fairly easily. She was naturally rhythmical, naturally well co-ordinated.

B. A boy is being taught about the internal combustion engine, with the aid of diagrams and an actual motor car engine. He learns how one can start the engine using a handle, and also how one can start it using a starting-motor powered by a battery. He thus acquires the ability to start suitably equipped engines in either of these two ways.

C. In a psychological laboratory a student is enabled 'to obtain voluntary control of what is for most persons an involuntary reflex'.[1]

In one experiment of this nature, the pupil of a man's eye was trained to contract at command. In the first stage of training, a bell was rung immediately before a light was shone in his eyes. After some trials, the sound of the bell alone would cause his pupil to contract. Then the man was instructed to close and open the circuit for both bell and light by closing and opening his hand at the verbal command of the experimenter. In this way verbal command became connected through the hand movement and the sound of the bell to the pupilary reflex. The next step in the experiment was to eliminate both the hand movement and the bell. This left only the vocal instruction of the experimenter as the conditioned stimulus, and the man's pupil now contracted to it alone. The last stage of the experiment consisted in having the subject himself repeat the verbal instructions, first aloud, then in a whisper and finally subvocally. Each of these forms of stimulation, it was found, could become the condition for the contraction of the pupil. So the man could, at the end of the experiment, effectively command his own pupilary reflex, and this ability was still present fifteen days later, without practice in the meantime.

Let us begin with the question : Is learning *how* to do something always a matter of learning *that* doing so-and-so brings about such-and-such an effect? Consider case B—the boy who learns how to start engines. Clearly the boy could pass on what he had learnt by word of mouth. Engines can be started either by turning the handle, or by using a starter-motor. But what about case A? Suppose the little girl is asked how she skips in time with the music. She can say 'Like this', and demonstrate her ability. But this is *showing,* not *saying,* how she does it. Indeed, it is not very clear what, other than a demonstration, can be meant by 'how she does it' in this situation. It is not as if she has to do something else to make herself skip as the boy has to turn the handle to make the engine start. We may give a meaning to 'how she does it' in terms of what goes on in her body : the impulses in the afferent and efferent nerves, the muscle-contractions and expansions, their timing in relation to one another, and so on. But we would be regarding the little girl in rather an odd light if we said that these 'goings-on' were things she *does*. It would be like saying that digesting her breakfast is something she does. In a sense it is, but it is not the sense in which eating her breakfast is something she does.

But cannot something be said on the following lines? For the little girl's feet to be off the ground when the skipping rope is in the 'down' position she has to be beginning her jump when it is in the horizontal position. To skip successfully she has to learn *that* beginning her jump when the skipping rope is horizontal has the effect that the rope passes under her feet.

I do not find this very convincing. For one thing, she could have learnt this and still not be able to time her jump. But I am not convinced that learning this is even a necessary, never mind a sufficient, condition of being able to skip. Perhaps I can make my point— which is that knowing *how* is not reducible to knowing *that*—more convincingly with examples of unlearnt abilities. Suppose I am asked how I clench my fist, or suck. A schoolboy may be told that what he is doing when he sucks milk up a straw is creating a lower pressure

63

at one end of the straw than there is at the other. This is the scientific explanation of the milk going up the straw. Similarly I may be told that what I am doing when I clench my fist is contracting certain muscles. But people can suck, and clench their fists, without knowing anything about pressures or muscles.

It might be said that acquiring the ability to do something, if it does not involve learning *that* (e.g. learning that doing so-and-so brings about such-and-such an effect), is not *learning* how to do it. The idea would be that learning is essentially an intellectual process. This idea does not seem to me to be in accord with our ordinary concept of learning. For better or worse we are not pure intellects. It seems to me desirable to retain a concept of learning which reflects this fact. There is what might be called 'purely bodily learning'. It plays a large part in the gymnast's skill, a smaller part in the surgeon's skill, but is essential to both.

Before going on to other questions about learning how to do something, let us notice some respects in which case C is like, and unlike, cases A and B.

(*i*) In case C—the pupil-contracting case—a stimulus (the subvocal command) produces a response (the contraction of the pupil). Case B—the engine-starting one—can also be described in stimulus-response terminology : a stimulus (turning the handle) produces a response (the engine starts). But the cases are not quite analogous. If the subvocal command is to bring about the pupil-contracting response a connection between the two has first to be induced. It was, in fact, induced by the stimulus-substitution procedure known as 'conditioning' (or, to be more precise, 'Pavlovian' or 'classical' conditioning). But it is conceivable that it should have been induced in other ways—perhaps simply by implanting a nerve between the speech muscles and the pupil-contracting muscles. This would be comparable to implanting a starter-motor and a starting button in the car, so that the engine responded to a stimulus other than manual cranking.

(*ii*) In case B the boy turns the handle, or presses the starting button, to make the engine start. It is the engine, not he, who starts. The pupil-contracting case seems different. The pupil which contracts is the pupil of the person who gives the subvocal command : it is part of him in a way in which the car, though the boy may own it, is not part of him. And yet the situation is not like that in case A. The person has to do something else (giving the subvocal command) to make his pupil contract. The little girl does not have to do something else to make her skipping occur. She simply skips.

Now let us ask ourselves : Does the man in case C learn to contract the pupils of his eyes? If we gave a negative answer to this question it would, I think, be for one, or both, of two reasons.

(*a*) In the sense in which skipping is something the little girl does, contracting the pupils of his eyes is not something the man does. He *makes* the pupils of his eyes contract. The fact that he can make them contract by a subvocal command, instead of by shining a light in them, does not mean that he contracts them *at will*. He no more contracts them at will than the boy starts the car at will (i.e. without turning the handle, or pushing the starting button). Strictly speaking, a person can be said to have learnt to do only what he does at will. Otherwise, what he has learnt is what to do to bring about a desired result. When we loosely speak of someone having learnt to start a car what we mean is that he has learnt what to do to get it to start.

(*b*) Whatever one does, in learning to do something, must itself really be something one *does,* something in which one is actively engaged. It cannot be simply something which happens to one. But 'being conditioned' is precisely not something one does. It is something which is done to one—either by oneself or, as is usually the case, by someone else.

Are these good reasons for denying that the man in case C learns to contract the pupils of his eyes?

I feel less sure about the second of them, so perhaps it would be as well to begin with that one.

There would seem to be two distinct things we may have in mind when we say of someone that he is learning, or has learnt, to do something. One is his acquiring the ability in question; the other is his having done something to acquire it. Are both these things necessary? Can a person be said to be learning to do something (for instance, to do a backward somersault) if whatever he is doing does not result in his acquiring the desired ability? Can a person be said to have learnt to do X if there is nothing he did previously which was 'learning to do X'?

I am inclined to give an affirmative answer to the last but one of these questions, and a negative answer to the last. But I do not think the precedent for these answers, in our everyday use of 'learn', is very strong. What we mean by 'learn' depends so much on the context, and even on the tense. In most contexts 'Has he learnt?' means 'Has he acquired the ability yet?'; but in some it means 'Did he acquire the ability by learning?'. In most contexts 'Is he learning?' means 'Is he engaged in the activity of learning?'; but in some it means 'Is he in fact acquiring the ability?'. It is because the word 'learn' may be used in these different but related ways that I do not feel confident about saying that an ability acquired by being conditioned is not an ability acquired by learning. It all depends on which of the features of the use of 'learn' one has in mind. I do not propose to legislate that we should always have both in mind.

This leaves us with the first supposed reason for denying that the man in case C learns to contract the pupils of his eyes—namely, that contracting the pupils of his eyes is not something he does, and hence not something he learns to do.

Is the implied distinction valid? If the pupils of someone's eyes contract through something he does how can it reasonably be denied that he contracts them? The experiment is described as one in which a man is enabled 'to obtain voluntary control of what is for most persons an involuntary reflex'. It can reasonably be denied, it was suggested, because contracting them is not something he does 'at will'. What does this mean?

One answer which, it might be thought, could hardly be wrong, is that it means that the immediate cause of their contraction is not his *willing* them to contract. This either gets us nowhere (willing them to contract = contracting them at will) or invites our acceptance of a new concept which has some of the features of the ordinary concept of action but lacks others (for instance, one cannot learn to 'will', or learn which 'acts of will' cause which movements). I reject this invitation, and accordingly say that to say that a person can do something 'at will' is not to say anything positive but is to *deny* that to do it he must do something else. To say that a person can do X at will is to deny that there is something else, Y, he must do if he is to do X, his doing Y being instrumental in his doing X. Thus, if a person can make his hair stand on end, but only by, say, brushing it upwards, he cannot stand it on end at will. And if a person can make the pupils of his eyes contract, but only by shining a light in them, or giving himself a subvocal command, he cannot contract them at will.

66

But has the man who has been conditioned learnt nothing? He may, indeed, have learnt nothing; for it is conceivable that he may not know that giving himself the subvocal command now has the effect that his pupils contract. On the other hand, he may know this, in which case we can say that he has learnt that he can now make his pupils contract in this new way. But he has not learnt to contract them, in the sense of now being able to contract them at will.

To sum up, the process of being conditioned, as it is exemplified in case C, is not itself an instance of someone learning something, either learning to do something, or learning that doing so-and-so brings about such-and-such an effect.

[II]

In the first half of this chapter I have taken conditioning to be a process of stimulus-substitution, whereby a reflex becomes associated with a new stimulus. This led to my giving a negative answer to the question 'Is being conditioned to do something learning to do it?' It would also lead to my giving a negative answer to the question, 'Could we have been conditioned to do the sort of things we have in fact learnt to do?'. But the term 'conditioning' may be used for less restricted processes, such as that sometimes called 'operant' conditioning to distinguish it from 'Pavlovian' or 'classical' conditioning. In this half of the chapter I propose to consider such processes. I shall begin with a very general question. For the question 'Could we have been conditioned, in any sense, to do the sort of things we have in fact learnt to do?' to have an affirmative answer, this very general question must have an affirmative answer. The question is 'Could we have been *caused* to do the sort of things we have in fact learnt to do?'

I want, in particular, to consider an argument for a negative answer to this question, which is based on what philosophers have recently been saying on such related topics as 'intention', 'motivation' and 'free action'. I shall call it the 'Action/Happening' argument, and formulate my own version of it.

Observing a small child occupied with clay and paper and scissors and matchsticks, I may ask 'What is he doing?' This may meet with the reply, 'Can't you see?' The answer to this is that there is a perfectly good sense in which 'what he is doing' may be in doubt when what is to be seen is not in doubt. If we ask him, he might have said 'I'm making a giraffe', but that this was what he was doing may not be obvious even when he has completed his task.

On the other hand, it might be said, I can see what he is doing in that I can see that he is cutting paper with scissors, pushing matchsticks into a lump of clay, etc. (These are things he does which are instrumental to his achieving his aim.)

In the light of what can be seen, it would, of course, be ridiculous to deny that the child was cutting paper with scissors. But it is not difficult to imagine cases in which even a description (in terms of what a person is doing) which seems not to go any way beyond what can be seen, can be false. He may not be doing anything; what we mistakenly interpret as an action may be convulsive, involuntary movements (as in Parkinson's disease), which he may even not know are taking place.

To the question 'What is he doing?' we have so far distinguished three replies. The first is in terms of his aim. He is making a giraffe. The second is in terms of what he is doing to achieve his aim. He is cutting paper with scissors, etc. The third is a denial that he is doing anything. It's Parkinson's disease. A fourth possible reply is in terms of a result of what he is doing in either of the first two senses, but a result to produce which was not his aim. For instance, he is making a mess (unwanted paper on the floor, etc.). Now although it was not his aim to make a mess he may have known that he could not make a giraffe without making a mess. In that case he will be 'morally' as well as causally responsible for the mess. If he did not know he would make a mess we say he made it unintentionally. If he did know he would make a mess we say neither that he made it intentionally nor that he made it unintentionally, but that although he knew he was bound to make a mess that was not his aim.

When animals, and particularly when human beings, are involved, it is natural for us to describe what we see in terms of what they are doing in the first two senses distinguished. In certain circumstances—for instance, when we are giving evidence in a court of law—we may be asked to report only on what we saw happen. It is then that the distinction is brought home to us between what is objectively there to be seen and our interpretation of it in terms of people's aims and what they do to achieve them. The importance of this distinction, in this context, is that two different interpretations may be possible of the same happening, one meaning that the accused person is guilty of an offence, the other that he is not guilty. It is up to the jury, not the people called to give evidence, to decide which interpretation is correct.

The first main point in the 'Action/Happening' argument is that a description of what is to be seen, *qua* happening, may be compatible with either of two incompatible descriptions of what is to be seen, *qua* what a person is doing. Another way of putting this would be to say that the concept of what a person is doing is not a concept of what is publicly observable : the person concerned is the final authority on what he is doing in a way in which no one is the final authority when it comes to what is happening or what is the result of what he is doing. The significance of this for causal explanation is that we know what it is to explain, causally, what happens, but it is not so clear what can be meant by causal explanation of what a person is doing.

One line that might be taken is to say that the causal explanation of someone's making a giraffe is his having the aim of making a giraffe. If this seems to be merely a linguistic device to retain the applicability of the concept of causation, we can talk, not of 'aims', but of 'intentions' or, better still, of 'desires'. He would not have made a giraffe unless he had felt a desire to make one. The point of talking of 'desires' instead of 'aims' is that desires may seem separated from (and therefore possible causes of) actions, in a way aims do not. Desires may even be locatable bodily feelings, as in the case of hunger, the desire for food.

The question is : If we spoke of desires, intentions, or aims as causes of actions, would we be explaining actions as we can explain happenings? This leads to the second main point in the 'Action/ Happening' argument. It is that whereas we can individuate the cause of a happening independently of its effects we cannot do this for the alleged causes of actions. Aims, intentions, and desires are essentially directed to some end, and cannot be individuated independently of that end. Therefore, whatever else they may be, they are not what might be called 'Humean' causes. (Hume held that if C is the cause of E then one cannot say, prior to experience of their conjunction, anything about E from a consideration of C alone.)

Another line that might be taken is to assimilate the question 'What is he doing?' (in the sense in which he is the final authority) to the question 'To what end or goal are the observed changes directed?' (in the sense in which, say, a psychologist with knowledge of psychological 'defence mechanisms' may be better placed than the person in whom the changes are taking place, to answer the question). Once this step is taken, as it has been by those psychologists who speak of 'purposive behaviour', 'goal-directed behaviour', 'means-end-readiness', etc. the report of the person concerned, as to what he is doing, loses its unique significance. An honest report will still be valuable, but it will no longer be regarded as settling the question. The person can be mistaken about what he is 'doing', about what his 'desires' are, and so on.

The advantage of this assimilation is, of course, that broadly the same kinds of explanation can be used for humans as are used for animals. The difference becomes an inconsequential one : to some extent humans know, and can say, to what goals their 'behaviour' is directed. There is an 'epiphenomenon' of consciousness. The disadvantage of the assimilation arises from its being our own actions which are reduced to 'behaviour'. We, as agents, are deposed, deprived of our freedom, made subservient to alien, blind, behaviouristic men, with wants replaced by needs, and private aims by publicly-ascertained goals.

All this having been said we must now return to the question : Is the 'Action/Happening' argument for a negative answer to the question 'Could we have been caused to do the sort of things we have in fact learnt to do?' valid? Attractive though the argument may be, I do not think it is valid. Its seeming validity arises from the equation, in the formulation of the question, of the ability to do something, with doing it. What is acquired by learning is an ability to do something. This is what is meant by talk of someone having learnt to do something. The question is, really, 'Could there be a causal explanation of our having acquired the sort of abilities we have in fact acquired by learning?' Once the question is reformulated in this way, the answer becomes obvious : the fact that an ability is acquired by learning is as compatible with an account being given of the conditions under which it is acquired as would be its being acquired by maturation or in any other way.

Now, to the question 'Could we have been conditioned to do the sort of things we have in fact learnt to do?' we earlier gave the answer 'No, if conditioning is taken to be a process of stimulus-substitution, whereby a reflex becomes associated with a new stimulus, for reflexes are not action.' The answer we have just given to the question 'Could there be a causal explanation of our having acquired the sort of abilities we have in fact acquired by learning?', however, raises the possibility of a different answer. It is: 'Yes, if by our having been conditioned is meant no more than that we acquire the abilities in question under certain conditions, and not under others.' The term 'conditioning' is not used by psychologists in this very wide sense. It is, however, sometimes used in a sense which is less restricted than that in which conditioning is a process of stimulus-substitution. This is the 'operant conditioning' to which I referred earlier. It is called 'conditioning' because of certain features it shares with classical conditioning. In both, responses are 'stamped in' by providing the subjects with things thought of by the experimenter as rewards. Such responses are said to be 'reinforced'. They differ in that in operant conditioning the response is not a reflex, but is a movement initiated by the subject. An example may make this clear. Suppose a hungry animal is in a box which contains no food but does contain three levers which it can press with its feet. On its tour of the box it discovers that these levers can be pressed. When it presses the right-hand one a pellet of food drops from a hole in the roof. When it presses the other two it is given a mild electric shock. After this has happened a number of times the animal goes straight to the right-hand lever (if food has more reinforcing effect than electric shocks).

Operant conditioning is sometimes called 'instrumental' conditioning, but this is a misnomer if it is taken to mean that the subject recognizes either that, or how, its response is instrumental in its obtaining the 'reward'. In so far as the subject does recognize these things, more is involved than simply its being conditioned.

The conclusion to be drawn from this is that if by 'conditioning' is meant *no more than* the 'stamping in' of a response then at least those abilities which do involve 'knowledge that' cannot be acquired by anyone simply by a process of being conditioned. Whether what I earlier called 'purely bodily learning' can be explained in terms of conditioning is another matter. In the example I used to introduce the notion of 'purely bodily learning'—the little girl learning to skip in time with music—there were certain features present (not least of which is that she saw what had to be done, and somebody doing it) which play no part in strict conditioning. How important such features are is a matter to be settled by the scientist, not by the philosopher.

NOTES

1. This phrase, and the account which follows, are taken from E. G. Boring, H. S. Langfeld, and H. P. Weld (Eds.) *Foundations of Psychology* (1948), pp. 44–5.

5

THE CONCEPT OF PLAY
R. F. Dearden

I. INTRODUCTION

'Play', educationalists often assert, 'is a serious business,' though at least on the face of it this is precisely what play is not. Is this perhaps just a deliberately paradoxical way of drawing our attention to the psychological, or even to the metaphysical, significance of play? Certainly there is a mass of psychological theorizing and observation available on this subject, while if we view play as does Froebel, through the spectacles of German Idealist philosophy, then it will be seen to have a metaphysical significance too. And if play can be viewed as having a significance as unexpected as that, then perhaps the assertion of its seriousness is not so much an interesting new fact about it as a moral demand that adults be less casual in the notice which they give to it.

But more puzzlement than this is occasioned in education by play. Parents and even children may be perplexed about it. Having learned from their parents to frame their expectations of school under the aspect of 'work', children are often surprised and sometimes disappointed to find that on going to school at five nothing very different may be expected of them from what they are accustomed elsewhere to regard as 'play'. How could that be appropriate in a school, a place to which one goes in order to be taught? No such perplexity arises where the pre-infant, nursery stage is concerned, since there never was a tradition of 'work' at that stage the memory of which could be the cause of reactionary discontent, and in fact the whole period is regarded by the more traditionally-minded as an educational write-off. Even if the appropriateness of play at the nursery stage is not disputed, the value of it may be. It may be questioned how play could possibly be an *educational process*, and the claim of nursery school mistresses to be 'teachers' may be seriously disputed.

It is plain, therefore, that in thinking about play in relation to education quite a number of puzzling questions raise themselves. For example, in what sense, if any, *could* play properly be called 'serious'? How do the various psychological theories of play relate to our ordinary concept of it? Could it be claimed at all defensibly to have a place in schooling once the nursery stage has been passed? And could the supervision of play possibly be regarded as 'teaching'? But logically prior to all these questions is the conceptual question : What is 'play'? Perhaps if we could get a little clearer about that, then the answer to some of the other questions just raised would be rather more obvious. The first task then must be to try to demarcate and characterize those among our activities that we have in mind when we talk about 'play'.

At first glance, it might seem a simple enough task to say what play is, but anyone who thinks so ought to try it. The Concise Oxford Dictionary gives twenty-four separately numbered sets of entries for the verb alone, and a multitude of idioms has developed round the word. A detailed linguistic inquiry might reveal all sorts of interesting analogies and affinities of one such idiom to another, but that sort of inquiry is no task for the philosopher. What he has to do is to try to pick out as best he can what seems to be the central concept round which these varied shifting meanings circle, and then count himself fortunate if he can set up criteria for the application of this concept which are at least sufficiently precise for his purpose.

2. FACT AND IDEAL

If the concept of play is to be demarcated at all clearly, then we must, to begin with, avoid the tendency which exists in some educational writing to restrict the concept just to those activities which fit into a certain *ideal* of child development. In this respect, 'play' shares with 'growth' a persistent ambiguity in such writing which leaves it always uncertain whether it is children as they are or children as they ought to be who are being described. Hitler grew, and play can be spiteful and destructive, yet clearly when play or growth are eulogized it is neither dictatorship nor nastiness that we are being encouraged to foster. This ambiguity between fact and ideal in the theory of child development has existed there ever since Rousseau launched it with a word which is the very paradigm of ambiguity : the word 'nature'. From Rousseau to the present day, many writers on child development have viewed themselves as describing something called 'education according to nature', or some variant on this such as 'natural learning'.[1] But there are at least three senses of 'nature' being run together when it is said that play is 'natural'.

The first sense is that of being spontaneous: the child bubbles into play activity, it does not have to be prompted in him, and this spontaneous activity is regarded as being naturally good, at least until the child has been corrupted by adults or by his environment. The second sense, especially dear to Rousseau, is that of being opposed to the artificialities of social convention and stems from the view that the simple life of the countryside is the best life for man. Dressing children in hussars' uniforms and regarding them as manikins are far from 'natural' in this sense. The third sense of 'nature' is that of the 'essence' of something. This notion is dominant in Froebel's view of play, where it is part of a metaphysical scheme which has its origins ultimately in Aristotle.[2] It implies a perfection of form towards which something is developing. On this view, living things, including children, are seen as having in themselves the seeds, as it were, of a potential unfolding and perfect flowering. Thus Froebel requires a kindergarten, or 'child-garden', where the essential nature of the child can be unfolded without stunting or distortion, whereas Rousseau describes Emile, at twelve years of age, as seeming (to the non-metaphysician that is) to be just a rough, vulgar little boy, whereas in fact he has unfolded 'the perfection of childhood'.

As a matter of history, children have benefited enormously from this confusion between fact and ideal. Through the reforms thus initiated children's play has come to be seen with fresh eyes, and educational psychology, which cannot get started without there being a prior conception of what is of educational value,[3] has been switched onto the investigation of children's play. But if we are ever to achieve clarity in discussions about play, the confusion between fact and ideal, between children as they actually are and children as we would have them be, must be dispelled. To some extent, the very research inspired by the reformers has itself served to dispel this confusion, especially the study of children's activities which starts from the less optimistic premises of psychoanalytic theory, so that a less value-loaded use of 'natural' is now more common. But to say that play is 'natural', in the sense just of something which can be counted on to appear, does nothing to explicate what is meant by 'play', though it may help to explain the forms which it takes. The upshot of this, therefore, is that the concept of 'play' is not to be equated with an ideal activity ambiguously described as 'natural'. Rough, quarrelsome, destructive, uncreative and unseemly play are all still 'play', and an adequate analysis of the concept must cover such cases quite as readily as others which may evoke in us smiles of approval.

3. CHILDREN'S ACTIVITIES

A useful next step will be to cite some examples of children's play, and to add some examples of activities of other sorts as a reminder that a 'child's interest' is *not* 'all in play', as Caldwell Cook once asserted it to be.[4] For a first example of children's play, we can take make-believe, in which the roles of adults and others are assumed and acted out. Thus children play at schools, mothers and fathers, nurses and patients, and so on. We might call this 'playing at' something or other. A second kind of play, 'playing with', centres round the manipulation of objects rather than acting out people's roles, as in play with sand, water, clay, bricks, soldiers, jig-saws and construction kits. As with role play, so with object play, representation can be as loose or precise as the child wishes. He may be a perfect mimic, or get no further than a crude identification in belief; he may labour to represent in clay with complete fidelity, or be content with a fingered blob. A third kind of play is predominantly physical, as in skipping, climbing, chasing, playing ball-games, skating and scooting. Play such as this may be freely made up or quite extensively rule-governed. Piaget's classic discussion of marbles, and the changing attitudes of children to the rules of the game as they pass through the primary school, illustrates this.[5] These three kinds of play, then, role play, object play and physical play, should provide sufficient examples against which to check any criteria of play which may later be suggested.

But children even of pre-infant school age engage in activities other than play. Increasingly, children like to do some 'work', in the form of helping adults in doing real tasks such as washing up, dusting, shopping and tidying up. Going to school is usually regarded, at least in part, also as 'work'. Work and play, however, do not, contrary to what we might too hastily assume, provide an exhaustive classification of children's activities. Routine activities such as washing, eating, dressing and getting ready for bed are neither work nor play, and neither are involvements in adult social activities, as in visiting, conversing, or 'going out'. Whatever the distinction might turn out to be, therefore, it is clear that there *is* a distinction between play and activities of other sorts, a distinction which, to avoid entanglements over what 'work' is and to avoid the misleading contrast of work with play, we can simply call for the moment that between play and non-play. That, at least, seems a safe distinction.

4. SOME SUGGESTED CRITERIA OF PLAY

In seeking to pick out the criteria implicit in applying the concept of 'play' one is not at a loss for want of precedents, but to review all of the suggestions that have been made would consume far too much time, so that only a few of the more representative and more widely canvassed of them will be considered here. A temptation that can often be found among these suggestions is that of pitching on one particular *sort* of play, or of allowing oneself to be steered by an ideal picture of 'the child' into noticing only those sorts of play that fit into that picture, but two questions need always to be asked of any such suggested criteria. First, are there any other sorts of play in which this feature must clearly be admitted to be absent? If there are, then it cannot be a condition necessary for applying the concept. An example of this mistake would be to suggest that 'play' implies some kind of make-believe, since plainly such forms of play as ball-games do not involve this. Secondly, are there any examples of non-play in which the suggested feature is present? If there are, then it cannot be sufficient for demarcating the concept. An example of this might be the suggestion that 'play' means being overtly active, since cooking and shopping involve overt activity but they are not play.

If we now turn to some actual suggestions that have been put forward, a massive sweeping away of possibilities can be effected right at the start by dismissing all suggestions which look to what children include in their play. It would be useless to wonder whether toys are always involved, for example, because the concept of a 'toy' cannot be explicated in terms of any perceptible properties possessed by an object, but is internally related to the concept of 'play' as being the concept of an object given a play use, whether special or temporary. A hammer may be father's 'tool' at one moment and his son's 'toy' at the next, but the hammer has not changed. Again, if we bracket together all the things that children play at, such as mothers and fathers, tea-parties, schools and so on, and look for some observable feature of behaviour which distinguishes them from the 'real' activities which they represent, we shall not find it, because whether this *is* representation or not is a question of the child's intention, of what he sees himself as doing, and not of the form which the activity takes.

Much more plausible as suggestions, however, are the various 'psychological' criteria of play, one of the most often canvassed of which is 'spontaneity'. A 'spontaneous' activity, in the sense required, seems to be one the origin or shape of which lies in the child's own unsolicited impulse. Such activity 'bubbles' out of children in a manner which is often unpredictable. This criterion, however, certainly could not be sufficient, since non-play activities may also be the objects of such spontaneous attraction. Parents often have to dampen spontaneous willingness to help in the performance of some task, such as painting or weeding, on account of the likelihood of a mess or an accident, while in other cases such spontaneous offers of help may be welcome. But neither is spontaneity a necessary condition, since the origin of play often lies in the suggestion of other children, while in some cases bored children may plead with adults to suggest what they might do. Moreover, the 'shape' of play, far from being spontaneously determined, is often stringently rule-governed, as we have seen. While 'spontaneity' doubtless picks out something which is often present in play, it therefore fails as a criterion for the application of the concept.

Another common 'psychological' approach to characterizing play is in terms of 'absorbed interest'. As Caldwell Cook once asserted: 'To do anything with interest, to get at the heart of the matter and live there active—that is Play.'[6] And it is true that children often do show a concentration and absorption in their play which resents interruption or interference. Such absorbed interest, however, may as readily be shown in non-play, as perhaps in writing a letter or in doing some kinds of school work, so that is cannot be sufficient, while on the other hand not all play is like this, so that it cannot be necessary either. Playing cricket, for example, can be quite boring, and children often play with something just because there seems nothing better to do. Again, the attractive feature in some sorts of play seems to be not so much absorbed interest as the containment of some such emotion as fear or excitement.

'Emotional satisfaction' is another common suggestion. Piaget[7] is in this area when he includes play under 'assimilation', as he calls it, by which he means here an activity orientated towards personal satisfaction rather than towards 'accommodation'. But although such satisfaction often is derived from much play, it is also derived from much else, so that it cannot be sufficient. And furthermore, there are intellectual forms of play, such as word and board games, which involve an exercise of wits rather than any obvious emotion, so that emotional satisfaction does not seem to be necessary either. However, this suggestion is one to which we shall later return.

We now seem to have been driven into the kind of impasse into which Wittgenstein was led in enquiring what it was that all games had in common : board-games, card-games, ball-games, Olympic games, solitary games like patience, ring-a-ring-a-roses and spontaneously made up games like throwing a ball against a wall. It does not seem to be amusement, or contest, or skill, or luck.

> What is common to them all?—Don't say : 'There *must* be something common, or they would not be called "games" '—but *look and see* whether there is anything common to all—For if you look at them you will not see something that is common to *all,* but similarities, relationships, and a whole series of them at that. To repeat : don't think, but look !⁸

To describe this state of affairs, in which there are many overlapping similarities but none overall, Wittgenstein coined the phrase 'family resemblances'. We might say, therefore, that the various activities we call 'play' do show a network of family resemblances, but no *overall* features or similarities. We may be even more strongly tempted to settle for this solution if we recall that not only children but also adults can properly be said to 'play', though adults' games are obviously more formalized and structured than are those of children. What is hopscotch likely to have in common with chess, for example, or bowls with playing at mothers and fathers? Yet we call them all 'play'. Wittgenstein says : 'don't think, but look'. But *looking* at play activities is just what we have been doing, though without much success; so that the suspicion must surely now arise that 'play' is not to be demarcated by looking for some feature present always in play activities, whether something open to immediate view or some felt quality of experience, but by making a move quite different from these usual ones.

5. PLAY AND SOCIAL LIFE

We can start by noticing that children do not have to be taught to play, in the way that they do have to be taught to keep themselves clean. The impulse to engage in activities we should call 'play' is there already, and in that sense is natural. But what children do have to be taught is *which* among their various activities count as 'play' and which do not, and they have to be taught the concept by adults who make the same distinction amongst their own activities. For example, the impulse to dabble with water, to pretend, and to chase need little or no encouragement, but the grouping together of such activities under a single concept labelled 'play', and the implied contrast with activities of other sorts, is an expression of how adults conceive some among the various activities which make up a form of social life. A promising move to make, therefore, would seem to be not to look at play by itself, as we have been doing, but to think of it in relation to social life generally. This is the move that I now want to make and to develop as a positive suggestion.

If we consider the activities which make up by far the largest part of adult life, the typical activities of adults that is to say, then a word which aptly characterizes them is 'serious'. They are serious in the sense that they are engaged in to further some purpose the omission of which would constitute neglect. Such purposes may be dictated by common prudence as being in our own interests, or they may be dictated by obligations and duties deriving perhaps from law, morality, religion or what is customarily regarded as proper to a particular social role. To say that the typical activities of adults are serious in this sense has got nothing to do with laughter or sobriety, or any expression on people's faces, but is an objective *evaluation* of certain activities. Whether particular individuals do or do not treat them as serious, they are serious, and a man who failed to regard them as such would be neglecting either his own interests or those of others. He would be neglecting the ordinary business of living, responsible attention to which is a condition of viability both for individuals and for society as a whole. In many cases a man who trifled here would be said to be 'playing at' whatever it was. In this way we condemn a man for 'playing at politics', or a woman ignores a man's attentions because he is 'only playing', or someone who ought to be getting on with a job is said to be 'playing around' or 'playing about'. A child's socialization largely consists in his being taught to recog-

nize, respect and by degrees to involve himself in these seriously purposeful activities which make up the main business of ordinary
living.

Of course, to say that the judgment of seriousness here is an objective evaluation is not to say that reappraisal is impossible, and a
person who disregarded the ordinary view might not be a trifler but
a person who genuinely disagreed with the usual judgment. Behind
the conception of what is serious in a form of life lies an understanding of ourselves and of our situation, a picture of the nature of reality which may in fact be mistaken in some respects : in thinking that
we have to propitiate the sea before sailing on it safely, or in thinking
that a communal dance is necessary to bring on rain, for example.
Though such activities might be thought to be part of the serious,
they would nevertheless rest on a mistake about people and their
situation. Behind our view as to what is serious, then, lies a picture
of reality which is the background against which our various purposes are pursued, though in a particular society this background is
likely to be so much taken for granted as to escape much remark.

Now the first thing that we can say about play is that the person
who plays does not *regard* his activity as being serious in this objectively evaluative sense. Play is neither the pursuit of purposes dictated by common prudence, nor is it the fulfilling of an obligation to
anybody. We could, therefore, scarcely neglect to play, but, being
free from the demands of the serious, we can do as we please. A
child at the sink, for example, may or may not be playing, depending
on how he regards his activity. If he does just as he pleases, then he
is playing; if he sees what he does as a task, so that not to remove
some egg from a spoon or not to finish would be neglect by the
norms of the task, then he is not playing. The same would be true of
an adult, except that since washing up would normally be a matter
of obligation for him, not taking it seriously would be 'playing' at it
in a condemnatory sense. We may move even further from the
serious, as in make-believe, and free ourselves from what we know
our real situation to be. Of course, even in pretending the real and
the serious are not completely lost sight of,[9] since that would be a
form of madness, but they are temporarily bracketed off and deliberately held in abeyance. A baby who had not yet learned to conceive
of his real situation could not properly be said to play, nor could a
completely autistic child who had no notion of the background
reality against which his activities took place.[10] Play is to be

contrasted with, and presupposes, the serious and the real, so that a child can properly be said to play only in proportion as he becomes aware of these.

Cannot play be serious then? Is it just false to say that 'play is a serious business'? For the moment, let us be content with the following. A boy may take the operation of his model railway or a man may take his golf very seriously indeed. Both may attach great importance to making the correct moves and in the correct order, be in earnest in the attention that he gives, be annoyed if things are not done properly, and so on. Consider the game of chess, for example, and one can clearly see the truth of saying that play may be serious. But the point to be noticed here is that this 'taking it seriously' is itself part of the game, while the game as a whole, considered not from the inside but in its relation to ordinary life, remains non-serious. The seriousness exhibited in play is not that dictated by prudence or obligation. We do not recognize our responsibilities by taking seriously our trains or our golf, or neglect to play at these things. However serious our attitude may be *within* play, objectively the activity remains non-serious in the sense that I have described. We may place ourselves under the spell of the serious as part of the game, but we remain free to break it without neglect either to our interests or to our obligations. If it ceased to be so, and we confused the pretend seriousness of play with the objectively serious, we should have to be reminded or reassured of the true nature of our activity. 'It's only play, you know,' we sometimes have to say to children, or 'It's only a game' to an adult, and the evaluative 'only' here stresses the contrast with the objectively serious. Rather differently, when we hear of Drake continuing with his bowls while the Armada approached, we may well be so perplexed as not to know quite what to think.

There is another way in which the non-seriousness of play can be brought out which derives from the fact that what is serious is not the same from society to society. Of course, if we visited another culture very different from our own we might still be able to recognize some play activities reliably enough, partly because of their overtness and partly because it is unimaginable that they could be serious. But many play activities represent the serious activities of a society, while others derive their content from a particular social tradition of child activity,[11] and these we might well not to be able reliably to recognize until we knew what was regarded as serious in that society. What looked like finger-play or a playful dance might be a religious ritual and therefore serious, while what looked like the purposeful use of an implement might be play with a toy. Such culture-relative play activities could not reliably be identified till we knew which of the forms of the social life concerned were regarded as serious.

Again, we might notice that in the frequent characterization of the activities of young animals as 'play' there seems once more to be implied the contrast between the serious and the non-serious. The serious business for animals includes hunting, feeding, grooming, escape, defence of a territory and so on, whereas young animals are conspicuously free from involvement in such serious activities. Of course, it is only analogies with human social life which are involved here, but the contrast I have been insisting on as distinctive of play does seem to be very clear in the very much simpler lives of animals.

A concept similar in some respects to that of 'play' is the concept of 'dreaming', though of course dreaming is not an activity. What is a dream? Immediately, we recollect particular dreams and try to identify features common to them all, just as we look for something common in all play. But just as there is nothing that could not be played at, so there is nothing that we could not dream.[12] The similarity to the 'serious' or to the 'real' in each case can be conceived of as being as exact as one pleases, so that 'content' will not serve as a criterion of demarcation. We might then shift to 'psychological qualities' and notice that there are indeed, just as in play, similarities often to be found among dreams in their felt qualities, qualities which may even lead the dreamer into the incoherent judgment 'this is a dream'. In the end, however, one is driven to the conclusion that dreams, like play, must be demarcated negatively, perhaps in some such way as that dreams are the experiences which we have while we are not awake, just as play is the activity which we engage in when we are free from the demands of the serious. Play, like dreaming in these respects, might be said to form a separate world.

A further feature of play which now comes into view, as an implication of its non-seriousness, is that it must be self-contained. No constraint is placed on play by a means-end relationship linked with the serious, as there would be in making something useful, or in movement with a purpose beyond the activity itself, and make-believe is still more obviously cut off. Even the rule-structures of games, elaborate as they may be, stand in disconnection from the serious and form no part of the legal system or our moral duty, quite unlike the bye-laws of the building or recreation ground in which the game might be played, or the moral rule of non-injury which would still have to be observed while playing. The only point which the rules of the game have is to make a game.[13] This self-contained character of play is further confirmed by noticing, with Huizinga,[14] that play typically has its special places, times and objects. It has its nurseries, play spaces and play grounds, its play periods with a clear start and finish, its toys and other apparatus. Play stands apart from the web of purposes which make up the serious, and in this sense is self-contained.

But now, if play is cut off from the serious in this way, so that its primary function cannot be to further people's interests, what reason have we to play? People often go to great trouble and expense to provide for themselves or others an opportunity to play, so what could be the reason for that? Whereas in stressing the non-serious and self-contained character of play it is made to seem something negative, as indeed it is in these respects, we now have to notice that the motive for engaging in it is the positive one that it is worthwhile in itself. We play, not thereby to achieve some further purpose or to fulfil some obligation, but just for what is involved in the activity itself. We do it 'for fun' as we say, which at one and the same time suggests both its non-seriousness and its intrinsic satisfactions. This, of course, is the feature of play being concentrated on by people who consider play by itself and suggest spontaneity, absorbed interest or emotional satisfaction as criteria of it. But these features cannot by themselves be sufficient and fall better into place once play has been located on the social map as non-serious and self-contained, for then it follows that its motivation could not be other than intrinsic to the activity itself. We play necessarily for what there is in the activity itself, whether it is the satisfaction of going down a slide, the absorbing interest of chess, the excitement of chasing, the fun of a party, the contained fear of being hunted by a 'lion', the amusement of mimicry, the struggle and possible victory of contest, or the engagement of our intellectual wits as in word games.

Play, then, is a non-serious and self-contained activity which we engage in just for the satisfaction involved in it, and this analysis is confirmed, I think, if one considers each of the three types of children's activities earlier distinguished, role play, object play and physical play, or indeed if one considers the various games which adults play. They are all of them non-serious, in that they have no purpose dictated by prudence, nor do they fulfil any kind of obligation. They are therefore all self-contained, both in having a clear start and finish and in having a point and structure purely internal to them, and as a further implication of their non-seriousness they are all engaged in for the intrinsic satisfactions which they give. Of course, this account of play could be complicated in all sorts of ways, for example by considering what to say of those people who have a professional interest in games, or those who play for the purpose of maintaining health or getting business contacts, but to chase such cases would be merely tedious. When one is trying to get somewhere, one does not pause to explore every lane and sidetrack.

Before leaving the question of what play is, however, something ought to be said about an important class of activities which on the face of it do satisfy the criteria suggested, yet which we should not call 'play'. These activities are the various arts and sciences when they are pursued quite apart from any obvious applications which they may have to the serious business of living. On the face of it, therefore, they could well be non-serious, but a closer look shows this not to be so. Though they often do give satisfaction to those who pursue them, the reason for pursuing them as worthwhile in themselves is rather that they seek to establish or to create something of objective value, whether this is some mathematical proof, scientific law or object of aesthetic merit. They are to be assessed not primarily by the satisfactions which they give, but by impersonal criteria of truth and of merit. Furthermore, though not themselves dictated either by prudence or by obligation, and hence not in that sense serious, they do have a very intimate connection with the serious in that they explore aspects of the conception of ourselves and of our situation which is the background against which our objective evaluations of seriousness are made.[15] They are concerned with the various sorts of 'reality' which are presupposed in asserting the validity of all such judgements.[16] The similarity of these activities to play, therefore, is no more than apparent.[17]

6. 'THEORIES' OF PLAY

The question which we can now go on to ask is where psychological theorizing and observation fit into this, especially in relation to children's play. Such theories have at various times been put forward as that play is a way of preparing for 'life' (the serious), or that it is a way of resolving difficulties and releasing emotions, while the analysts of dreams have seen also in play the sometimes bizarre comments of one mode of experience upon another. Observation of play directed to seeing what kinds of learning take place in it has discovered progress in speech, in co-operation with others, in gaining awareness of one's strengths and capabilities, in gaining familiarity with the physical properties of things, and so on. These, then, are just some of the ways in which psychology bears upon play.

Now commentaries such as these tell us nothing about the *concept* of play; indeed, a knowledge of the 'meaning' of play, in this conceptual sense of 'meaning', is a presupposition and not the outcome of these inquiries. It is not the concept of play which is observed, theorized about and reported upon, but the particular things done by children at play. If it were otherwise, then the vast majority of language-users, who know nothing of theories of play, would be uttering a senseless noise in using the word at all, and furthermore it is hard to see how the theorist himself would have as his initial datum a *class* of activities to theorize about. Since our inquiry so far has been concerned with the *concept* of play, it is therefore not to be upset by any findings of psychology about the particular things done by children at play.

A second point about these observations and theorizings is that they tell us nothing of what children 'do', in the sense of 'do' in which a person knows what he is doing. For example, if we asked a child with a doll what she was 'doing', an appropriate reply might be 'feeding her', 'changing her clothes', 'telling her she has been naughty', and so on. If, however, she replied that she was 'preparing for motherhood', 'learning the role of mother' or 'effecting a therapeutic release of aggression', we should not only be staggered at the precocity of her language but forced to conclude that this was not play at all, since consciously preparing for life and deliberately sought therapy both fall under the aspect of the serious. The theorist, then, not only tells us nothing of what is meant by 'play', but he tells us nothing of what children are aware of doing in playing. What he does tell us something about is the *function* of play in growing up, and this distinction between what is meant by 'play' and what children see themselves as doing on the one hand, and what an intelligent observer perceives to be the function of their play on the other, is crucially important in trying to clear up some of the confusions which were mentioned at the outset. Something more must therefore be said about an observer's description of the function of play.

When we consider the 'function' of something, we are considering what is effected or brought about by it, but this may be viewed in at least three ways. We may be considering what *ought* to be brought about, or what people *think* is brought about, or what is *in fact* brought about, and these three do not always coincide. For example, perhaps the function of a particular priest ought to be to minister to his flock, whereas he thinks of his job in terms of providing himself with a comfortable living, while a Marxist observer sees it as in fact diverting social discontents from their proper object. Where play is concerned, the psychologist is like the Marxist in this example. He does not regard play as the child himself or the ordinary adult does, but detects in it various kinds of unsuspected and non-obvious functional significance, such as its therapeutic function and its learning function. What has to be especially noticed here is that the effect of this is partially to undercut the non-seriousness implied by the concept. Play, it was suggested, is an activity engaged in when our attention is released from the serious, and this must remain true if theorists are to be left with a distinguishable activity to theorize about. But the functional significance of play revealed by the theorist puts it in a quite different light as being, from *his* point of view, indeed 'a serious business'. Whether play is viewed therapeutically, or in terms of learning, or even as the first act in Froebel's metaphysical drama of unfolding,[18] it is then seen by the *observer* as serious.

It is this new dimension of seriousness revealed by the theorist which produces such paradoxes as that 'play is a serious business', or that 'play is the child's work'. Such a result is not uncommon when a concept antedates psychological discoveries relevant to its application. For example, 'responsibility' and 'punishment' are other concepts which have been made uncertain in their application in this way. While theorists tell us nothing of what 'play' means, therefore, or of what children are conscious of doing, what they do reveal is something about the unsuspected functions of play, functions which link it with the serious in such a way as to place adult observers of it under an obligation in regard to it, for neglect suitably to provide for it could have results which must, on already existing assumptions, be regarded as harmful. This, of course, is to take it for granted that the theories and observations concerned are true, a question on which a philosopher may not be competent to decide. But taking this for granted, I want now to turn to consider, in the light of its functional significance, play as a possible educational process.

7. PLAY AND EDUCATION

If a parent thinking of sending a child to a nursery school knows only that children 'play' there, then the activities of the nursery school are smartly marshalled under the non-serious. Why should anyone go to the trouble or expense, it might be thought, of arranging for children just to 'play', when they can do that perfectly well elsewhere, in the garden, street, or park for example? Various answers could be given to this, such as that in a well-run nursery children are safe and their health is looked after, that there are many opportunities to work out personal difficulties and to achieve some sort of balanced emotional development, that children learn to talk to each other freely, to share, co-operate, help others and so on. Above all, it might be said, a child who goes to a nursery has a greater chance of being secure and happy. But while each of these things that have just been mentioned is very important, and nothing that I shall say will minimize its importance, it is not education. The concept of 'education' does indeed imply, as Professor Peters has shown,[19] some kind of improvement, but not any kind of improvement. Certainly seeing that children develop safely, in good health, without unsolved emotional difficulties and in happy interaction with other children is a commendable function for anyone to perform, and certainly many kinds of improvements may take place under such a regime, but there is nothing specifically educational here. There is nothing here which is even aimed at later achieving the kind of cognitive perspective, or building up of a differentiated understanding, which is one criterion for picking out a process as being educational.[20] And indeed where a good many nurseries are concerned, such as those run by health authorities or by private individuals, there is no claim to be doing anything specifically of educational value, unless perhaps it is that a good basis for later making a start at educating children is being laid.

In some nurseries, however, play is regarded in such a way as to lay claim to being thought of as an educational process; the staff regard themselves as teachers and the institution itself is regarded as a school. Not all nurseries are or claim to be nursery schools, but these do. An objection that might immediately be made to this is that there is little or no set instruction given in such institutions, so how can the staff be regarded as teachers? The answer to this is that the concept of 'teaching' is much wider than that of 'instructing', which implies an imparting or telling of what is to be learned. 'Teaching' leaves it open how learning will be brought about, the only restrictions placed on possible forms of teaching being derivative from what it is to learn some particular thing. For the staff of a nursery school to claim to be 'teachers', therefore, it is by no means necessary that they should give set instruction in anything: many other forms of teaching remain open to them, such as arranging carefully selected activities, asking leading questions, commenting on things being done and making suggestions about them, and so on.[21] It is really very easy to show that the staffs of such schools could be said to 'teach', therefore. But once again, not all teaching by any means is educational, so that to show that nursery school teachers are indeed teachers does not imply that they educate, or that play is an educational process. Teaching someone to tie his shoe-laces, for example, is useful, but hardly scores as an educational success.

For the play activities which are arranged in a nursery, or indeed in an infant school, to be regarded as specifically educational, and not just useful, therapeutic, or happiness-producing, it would have to be shown that they are continuous with the development of the kind of differentiated understanding which has been referred to as giving 'cognitive perspective' to one's experience. And since it is no accident that such a development is what is to be sought during the more formal schooling which follows the nursery stage, we can say that if the activities of the nursery are to be regarded as educational, then they must be continuous with what is to be sought in later schooling, and not just arranged with an eye to health and safe amusement. Guided in that way by a directional framework of values formed with an eye on what is to follow in later schooling, and guided by a theoretical knowledge of how play can be so arranged as to have this learning function, the adults who supervise such play would indeed be teachers and would also have arranged an educational situation. The learning which it is the function of such play to develop may be more chancy than in the more familiar instructional setting common in formal schooling, but it is much less chancy and unselected than is what is learned in unsupervised play, or play supervised by adults who lack the requisite theoretical knowledge to be aware of the possible educational functions of it. But of course, I have only described how things would have to be for the play activities of a nursery to be regarded as educational; whether any particular institution satisfies this description is a further question which only knowledge of that institution would enable one to answer.

In conclusion, however, it must be said that it is doubtful whether much of *substantial* educational value could be learned by a process of unconscious 'picking up' during play activities. So much of school learning must be more deliberate than that, in requiring practice, for example. This is not to say that all activity which could *properly* be called play ought quite suddenly to cease in school at, say, six years of age, but that by then it should be gradually giving way to activities which children themselves regard as serious, and therefore not as play. Such activities may well be interesting and enjoyable, but to call them 'play' is to fail to take children as seriously as they are then coming to take themselves, and it is unnecessarily to invite the hostility of adults to what are in fact enlightened methods of setting about the serious business of education.

NOTES

1. Other variants are discussed in Hardie, C. D., *Truth and Fallacy in Educational Theory* (1942), Ch. 1.

2. Popper, K. R., *The Open Society and its Enemies* (1945), Vol. 2, Ch. 11.

3. Best, E., 'Common Confusions in Educational Theory' in *Philosophical Analysis and Education* (1965), ed. Archambault, R. D.

4. Caldwell Cook, H., *The Play Way* (1917), p. 3.

5. Piaget, J., *The Moral Judgement of the Child* (English Edn. 1932).

6. Caldwell Cook, H., op. cit., p. 9.

7. Piaget, J., *Play, Dreams and Imitation in Childhood* (Eng. trans. 1951).

8. Wittgenstein, L., *Philosophical Investigations* (1953), Sect. 66.

9. Austin, J. L., 'Pretending' in *Proceedings of the Aristotelian Society* (1956–7).

10. Cf. Kenny, A., *Action, Emotion and Will* (1963), pp. 42–3 on the possible impropriety of attributing to babies emotions such as fear or love.

11. Opie, I. and Opie, P., *Lore and Language of Schoolchildren* (1959).

12. Descartes, *Meditations*, Ch. 1.

13. Toulmin, S. E., *The Place of Reason in Ethics* (1950), Ch. 6, Sect. 6.

14. Huizinga, J., *Homo Ludens* (English edn. 1949).

15. Peters, R. S., *Ethics and Education* (1966), Ch. 5.

16. On this use of 'reality' see Toulmin, S. E., op. cit., Ch. 8.

17. Cf. Oakeshott, M., 'The Voice of Poetry in the Conversation of Mankind' in *Rationalism in Politics* (1962), pp. 197–202.
18. Froebel, F., *The Education of Man* (1826).
19. Peters, R. S., op. cit., Ch. 1.
20. Peters, R. S., ibid.
21. On the ways in which a teacher can give this kind of informal guidance see for example, Gardner, D. E. M. and Cass, J. E., *The Role of the Teacher in the Infant and Nursery School* (1965).

6

RULES AND ROUTINES
Max Black

I take it for granted that education consists in large part of a sustained effort to generate capacities for skilful performance. Even 'theoretical knowledge' of facts and principles, if it is to be of any value, must be manifested in certain modes of activity. All education aims, in the first instance, at 'know-how'.

Two distinct ideals of intelligent and skilful performance have an immediate appeal. The first is of graceful, free-flowing, action unimpeded by self-conscious reference to instructions. One thinks immediately of the natural movements of animals—but also of certain exercises of high skill: Menuhin's playing the violin as if it were as easy as breathing. Action of this kind gives an impression of freedom from conscious effort or calculation: the musician 'loses himself in the music', though with intense control and awareness. A contrasting ideal is of deliberate calculating action according to an articulated program. An example might be a mathematician expounding a formal proof in public, with each step explicitly defended by cited reasons. Absence of ease and grace in such a performance is compensated by a high degree of 'rationality'. 'Free-flowing' activity, at its best, looks like a dance: 'rational' activity, at its worst, like drill.[1]

The antithesis between 'dance' and 'drill', between free-flowing and calculated action is too vague to have much value as a guide to education. Instead of pursuing it, I shall try to take a hard look at a particular type of 'calculated action', characterized by the presence of governing *rules*. My object is to become somewhat clearer than I now am about the nature and the educational significance of such 'rule-governed action'.

1

Consider the differences between two familiar activities: doodling (D) and completing an income tax form (F). Both may be intentional and voluntary, but seem to have almost nothing else in common. About F, we can say the following things, none of which are true of D:

(1) It makes sense to say of one of the steps taken in F that it was a *mistake*, or that it was *wrong*.

(2) Nobody can be regarded as doing F unless he would treat certain entries as mistakes, and would try to *correct* them.

(3) Each step in F has an *intrinsic reason*,[2] which can be offered as an explanation, clarification, or defence of what he is doing.

(4) Nobody can count as doing F unless he treats as obvious reasons that justify what he is doing.

(5) It makes sense of a particular instance of F to say that it is *unfinished* or incomplete.

(6) In order to be doing F, the agent must have the completion of the task as an end in view.

(7) Anybody doing F must know *how to do it*, which implies that he could do F on other occasions and could show another person how to do it.

(8) To do F is to make repeated reference to the *instructions* for doing F, each of them being treated as an injunction to be followed, 'obeyed'.

Now it would be absurd to say of a doodler, that he had made a wrong stroke, was trying to correct it, had a good or bad reason for doing it that way, had left the doodle unfinished, knew how to teach doodling, or was following instructions for doodling.[3] To doodle is to do as one pleases, in the spirit of the Abbey of Theleme, under the sole sway of pleasure; but to follow instructions, as in F, is to enter the realm of right-and-wrong, justification by reasons, standards of completeness, and built-in generality of procedure—in short to behave rationally.

Completing an income tax form is a perspicuous instance of *rule-invoking* (or explicitly rule-governed) action. In the only sense that needs consideration here,[4] a rule is a *general instruction*, expressed in a formula that states *what is to be done* in order to achieve some stated or understood end in view. A standard formula for such a rule is: 'In order to arrive at E, do $A1$ $A2$ . . . . , in such-and-such a sequence and in such-and-such combinations.' A rule is a recipe for a designated achievement.

Of the eight features of rule-invoking action listed above, the last encompasses all the others. For instance, following the rule in question is necessarily being ready and able to treat some acts as mistaken (point 2): the rule defines classes of actions that are correct *according to the rule* and there is no logical gap between obeying the rule and obeying the rule correctly.[5] On the other hand, none of the first seven points separately, nor all of them together, suffice to define rule-invoking action. A man may do something wrong because he fails to respond correctly to a specific command (*not* a rule!); my reason for drinking may be that I am thirsty, but it would be perverse to insist that I am following a rule, and so on. Even a man whose actions conform to all seven of the points, need not be regarded as rule-governed in his behaviour.

What, then, is it to *obey* a rule explicitly invoked?

2

Of course, the rule must be understood and the agent must try to do as the rule prescribes. Is there anything more? Must we suppose some distinctive act of 'obedience' intervening between understanding and acting? In general, not. Cases where an agent reads a recipe, hesitates, says aloud 'I'll use it,' and then proceeds to do so might plausibly be regarded as including distinctive acts of 'obedience'. But this is unusual. Very likely, the cook reads the recipe and at once starts arranging the ingredients for a Dundee cake without any intervening act of recipe-adoption. *Obedience to the rule is shown by trying to do as instructed.* If this were not so, somebody could read the instructions, do exactly as he was told (with repeated reference to the explicit instructions) and still be able to claim that he 'simply chose to do what the recipe required' without really obeying it. The claim would be absurd : here actions really do speak louder than words and their force cannot be cancelled by a protest or a mental reservation.

Knowing how to respond to a rule *as a rule* is something that has to be learned : it is not a natural aptitude like breathing, but a distinctively human mode of behaviour. The practice of giving and receiving rules involves a complex pattern of demands, objections, claims, and defences, that we overlook only because we were initiated into it so long ago. It is no more 'natural' than the practice of playing games according to fixed rules. (We can easily imagine human beings unable to understand what it is to play conventional games; a human society lacking the 'practice' of rule-giving admittedly strains the imagination.) This prior initiation and training, itself not induced by rule-invocation, makes it possible for an agent to *obey* a rule.[6]

It is this earlier training, not some distinctive act of 'obedience', that is essential for *following* a rule.[7]

This view of the matter has an important consequence. Participation in the rule-giving-and-receiving practice depends, as in all human institutions, upon a general presumption of *justifiable trust*. Unless rule-givers were usually trustworthy and rules for the most part 'worked', there could be no viable institution of rule-using. (For the same reasons, if adults lied to their children, irresponsibly and unsystematically, most of the time, the children could never learn to talk.)

The general presumption of trust generates more specific presumptions concerning presented rules. It is impossible (logically impossible, I think) for anybody to follow an instruction, *qua* rule of action, while thinking it detrimental to the end in view. If, so thinking, he performs the acts prescribed, he is transforming the rule into a rule for for another purpose—or into something other than a rule. Sceptical as I am about the accuracy of cook books, I can still *follow* a recipe for haggis for want of a better alternative. But if I think the printed recipe will produce only a nasty inedible mess, I cannot *accept* it as a rule for making haggis. (If I 'go through the motions', my motive may be curiosity, the desire not to offend a Scotch friend, or something else; I am then 'obeying' the rule only in some Pickwickian sense.) Obedience to a rule demands *some* confidence in the rule-giver.

No teacher needs to be told that the requisite confidence—the *consent of the taught*, as we might say—is often lacking: the child, acting under duress, does not really think that Teacher is usually right, or that the instructions thrust upon him really 'work' (too often they don't!). The intended instructions are then responded to as *orders* or commands, to be obeyed (in another sense of that word). The task changes into that of 'passing the test'—or, more generally, 'satisfying Teacher'. This, too, is education of a sort—education in how to coexist with arbitrary authority.

3

Rules, general instructions, purport to specify *good* ways to approach stated or assumed objectives (ends in view). A given rule may be defective in two distinct ways: by leading away from the end in view or by being unsuitable for use—roughly speaking, by being misdirected or by being inefficient. Similarly for other instruments: a hammer may be a poor one because it is too flimsy to drive nails home, or else because it is too heavy to be handled. The apocryphal rule for counting sheep by adding the number of feet and dividing by four is not misdirected, but is plainly inefficient. Let us call a rule that is not misdirected, that does prescribe actions conducive to the end in view, *right*; and a rule that is both right and efficient a *good* one. The goodness of rules is plainly a matter of degree.

Overlooking the vagueness in the notions of rules being 'right' or 'efficient', we can say that a question about the goodness of a given rule is determinable, in principle, by appeal to logic or to matters of fact. We can *prove* that hugging the wall of a maze will eventually lead to an exit; but it is a matter of experience that bread stays fresh in a refrigerator. Whether a rule is good is a cognitive issue, demanding knowledge, not decision or commitment. That is why rules can be freely adopted, when taken to be right and efficient, with no ultimate reliance upon authority. Given a chosen end in view and determinate skill, the rule's credentials are, in the end, rooted in the nature of the external world. Hence the step from a rule ('something to be done') to a corresponding principle ('the way things are') may need only a change of grammatical mood.

There is, to be sure, a certain duplicity in rules. The imperative mood in which they are naturally formulated suggests some external source whose special knowledge or expertise lends weight to the rule, giving it something of the force of recommendation, piece of advice, or even an order. ('Do such-and-such, because *I* say so, with proper authority.') Indeed, the practical point of obeying rules issuing from another is to relinquish initiative and responsibility for the time being. While I follow the recipe, my role as agent shrinks to the simpler and more passive one of *doing as I am told*—as if an experienced chef stood at my elbow. My interest shifts from the primary task of baking a cake to the secondary one of correctly following instructions, which is so much easier.[8] I act upon authority—and wish to. But such submission is, in the long run, wholesome only if eventually subjected to criticism. Sooner or later, provisional submission to the authority of rules must be tested by logic and against the facts. As justice must not only be done, but must be *seen* to be done, so also the goodness of rules (in any educational programme aspiring to be rational) must in the end be *shown*—and not indefinitely assumed by an act of trust.

4

A man who deliberately obeys, 'invokes', a rule can cite that rule as a *reason* for his action; one who blindly follows a routine, behaves regularly, cannot offer a reason of that kind—and may be able to offer no reasons at all. ('Why are you taking the walking stick?' 'Because I want to!' That tells us nothing : we know that he was not taking it inadvertently.)

Reasons for actions are typically offered in order to defend or to justify the actions; to render them intelligible; or to amplify their descriptions, by reference to intention, motive or purpose. In performing such meta-activities (as they might be called), the rule-invoking agent has intellectual resources unavailable to somebody performing superficially similar actions, routinely, blindly, 'out of mere habit' or even 'unaware'. Let us say, for short, that rule-invoking-action is potentially and distinctively *self-critical*. (By 'self-criticism' I mean the processes of justification, explanation and verbal elaboration already alluded to.) Paradoxically, the constraints imposed by adherence to a rule are balanced by greater scope and freedom to act at the 'meta'-level. (This is why metamathematics demands *formalized* object-languages; and also why a sonnet in traditional form is easier to criticize than a piece of free verse.)

Reasons can render actions intelligible. When we say, of another's action, 'We don't know what he is doing' or, sometimes, more explicitly, 'We don't *understand* what he is doing', we can sometimes be enlightened by a statement of the agent's reasons and their supposed connection with his end in view. Given the rule invoked— if there is such a rule—we can make immediate sense of what is being done, whatever our ultimate reservations about the goodness of the rule employed. Conversely, where rule-connected reasons cannot be given, because the behaviour in question is a blind routine, *this* mode of understanding is excluded—although causal explanation may still be available.[9]

Now apply this to a man's view of his own action. If invoking a rule, he understands up to a point precisely what he is doing—that is, treating the given rule as defining a good procedure for achieving an accepted end in view. But when a man's behaviour is blind routine, there is an important sense in which he does not know *what* he is doing, or *why* he is doing it. This need not be discreditable if there is nothing to explain, nothing to understand; but is generally taken to be so, in moderation, where reasons might be given, by reference to an appropriate rule. A man unable to supply reasons when appropriate reasons are available falls short of acting with full rationality. The tie between rule-governed behaviour and rationality goes far to explain and to justify educational emphasis upon such behaviour.

5

I have been using the expression 'rule-invoking action' to apply, in the first instance, to episodes in which attention is paid to printed or written instructions. It is natural to include under the same rubric the analogous cases in which the agent *recites* the rule to himself, aloud or 'in his head'. A rule thus recited may be remembered as issuing from some authority—or may simply have been discovered by the agent himself. These new cases are clearly 'rule-governed'.

Less clear, but in some ways more interesting, are actions satisfying most of the criteria for rule-invocation listed in Section 2 above, but in which there is no discernible explicit reference *to* any rule. A man who can still remember how to solve quadratic equations, as he was taught to do in school, does not perform the task with an open Algebra book at his elbow, nor is he heard to mutter 'Must do this; then do that . . . ' Indeed either of these would indicate imperfect mastery of the relevant rule of procedure, would be a sure sign that the rule had not fully entered into *his own possession*.

The well-taught solver of quadratic equations should have little trouble in formulating the controlling rule of procedure upon demand. But if he has trouble in describing his procedure, we may be able to do it for him. In either case, if all goes well, he will immediately *accept* the verbal formulation : he will say perhaps, 'Yes—that is what I was doing all along!' Solving the equation is a very clear case of what I propose to call *rule-accepting* action. For paradigm instances of rule-acceptance, it is essential that the correct formulation of the rule seem obvious (and hence easy to find) and that once formulated it will be accepted unhesitatingly by the agent himself. The harder it is to formulate the rule, and the more reluctant the agent is to receive it, the less inclined we ought to be to treat the episode as a clear case of rule-acceptance.

There is a deliberate ambiguity in the label 'rule-accepting', between 'accepting the rule *all along*' and 'accepting the rule *retroactively*'. I think there is no harm in it. Some writers would speak of 'implicitly rule-governed action' and of 'subconscious' or even 'unconscious' awareness of the rule. The accompanying imagery of the rule concealed in the wings, waiting to be brought before the footlights of consciousness—out of sight, but not out of mind, as it were—is admissible if not taken too seriously.[10] However we choose to think about this, we shall need to grant the following points: (1) rule-accepting action, prior to its verbal articulation, already possesses most of the interesting features of rule-invoking action (correction of 'mistakes', etc.); (2) it can readily be transformed[11] into potentially rule-invoking behaviour by supplying the rule; (3) once this is done, the full resources of the self-critical 'meta-activities' become available to the agent himself.

6

What shall we say, now, about actions manifesting many of the distinctive features of 'rule-governed behaviour' in which, however, the agent *cannot* formulate the rule and cannot or will not accept the verbal formula supplied by another? Take the case of a man riding a bicycle, without conscious effort or more than peripheral awareness of what he is doing. Professor Michael Polanyi has provided what he calls 'the rule observed by the cyclist',[12] but his formulation occupies ten lines and contains reference to such technical notions as 'angle of unbalance', 'square of the speed' and 'inverse proportionality'. Obviously, the ordinary cyclist could not even understand the rule—and, if he did, would be unable to follow it (as Polanyi himself points out).

This type of case needs to be sharply distinguished from those already discussed. If we call such action *rule-covered,* as I would propose, we ought to take that to mean only that an outside analyst can give a certain kind of description of it—can view it *sub specie regulae*, as it were. This kind of verbal articulation is of no value, by way of 'self-criticism', to the agent himself, although it may have considerable importance elsewhere. (If we want to simulate rule-covered action by machines, we need to formulate the rule, in order to supply the machine with a programme. In general, many logically equivalent programmes could be contrived. If we thought of the human agent as '*really* following *one* of these programmes', we would have the embarrassment of choosing among equivalent rules, none of which the agent himself would accept.)

Rule-covered behaviour, as defined above, is easily confused with cases in which the agent's justified refusal to adopt a proposed 'articulation' is due to inadequacy of the language of description.

Consider the following illustration. A beginner's book on chess might contain the rule : 'A Knight moves from one corner of a rectangle composed of three squares by two to the diagonally opposite corner, if that square is unoccupied, without regard for any other pieces in that rectangle.' In moving a Knight, a very slow-witted learner might perhaps be heard reciting this clumsy formula; a somewhat brisker chap might be observed using a finger to trace out a 3 by 2 rectangle and checking that the diagonally opposite square is empty before moving. (In our terminology, the first action would be 'rule-invoking', the second 'rule-accepting'.) But anybody who *had* to do either of these things would never make much of a chess player. If all goes well, a kind of *phenomenological compression* of the original formula occurs: a reduction to essentials, as it were. The player comes to *see* the target square as available for the Knight —and, indeed, at the same time, to see the other available squares, arranged in a constellation of related positions. (The 'assimilation' of the original formula demanded may require hard work and much practice, with varying degress of success. Even with experienced players, 'blindness' to possibilities is not uncommon.) The phenomenological prominence of the target-square now functions as a criterion, and the criteria embodied in the original formula may be so effectively suppressed that 'verbal articulation' may be disconcertingly difficult. (Consider how easy it may be to tie a reef knot—and how hard to say *what* one does.)

In such cases, the agent's resistance to a proposed articulation (which usually looks absurdly complex) may arise from his use of a private symbolism of visual cues, that has ousted the public and official terminology of the original instructions. Such symbolism is not 'private' in the philosopher's technical sense of unintelligibility in principle to another. The structuring of a chess player's visual field, at which I have hinted, might be shown in a 'public' diagram —for instance, in a film of a lone Knight on a chessboard, upon which the 'target squares' are suddenly made 'prominent' (by being brought into relief by being outlined, changing colour, etc). If such a non-verbal diagram were correctly understood, it would serve the function of the 'verbal articulation' in rule-accepting behaviour. I shall speak in such cases of *rule-guided action*.

Rule-guided action, that is appropriately articulated by non-verbal symbolism, and the intuitive transformation or 'condensation' that makes it possible, seems to me of fundamental importance to educational method. (In spite of the efforts of Gestalt psychologists, it is still an unjustly neglected field of research.) It is connected in the most intimate way with the learner's necessary effort to impose a memorable order upon what looks initially like a chaos of unrelated items.[13] Whatever the topic—a mathematical proof, the conjugation of a verb, the salient features of the Industrial Revolution—the data must be 'rendered down', simplified, structured, if they are to be assimilated, remembered and properly used. Only in this way does '*the* rule' for achieving something become '*my* rule'.

8

Much of my discussion has turned, one way or another, upon the possibility of a verbal formulation of a rule. It may be as well, therefore, to consider certain fundamental limitations upon such 'articulation'. (I shall neglect some obvious practical limitations arising from lack of skill on the part of teacher or learner.)

The first limitation may be introduced by as trivial an example as that of somebody knitting a scarf. Whether or not the knitter resorts to printed instructions, *we* can certainly articulate a governing rule : say 'Knit plain and purl for a hundred stitches, then turn and continue' (call this formula A). Now the correct application of formula A is itself a rule-governed activity which might be articulated by another formula, B say, explaining how to make 'plain' and 'purl' stitches, and so on. (Cf. the 'Instructions' sometimes appended to official forms, telling one how to do what one has been told to do!) Could one then not envisage a further formula, C, articulating the mode of application of B, and so on without end?

The infinite regress that threatens here is factitious. The chain of rules will quickly terminate, for want of an adequate vocabulary. The nearer we come to what is readily *seen* by an apt learner, the harder it becomes to articulate the governing rule and a point is soon reached at which the effort of attending to the verbal formula positively interferes with the primary performance. (Try saying *what* you are doing while knitting—or while running downstairs.)

Of course, sensible men soon abandon *saying* in favour of *showing* : however hard it may be to teach knitting by example, it is incomparably harder to do so by talking about it.

This point can be generalized : successful use of articulated rules presupposes mastery of skills (rule-governed performances) not controlled by *explicit* rules. Hence, 'practice' must precede the critical activity of rule formulation. Only in this way can the intellectual and educational values of rule-formulation be realized : without the prior foundation of more or less 'blind' practice and experience, the rules degenerate into sterile verbalism.

9

I have tried to perform a preliminary survey—rough, but serviceable—of the complex notion of 'rule-governed behaviour'. One moral I would like to draw is that the learner and the teacher are never faced with a stark choice between blind, unconscious, mastery ('rule-covered behaviour' or the even more primitive outcome of 'conditioning') and self-conscious adherence to explicitly formulated principles ('rule-invoking behaviour'). Between these extremes, we have been able to discern types of intelligent and skilful performance ('rule-accepting' and 'rule-guided' behaviour), which combine the virtues of 'free-flowing' and 'prescribed' behaviour. Here, ideally, there is no longer any conflict between the two ideals I invoked at the outset, and submission to the discipline of rules, freely adopted, becomes indistinguishable from the freedom of self-realization.

In working for this ideal harmony, a good teacher will be sensitively alert to the supreme importance of timing—the rhythm of alternation between the different modes of action. He will not shrink from brute conditioning, to lay a necessary foundation of primitive habits of response. But unless he wants his pupils to be no better than trained circus animals, he will try, at the right time, to change blind response into self-directed control by justified rules. He will be willing to break down primitive habits by analysis and criticism, if only for the sake of ultimately inducing higher levels of performance. (The ideal cycle, indefinitely repeated, will be from 'rule-covering behaviour' to 'rule-invoking behaviour' and then to 'rule-accepting behaviour' and 'rule-guided' behaviour.)

There are, alas, no firm rules for what is 'the right time'. Rules are defeasible, hedged about with *ceteribus paribus* clauses to be applied at the discretion of their users. But there are no useful rules for the application of discretion, tact or judgment. A sub-title for this essay might have been 'In Defence of Rules and Principles'. I have hoped it might be read by those who will know that there is a time for throwing rule-books away.

NOTES

1. But consider the following description : 'A moment before they had been swaying drunk. The touch of arms sobered them : they went through the manual from A to Z before us perfectly. More than mechanically perfect it was : a living, intelligent pattern and poem of movement' (T. E. Lawrence, *The Mint,* Jonathan Cape, 1955, p. 186). Drill *can* have the aesthetic grace of a 'dance'.

2. I shall not try to define this. If asked why I am entering my age on the form, I should be giving an intrinsic reason if I said 'Because the instruction asks for it.' An extrinsic reason would be : 'Because I am afraid of the penalty for omission.'

3. This must not be taken too literally, of course. One can, more or less playfully, treat even doodling as a kind of task. But the artificiality is patent.

4. Further discussion of the concept of a rule is to be found in Chapter 6 of my *Models and Metaphors* (Ithaca, N.Y., 1962).

5. This is an important reason why imputation of rule-governed behaviour involves the presence of more than mere irregularity of behaviour. Sometimes I push at a door marked 'push', sometimes not; I may or may not take my walking stick when I go for a stroll. Both types of deviation from simple regularity might be predictable by some causal theory. What distinguishes the first from the second as 'rule-governed' is the way in which the agent *treats* the deviation. If I curse when I realize I have left the stick behind, insist on going back for it, etc. that is *some* evidence that I am conforming to a rule.

6. If the reader thinks that reference to prior initiation into the 'practice' shifts the burden of conceptual clarification without disposing of it, I would agree. Much more needs to be done by way of clarifying the nature of the practice.

7. I have no space to discuss *disobedience* to rules (a mode of behaviour of some interest to teachers). It may be enough to make the obvious point that disobedience or violation implies a kind of weak recognition of the rule : you cannot break a rule (in the primary sense of 'break') without knowing what the rule is and understanding its pretensions to validity. The innocent can misbehave, but cannot break rules. It is tempting, but mistaken, to say that the violator stands the rule on its head, replacing it by an opposed rule, on the principle of 'Your right

shall be my wrong'. But rule-breaking need not be done to rule (wrong-doing need not be principled): the rule can simply be ignored (suppressed, forgotten.) Active and principled disobedience is a backhanded kind of tribute paid to the rule by the rule-breaker.

8. The consequent division and deflection of attention may have something to do with the jerky, angular or monotonous rhythm of *prescribed* behaviour, that is so much despised by admirers of the free-flowing and spontaneous. Deflected attention has obvious dangers: it is all too easy to get too interested in the recipe and to forget about the cake. Any schoolroom can provide examples.

9. Reasons may be given, sometimes, for intentional or purposive action that is not rule-governed. This is too large a topic to be pursued here.

10. If the reader is strongly inclined to think that the conception of implicit or sub-conscious obedience *must* be right, let him consider the following. My regular practice of washing in the morning is *as if* I were obeying a command. Am I to be taken as obeying an implicit *command*?

11. Verbal articulation will *change* the performance, in subtle or massive ways. Indeed its main point will often be to correct and to improve the performance.

12. Michael Polanyi, *Personal Knowledge* (London, 1958), p. 49.

13. See, for instance, Polanyi's discussion of 'the kind of topographic knowledge which an experienced surgeon possesses of the regions on which he operates' (op. cit., p. 89). It seems to me unduly pessimistic to call such knowledge 'ineffable'.

7

TEACHING AND TRAINING
Gilbert Ryle

I have no teaching tricks or pedagogic maxims to impart to you, and I should not impart them to you if I had any. What I want to do is to sort out and locate a notion which is cardinal to the notions of teaching, training, education, etc. about which too little is ordinarily said. This notion is that of *teaching oneself* which goes hand in glove with the notion of *thinking for oneself*. You will all agree, I think, that teaching fails, that is, either the teacher is a failure or the pupil is a failure, if the pupil does not sooner or later become able and apt to arrive at his own solutions to problems. But how, in logic, can anyone be taught to do untaught things? I repeat, how, in logic, can anyone be taught to do untaught things?

To clear the air, let me begin by quickly putting on one side an unimportant but familiar notion, that of the self-taught man. Normally when we describe someone as a self-taught man we think of a man who having been deprived of tuition from other teachers tries to make himself an historian, say, or a linguist or an astronomer, without criticism, advice or stimulation from anyone else, save from the authors of such textbooks, encyclopaedia articles and linguaphone records as he may happen to hit on. He hits on these, of course, randomly, without having anyone or anything to tell him whether they are good ones, silly ones, old-fashioned ones or cranky ones. We admire the devotion with which he studies, but, save for the rare exception, we pity him for having been the devoted pupil only of that solitary and untrained teacher, himself. However, I am not interested in him.

What I am interested in is this. Take the case of an ordinary unbrilliant, unstupid boy who is learning to read. He has learned to spell and read monosyllables like 'bat', 'bad', 'at', 'ring', 'sing' etc. and some two-syllable words like 'running', 'dagger' and a few others. We have never taught him, say, the word 'batting'. Yet we find him quite soon reading and spelling unhesitantly the word 'batting'. We ask him who taught him this word and, if he remembers, he says that he had found it out for himself. He has learned from himself how the word 'batting' looks in print, how to write it down on paper and how to spell it out aloud, so in a sense he has taught himself this word—taught it to himself without yet knowing it. How can this be? How can a boy who does not know what 'b-a-t-t-i-n-g' spells teach himself what it spells?

In real life we are not a bit puzzled. It is just what we expect of a not totally stupid child. Yet there is the semblance of a conceptual paradox here, for we seem to be describing him as at a certain stage being able to teach himself something new, which *ipso facto* was not yet in his repertoire to teach. Here his teacher was as ignorant as the pupil, for they were the same boy. So how can the one learn something from the other?

What should we say? Well, clearly we want to say that the prior things that we *had* taught him, namely words like 'bat', 'bad', 'rat' and longer words like 'butter', 'running' etc. enabled him and perhaps encouraged him to make a new bit of independent, uncoached progress on his own. We had taught him *how* to read some monosyllables, *how* to run some of them together in dissyllables, and so on. We had taught him a way or some ways of coping with combinations of printed letters, though not in their particular application to this new word 'batting'. He had made this particular application himself. So to speak, we had previously from the deck shown him the ropes and now he climbs one of them with his own hands and feet; that is to say, not being totally stupid, he was able and ready to employ this slightly general knowledge that we had given to him on a new concrete and particular problem that we had not solved for him. We had given him the wherewithal with which to think it out for himself—and this thinking out was his doing and not ours. I could just as well have taken an example from the much more sophisticated stratum where a brilliant undergraduate makes a good philosophical move that no one else has ever taught him, and maybe no one else has ever made.

Naturally, most often the boy or the undergraduate, if asked Who taught you that? would reply not that he had taught it to himself or that he had learned it from himself, but rather that he had found it out or thought it out or worked it out for himself. Just this brings out a big part of what interests me, namely, that though in one way it is obviously impossible for one person's own discovery, whether trivial or important, to be simply what someone else had previously taught him—since it would then not be his discovery—, yet in another way it is and ought to be one main business of a teacher precisely to get his pupils to advance beyond their instructions and to discover new things for themselves, that is, to get them to think things out for themselves. I teach Tommy to read a few words like 'bat', 'run' and 'running' in order that he may then, of his own motion, find out how to read lots and lots of other words, like 'batting', that we have not taught to him. Indeed we do not deem him really able to spell or read until he can spell and read things that he has not been introduced to. Nor, to leave the schoolroom for the moment, do I think that Tommy has learned to bicycle until he can do things on his bicycle far more elaborate, speedy, tricky and delicate than the things I drilled him in on the first morning. I taught him the few elements on the first morning just in order that he might then find out for himself how to cope with hosts of non-elementary tasks. I gave him a few stereotyped exercises, and, as I had hoped and expected, in a couple of days he had developed for himself on this basis a fair wealth of boyish skills and dexterities, though he acquired these while I was away in London.

However, there remains a slight feeling of a puzzle or paradox here, and it comes, I think, from this source. A familiar and indispensable part or sort of teaching consists in teaching by rote lists of truths or facts, for example the proposition that 7×7 is 49, etc., the proposition that Waterloo was fought in 1815, etc., and the proposition that Madrid is the capital of Spain, etc. That the pupil has learned a lesson of this propositional sort is shown, in the first instance, by his being able and reasonably ready to reproduce word-perfectly these pieces of information. He gets them by heart, and he can come out with them on demand. Now every teacher knows that only a vanishingly small fraction of his teaching-day really consists in simply reciting lists of such snippets of information to pupils, but very unfortunately, it happens to be the solitary part which un-schooled parents, Sergeant Majors, some silly publicists and some educationalists always think of when they think of teaching and learning. They think or half-think that the request 'Recite what you have learned in school today, Tommy' is a natural and proper one, as if all that Tommy could or should have learned is a number of memorizable propositions; or as if to have learned anything consisted simply in being able to echo it, like a gramophone. As you all know, most teaching has nothing whatsoever in common with this crude, semi-surgical picture of teaching as the forcible insertion into the pupil's memory of strings of officially approved propositions; and I hope to show before long that even that small and of course indispensable part of instruction which is the imparting of factual information is grossly mis-pictured when pictured as literal cramming. Yet, bad as the picture is, it has a powerful hold over people's general theorizings about teaching and learning. Even Tommy's father, after spending the morning in teaching Tommy to swim, to dribble the football or to diagnose and repair what is wrong with the kitchen clock, in the afternoon cheerfully writes to the newspapers letters which take it for granted that all lessons are strings of memorizable propositions. His practice is perfectly sensible, yet still his theory is as silly as it could be.

Perhaps the prevalence of this very thin and partial notion of teaching and learning inherits something from the teaching and learning that are done in the nursery, where things such as 'Hickory Dickory Dock' and simple tunes are learned by heart from that mere vocal repetition which enables the parrot to pick them up too.

Well, in opposition to this shibboleth, I want to switch the centre of gravity of the whole topic on to the notions of Teaching-to so and so, and Learning-to so and so, that is, on to the notion of the development of abilities and competences. Let us forget for a while the memorization of truths, and, of course, of rhymes and tunes, and attend, instead, to the acquisition of skills, knacks and efficiencies. Consider, for example, lessons in drawing, arithmetic and cricket— and, if you like, in philosophy. These lessons cannot consist of and cannot even contain much of dictated propositions. However many true propositions the child has got by heart, he has not begun to learn to draw or play cricket until he has been given a pencil or a bat and a ball and has practised doing things with them; and even if he progresses magnificently in these arts, he will have little or nothing to reply to his parents if they ask him in the evening to recite to them the propositions that he has learned. He can *exhibit* what he has begun to master, but he cannot *quote* it. To avoid the ambiguity between 'teach' in the sense of 'teach that' and 'teach' in the sense of 'teach to' or 'teach how to', I shall now sometimes use the word 'train'. The drawing-master, the language-teacher or the cricket-coach *trains* his pupils in drawing or in French pronunciation or in batting or bowling, and this training incorporates only a few items of quotable information. The same is true of philosophy.

Part, but only part of this notion of training is the notion of drilling, i.e. putting the pupil through stereotyped exercises which he masters by sheer repetition. Thus the recruit learns to slope arms just by going through the same sequence of motions time after time, until he can, so to speak, perform them in his sleep. Circus-dogs and circus-seals are trained in the same way. At the start piano-playing, counting and gear-changing are also taught by simple habituation. But disciplines do not reduce to such sheer drills. Sheer drill, though it is the indispensable beginning of training, is, for most abilities, only their very beginning. Having become able to do certain low-level things automatically and without thinking, the pupil is expected to advance beyond this point and to employ his inculcated automatisms in higher level tasks which are not automatic, and cannot be done without thinking. Skills, tastes and scruples are more than mere habits, and the disciplines and the self-disciplines which develop them are more than mere rote-exercises.

His translators and commentators have been very unjust to Aristotle on this matter. Though he was the first thinker and is still the best, systematically to study the notions of ability, skill, training, character, learning, discipline, self-discipline, etc. the translators of his works nearly always render his key-ideas by such terms as 'habit' and 'habituation'—as if, for example, a person who has been trained and self-trained to play the violin, or to behave scrupulously in his dealings with other people acts from sheer habit, in the way in which I do tie up my shoelaces quite automatically and without thinking what I am doing or how to do it. Of course Aristotle knew better than this, and the Greek words that he used are quite grossly mistranslated when rendered merely by such words as 'habit' and 'habituation'. The well-disciplined soldier, who does indeed slope arms automatically, does not also shoot automatically or scout by blind habit or read maps like a marionette.

Nor is Tommy's control of his bicycle merely a rote-performance, though he cannot begin to control his bicycle until he has got some movements by rote. Having learned through sheer habit-formation to keep his balance on his bicycle with both hands on the handlebars, Tommy can now try to ride with one hand off, and later still with both hands in his pockets and his feet off the pedals. He now progresses by experimentation. Or, having got by heart the run of the alphabet from ABC through to XYZ, he can now, but not without thinking, tell you what three letters run *backwards* from RQP, though he has never learned by heart this reversed sequence.

I suggest that our initial seeming paradox, that a learner can sometimes of himself, after a bit of instruction, better his instructions, is beginning to seem less formidable. The possibility of it is of the same pattern as the familiar fact that the toddler who has this morning taken a few aided steps, tries this afternoon with or without success to take some unaided steps. The swimmer who can now keep himself up in salt water, comes by himself, at first with a bit of extra splashing, to keep himself up in fresh water. How do any formerly difficult things change into now easy things? Or any once untried things into now feasible ones? The answer is just in terms of the familiar notions of the development of abilities by practice, that is trying and failing and then trying again and not failing so often or so badly, and so on.

Notoriously a very few pupils are, over some tasks, so stupid, idle, scared, hostile, bored or defective, that they make no efforts of their own beyond those imposed on them as drill by their trainer. But to be non-stupid, vigorous and interested *is* to be inclined to make, if only as a game, moves beyond the drilled moves, and to practise of oneself, e.g. to multiply beyond 12 × 12, to run through the alphabet backwards, to bicycle with one hand off the handlebar, or to slope arms in the dark with a walking-stick when no drill-sergeant is there. As Aristotle says 'the things that we have got to do when we have learned to do them, we learn to do by doing them.' What I can do today I could not do easily or well or successfully yesterday; and the day before I could not even try to do them; and if I had not tried unsuccessfully yesterday, I should not be succeeding today.

Before returning to go further into some of these key notions of ability, practice, trying, learning to, teaching to, and so on, I want to look back for a moment to the two over-influential notions of teaching *that* so and so, i.e. telling or informing, and of learning *that* so and so, i.e. the old notion of propositional cramming. In a number of nursery, school and university subjects, there are necessarily some or many true propositions to be accumulated by the student. He must, for example, learn that Oslo is the capital of Norway, Stockholm is the capital of Sweden and Copenhagen is the capital of Denmark. Or he must learn that the Battle of Trafalgar was fought in 1805 and that of Waterloo in 1815. Or that $7 + 5 = 12$, $7 + 6 = 13$, $7 + 7 = 14$, etc.

At the very start, maybe, the child just memorizes these strings of propositions as he memorizes 'Hickory Dickory Dock', the alphabet or 'Thirty days hath September'. But so long as parroting is all he can do, he does not yet know the geographical fact, say, that Stockholm is the capital of Sweden, since if you ask him what Stockholm is the capital of, or whether Madrid is the capital of Sweden, he has no idea how to move. He can repeat, but he cannot yet use the memorized dictum. All he can do is to go through the memorized sequence of European capitals from start through to the required one. He does not qualify as knowing that Stockholm is the capital of Sweden until he can detach this proposition from the memorized rigmarole; and can, for example, answer new-type questions like 'of which country out of the three, Italy, Spain and Sweden is Stockholm the capital?' or 'Here is Stockholm on the globe—whereabouts is Sweden?' and so on. To know the geographical fact requires having taken it in, i.e. being able and ready to operate with it, from it, around it and upon it. To possess a piece of information is to be able to mobilize it apart from its rote-neighbours and out of its rote-formulation in unhackneyed and *ad hoc* tasks. Nor does the pupil know that $7 + 7 = 14$ while this is for him only a still undetachable bit of a memorized sing-song, but only when, for example, he can find fault with someone's assertion that $7 + 8 = 14$, or can answer the new-type question. How many 7s are there in 14?, or the new-type question 'If there are seven boys and seven girls in a room, how many children are in the room?' etc. Only then has he taken it in.

In other words, even to have learned the piece of information *that something is so* is more than merely to be able to parrot the original telling of it—somewhat as to have digested a biscuit is more than merely to have had it popped into one's mouth. Can he or can he not infer from the information that Madrid is the capital of Spain that Madrid is not in Sweden? Can he or can he not tell us what sea-battle occurred ten years before Waterloo?

Notice that I am not in the least deprecating the inculcation of rotes like the alphabet, the figures of the syllogism, 'Hickory Dickory Dock', the dates of the Kings of England, or sloping arms. A person who has not acquired such rotes cannot progress from and beyond them. All that I am arguing is that he does not qualify as knowing even that Waterloo was fought in 1815 if all that he can do is to sing out this sentence inside the sing-song of a memorized string of such sentences. If he can only echo the syllables that he has heard, he has not yet taken in the information meant to be conveyed by them. He has not grasped it if he cannot handle it. But if he could not even echo things told to him, *a fortiori* he could not operate with, from or upon their informative content. One cannot digest a biscuit unless it is first popped into one's mouth. So we see that even to have learned a true proposition is to have learned *to do* things other than repeating the words in which the truth had been dictated. To have learned even a simple geographical fact is to have become able to cope with some unhabitual geographical tasks, however elementary.

We must now come back to our central question : How is it possible that a person should learn from himself something which he previously did not know, and had not, e.g., been taught by someone else? This question is or embodies the apparently perplexing question : How can one person teach another person to think things out for himself, since if he gives him, say, the new arithmetical thoughts, then they are not the pupil's own thoughts; or if they are his own thoughts, then he did not get them from his teacher? Having led the horse to the water, how can we make him drink? But I have, I hope, shifted the centre of gravity of this seeming puzzle, by making the notions of *learning-to* and *teaching-to* the primary notions. In its new form the question is: How, on the basis of some tuition, can a person today get himself to do something which he had not been able to do yesterday or last year? How can competences, abilities and skills develop? How can trying ever succeed? We are so familiar, in practice, with the fact that abilities do develop, and that tryings can succeed that we find little to puzzle us in the idea that they do.

Looked at from the end of the teacher the question is: How can the teacher get his pupil to make independent moves of his own? If this question is tortured into the shape : How can the teacher make or force his pupil to do things which he is not made or forced to do? i.e. How can the teacher be the initiator of the pupil's initiatives? the answer is obvious. He cannot. I cannot compel the horse to drink thirstily. I cannot coerce Tommy into doing spontaneous things. Either he is not coerced, or they are not spontaneous.

As every teacher, like every drill-sergeant or animal trainer knows in his practice, teaching and training have virtually not yet begun, so long as the pupil is too young, too stupid, too scared or too sulky to respond—and to respond is not just to yield. Where there is a modicum of alacrity, interest or anyhow docility in the pupil, where he tries, however faintheartedly, to get things right rather than wrong, fast rather than slow, neat rather than awkward, where, even, he registers even a slight contempt for the poor performances of others or chagrin at his own, pleasure at his own successes and envy of those of others, then he is, in however slight a degree, co-operating and so self-moving. He is doing something, though very likely not much, and is not merely having things done to him. He is, however unambitiously and however desultorily, attempting the still difficult. He has at least a little impetus of his own. A corner, however small a corner of his heart is now in the task. The eager pupil is, of course, the one who, when taught, say, to read or spell a few words like 'at', 'bat' and 'mat' travels home on the bus trying out, just for fun, all the other monosyllables that rhyme with 'at', to see which of them are words. When taught to read and spell a dis-syllable or two, he tries his hand, just for fun and often but not always unsuccessfully, on the polysyllables on the advertisement-hoardings; and just for fun he challenges his father to spell long words when he gets home. He does this for fun; but like much play it is spontaneous self-practising. When he returns to school after the holidays, although his spelling and reading are now far in advance of their peak of last term, he will stoutly deny that he has done any work during the holidays. It has not been work, it has been absorption in a new hobby, like exercising a new limb.

His over-modest teacher may say that he has taught this boy next to nothing—nor has he, save for the very beginnings of everything.

However, we should remember that although a total absence of eagerness or even willingness spells total unteachability, the presence of energy, adventurousness and self-motion is not by itself enough. The wild guesser and the haphazard plunger have freedom of move-ment of a sort, but not of the best sort. Learning how to do new and therefore more or less difficult things does indeed require trying things out for oneself, but if this trying-out is not controlled by any testing or making sure, then its adventurousness is recklessness and not enterprise. He is like the gambler, not like the investor. The moves made, though spontaneous, are irresponsible and they yield no dividends. Nothing can be learned by him from their unsuccesses or from their occasional fortuitous successes. He shoots away, but learns nothing from his misses—or from his fluke hits.

It is just here, with the notion of taking care when taking risks, that there enters on the scenes the cardinal notion of *method*, i.e. of techniques, *modi operandi*, rules, canons, procedures, knacks, and even tricks of the trade. In doing a thing that he has never done before, a person may, but need not, operate according to a method, sometimes, even according to a sheer drill that he has adhered to before. If he does, then his action is still an innovation, although the pattern of his action is a familiar and inculcated one. The poet composes a sonnet, taking care to adhere to the regulation 14 lines, to the regulation rhyming scheme, to the regulation metrical pattern, or else perhaps to one of the several permitted patterns—yet, nonetheless, his sonnet is a new one. No one has ever composed *it* before. His teacher who taught him how to compose sonnets had not and could not have made him compose this sonnet, else it would be the teacher's and not the pupil's sonnet. Teaching people how to do things just *is* teaching them methods or *modi operandi;* and it is just because it is one thing to have learned a method and another thing to essay a new application of it that we can say without paradox that the learner's new move is his own move and yet that he may have learned the *how* of making it from someone else. The cook's pudding is a new one and piping hot, but its recipe was known to Mrs. Beeton in the days of Queen Victoria.

Well, then, what sort of a thing is a method? First for what it is not. Despite what many folk would say, a method is not a stereotyped sequence-pattern or routine of actions, inculcatable by pure rote, like sloping arms or going through the alphabet. The parrot that can run through 'Hickory Dickory Dock' has not learned how to do anything or therefore how not to do it. There is nothing that he takes care not to do.

A method is a learnable way of doing something, where the word 'way' connotes more than mere rote or routine. A way of doing something, or a *modus operandi,* is something general, and general in at least two dimensions. First, the way in which you do a thing, say mount your bicycle, can be the way or a way in which some other people or perhaps most other people mount or try to mount their bicycles. Even if you happen to be the only person who yet does something in a certain way, it is possible that others should in future learn from you or find out for themselves the very same way of doing it. *Modi operandi* are, in principle, public property, though a particular action performed in this way is my action and not yours, or else it is your action and not mine. We mount our bicycles in the same way, but my bicycle-mounting is my action and not yours. You do not make my mincepies, even though we both follow the same Victorian recipe.

The second way in which a method is something general is the obvious one, that there is no limit to the number of actions that may be done in that way. The method is, roughly, applicable anywhere and anywhen, as well as by anyone. For however many people are known by me to have mounted their bicycles in a certain way, I know that there could have been and there could be going to be any number of other bicycle-mountings performed by myself and others in the same way.

Next, methods can be helpfully, if apparently cynically, thought of as systems of avoidances or as patterns of 'don'ts'. The rules, say, of English grammar do not tell us positively what to say or write; they tell us negatively not to say or write such things as 'A dog *are* . . . ' and 'Those dogs *is* . . . ', and learning the art of rock-climbing or tree-climbing is, among hundreds of other things, learning never, or hardly ever, to trust one's whole weight to an untried projection or to a branch that is leafless in summer time.

People sometimes grumble at the Ten Commandments on the score that most of them are prohibitions, and not positive injunctions. They have not realized that the notice 'Keep off the grass' licenses us to walk anywhere else we choose; where the notice 'Keep to the gravel' leaves us with almost no freedom of movement. Similarly to have learned a method is to have learned to take care against certain specified kinds of risk, muddle, blind alley, waste, etc. But carefully keeping away from this cliff and from that morass leaves the rest of the countryside open for us to walk lightheartedly in. If I teach you even twenty kinds of things that would make your sonnet a bad sonnet or your argument a bad argument, I have still left you an indefinite amount of elbow-room within which you can construct your own sonnet or argument, and this sonnet or argument of yours, whether brilliant or ordinary or weak, will at least be free of faults of those twenty kinds.

There exists in some quarters the sentimental idea that the teacher who teaches his pupils how to do things is hindering them, as if his apron-strings coerced their leg-movements. We should think of the inculcation of methods rather as training the pupils to avoid specified muddles, blockages, sidetracks and thin ice by training them to recognize these for what they are. Enabling them to avoid troubles, disasters, nuisances and wasted efforts is helping them to move where they want to move. Road signs are not, for the most part, impediments to the flow of traffic. They are preventives of impediments to the flow of traffic.

Of course we can easily think of silly ways of doing things which continue to be taught by grown-ups to children and adhered to by the grown-ups themselves. Not all methods are good methods, or all recipes good recipes. For example, the traditional ban on splitting the infinitive was a silly rule. But the gratuitous though trivial bother of conforming to this particular veto was negligible compared with the handicap that would be suffered by the child who had never been taught or picked up for himself any of the procedures for composing or construing sentences. He would have been kept back at the level of total infancy. He could not say or follow anything at all if, for example, he had not mastered conjunctions, or even verbs, and mastering them involves learning how *not* to make hashes of them.

How does one teach methods or ways of doing things? Well, there is no simple answer to this. Different arts and crafts require different kinds of disciplines; and in some one particular field, say drawing, one teacher works very differently from another. Sometimes a little, sometimes a lot can be told; there is much that cannot be told, but can be shown by example, by caricature and so on. But one thing is indispensable. The pupil himself must, whether under pressure or from interest or ambition or conscientiousness, practise doing what he is learning how to do. Whether in his exercises in the art he religiously models his strokes after Bradman, or whether he tries to win the praise or avoid the strictures or sarcasms of a feared, respected or loved coach, he learns by performing and improves by trying to better his own and his fellows' previous performances by eradicating their faults. The methods of operating taught to him become his personal methods of operating by his own criticized and self-criticized practice. Whether in spelling, in Latin grammar, fencing, arithmetic or philosophy, he learns the ropes, not much by gazing at them or hearing about them, but by trying to climb them—and by trying to climb them less awkwardly, slowly and riskily today than he did yesterday.

So far I have been, for simplicity, dividing the contributions of the teacher and the pupil by saying that the teacher in teaching how to so and so is teaching a method or way of operating, while the pupil keeps his initiative by making his own at the start somewhat arduous, because new applications of that method. The teacher introduces the pupil to the ropes, but it is for the pupil to try to climb them.

But now we should pay some attention to the fact that pretty soon the pupil has become familiar with the quite general fact that for lots and lots of widely different kinds of operations—spelling, say, skating and bowling at cricket—there exist different *modi operandi*. There are spelling-mistakes and there are bowling-faults, and neither spelling nor bowling can go right unless these faults are systematically avoided. So now, when he undertakes an altogether new kind of operation, canoeing, say, he from the start expects there to be *modi operandi* here too. This too will be a thing that he will have to learn how to do, partly by learning how not to do it. But this time, it may be, there is no one to teach him, and not even any other canoeist to imitate. He has got to find out for himself the way, or anyhow a way, of balancing, propelling and steering his canoe. Well, at first he tries a lot of random things, and nearly all of them end in immersion or collision; but he does after a time find out some ways of managing his craft. He may not achieve elegance or speed, but he does find out how not to topple over and how not to run into obstacles. He is trained, this time purely self-trained, regularly to avoid some kinds of faulty watermanship. But it is because he had previously learned by practice, coaching and imitation the 'hows' of lots of other things such as tree-climbing, spelling and skating, that he now takes it for granted that canoeing has its 'hows' as well, which similarly can be learned by practice, trial and error, and looking for ways of avoiding the repetition of errors. Here, as elsewhere, he has to study in order to improve; but this time he has nothing to study save his own unsuccesses and successes.

His more reckless and impatient brother, though full of go, just makes a dash at it, and then another quite different dash at it, and learns nothing or almost nothing from the failures which generally result, or even from the successes which sometimes just happen to result. He is not a self-trainer.

The third brother is uninterested, slow in the uptake, scared or idle. He never chances his arm. He tries nothing, and so initiates nothing either successfully or unsuccessfully. So he never learns to canoe; never, perhaps, even regrets not having learned it or envies those who have. There is no question of his training himself in this particular art, or even, if he is a very bad case, of his being trained by anyone else; just as there was fifty years ago no real question of me training myself or of my being trained by anyone else in the arts of cricket or music.

The supreme reward of the teacher is to turn out from time to time the student who comes to be not merely abreast of his teacher but ahead of him, the student, namely, who advances his subject or his craft not just by adding to it further applications of the established ways of operating, but by discovering new methods or procedures of types which no one could have taught to him. He has given to his subject or his craft a new idea or a battery of new ideas. He is original. He himself, if of a grateful nature, will say that his original idea just grew of itself out of what he had learned from his teachers, his competitors and his colleagues; while they, if of a grateful nature, will say that the new idea was his discovery. Both will be right. His new idea is the fruit of a tree that others had planted and pruned. It is really his own fruit and he is really their tree.

We started off with the apparent paradox that though the teacher in teaching is doing something to his pupil, yet the pupil has learned virtually nothing unless he becomes able and ready to do things of his own motion other than what the teacher exported to him. We asked; How in logic can the teacher dragoon his pupil into thinking for himself, impose initiative upon him, drive him into self-motion, conscript him into volunteering, enforce originality upon him, or make him operate spontaneously? The answer is that he cannot— and the reason why we half felt that he must do so was that we were unwittingly enslaved by the crude, semi-hydraulic idea that in essence to teach is to pump propositions, like 'Waterloo, 1815' into the pupils' ears, until they regurgitate them automatically.

When we switched from the notion of 'hydraulic injection' to the notion of 'teaching to' or 'teaching how to', the paradox began to disappear. I can introduce you to a way or the way of doing something, and still your actual essays in the exercise of this craft or competence are yours and not mine. I do not literally make you do them, but I do enable you to do them. I give you the *modus operandi*, but your operatings or tryings to operate according to this *modus* are your own doings and not my inflictings and the practising by which you master the method is your exertion and not mine. I have given you some equipment against failing, *if* you try. But that you try is not something that I can coerce. Teaching is not gate-shutting but gate-opening, yet still the dull or the scared or the lame calf does not walk out into the open field. All this does not imply the popular sentimental corollary that teachers should never be strict, demanding, peremptory or uncondoning. It is often the hard task-master who alone succeeds in instilling mistrust of primrose paths. The father may enlarge the child's freedom of movement by refusing to hold his hand, and the boxing-instructor or the philosophy-tutor may enlarge his pupil's powers of defence and attack by hitting him hard and often. It is not the chocolates and the sponge-cakes that strengthen the child's jaw-muscles. They have other virtues, but not this one.

8

PHILOSOPHICAL MODELS OF TEACHING
Israel Scheffler

I. INTRODUCTION

Teaching may be characterized as an activity aimed at the achievement of learning, and practised in such manner as to respect the student's intellectual integrity and capacity for independent judgment. Such a characterization is important for at least two reasons : First, it brings out the intentional nature of teaching, the fact that teaching is a distinctive goal-oriented activity, rather than a distinctively patterned sequence of behavioural steps executed by the teacher. Secondly, it differentiates the activity of teaching from such other activities as propaganda, conditioning, suggestion, and indoctrination, which are aimed at modifying the person but strive at all costs to avoid a genuine engagement of his judgment on underlying issues.

This characterization of teaching, which I believe to be correct, fails, nevertheless, to answer certain critical questions of the teacher : What sort of learning shall I aim to achieve? In what does such learning consist? How shall I strive to achieve it? Such questions are, respectively, normative, epistemological, and empirical in import, and the answers that are provided for them give point and substance to the educational enterprise. Rather than trying to separate these questions, however, and deal with each abstractly and explicitly, I should like, on the present occasion, to approach them indirectly and as a group, through a consideration of three influential models of teaching, which provide, or at any rate suggest, certain relevant answers. These models do not so much aim to *describe* teaching as to *orient* it, by weaving a coherent picture out of epistemological, psychological, and normative elements. Like all models, they simplify, but such simplification is a legitimate way of highlighting what are thought to be important features of the subject. The primary issue, in each case, is whether these features are indeed critically important, whether we should allow our educational thinking to be guided by a model which fastens upon them, or whether we should rather reject or revise the model in question. Although I shall mention some historical affiliations of each model, I make no pretence to historical accuracy. My main purpose is, rather, systematic or dialectical, that is, to outline and examine the three models and to see what, if anything, each has to offer us in our own quest for a satisfactory conception of teaching. I turn, then, first to what may be called the 'impression model'.

2. THE IMPRESSION MODEL

The impression model is perhaps the simplest and most widespread of the three, picturing the mind essentially as sifting and storing the external impressions to which it is receptive. The desired end result of teaching is an accumulation in the learner of basic elements fed in from without, organized and processed in standard ways, but, in any event, not generated by the learner himself. In the empiricist variant of this model generally associated with John Locke, learning involves the input by experience of simple ideas of sensation and reflection, which are clustered, related, generalized, and retained by the mind. Blank at birth, the mind is thus formed by its particular experiences, which it keeps available for its future use. In Locke's words (Bk. II, Ch. I, Sect. 2 of the *Essay Concerning Human Understanding*):

> Let us then suppose the mind to be, as we say, white paper, void of all characters, without any ideas; how comes it to be furnished? Whence comes it by that vast store, which the busy and boundless fancy of man has painted on it with an almost endless variety? Whence has it all the materials of reason and knowledge? To this I answer, in one word, From experience; in that all our knowledge is founded, and from that it ultimately derives itself. Our observation, employed either about external sensible objects, or about the internal operations of our minds, perceived and reflected on by ourselves, is that which supplies our understandings with all the materials of thinking. These two are the fountains of knowledge, from whence all the ideas we have, or can naturally have, do spring.

Teaching, by implication, should concern itself with exercising the mental powers engaged in receiving and processing incoming ideas, more particularly powers of perception, discrimination, retention, combination, abstraction, and representation. But, more important, teaching needs to strive for the optimum selection and organization of this experiential input. For potentially, the teacher has enormous power; by controlling the input of sensory units, he can, to a large degree, shape the mind. As Dewey remarked,[1]

> Locke's statements...seemed to do justice to both mind and matter.... One of the two supplied the matter of knowledge and the object upon which the mind should work. The other supplied definite mental powers, which were few in number and which might be trained by specific exercises.

The process of learning in the child was taken as paralleling the growth of knowledge generally, for all knowledge is constructed out of elementary units of experience, which are grouped, related, and generalized. The teacher's object should thus be to provide data not only useful in themselves, but collectively rich enough to support the progressive growth of adult knowledge in the learner's mind.

The impression model, as I have sketched it, has certain obvious strong points. It sets forth the appeal to experience as a general tool of criticism to be employed in the examination of all claims and doctrines, and it demands that they square with it. Surely such a demand is legitimate, for knowledge does rest upon experience in some way or other. Further, the mind is, in a clear sense, as the impression model suggests, a function of its particular experiences, and it is capable of increased growth with experience. The richness and variety of the child's experiences are thus important considerations in the process of educational planning.

The impression model nevertheless suffers from fatal difficulties. The notions of absolutely simple ideas and of abstract mental powers improvable through exercise have been often and rightly criticized as mythological:[2] Simplicity is a relative, not an absolute, concept and reflects a particular way of analysing experience; it is, in short, not given but made. And mental powers or faculties invariant with subject matter have, as everyone knows, been expunged from psychology on empirical as well as theoretical grounds. A more fundamental criticism, perhaps, is that the implicit conception of the growth of knowledge is false. Knowledge is not achieved through any standard set of operations for the processing of sensory particulars, however conceived. Knowledge is, first and foremost, embodied in language, and involves a conceptual apparatus not derivable from the sensory data but imposed upon them. Nor is such apparatus built into the human mind; it is, at least in good part a product of guesswork and invention, borne along by culture and by custom. Knowledge further involves *theory,* and theory is surely not simply a matter of generalizing the data, even assuming such data organized by a given conceptual apparatus. Theory is a creative and individualistic enterprise that goes beyond the data in distinctive ways, involving not only generalization, but postulation of entities, deployment of analogies, evaluation of relative simplicity, and, indeed, invention of new languages. Experience is relevant to knowledge through providing tests of our theories; it does not automatically generate these theories, even when processed by the human mind. That we have the theories we do is, therefore, a fact, not simply about the human mind, but about our history and our intellectual heritage.

In the process of learning, the child gets not only sense experiences but the language and theory of his heritage in complicated linkages with discriminable contexts. He is heir to the complex culture of belief built up out of innumerable creative acts of intellect of the past, and comprising a patterned view of the world. To give the child even the richest selection of sense data or particular facts alone would in no way guarantee his building up anything resembling what we think of as knowledge, much less his developing the ability to retrieve and apply such knowledge in new circumstances.

A *verbal* variant of the impression model of teaching naturally suggests itself, then, as having certain advantages over the *sensory* version we have just considered : What is to be impressed on the mind is not only sense experience but language and, moreover, accepted theory. We need to feed in not only sense data but the correlated verbal patterning of such data, that is, the *statements* about such data which we ourselves accept. The student's knowledge consists in his stored accumulation of these statements, which have application to new cases in the future. He is no longer, as before, assumed capable of generating our conceptual heritage by operating in certain standard ways on his sense data, for part of what *we* are required to feed into his mind is this very heritage itself.

This verbal variant, which has close affinities to contemporary behaviourism, does have certain advantages over its predecessor, but retains grave inadequacies still, as a model of teaching. To *store* all accepted theories is not the same as being able to *use* them properly in context. Nor, even if some practical correlation with sense data is achieved, does it imply an understanding of what is thus stored, nor an appreciation of the theoretical motivation and experimental evidence upon which it rests.

All versions of the impression model, finally, have this defect: They fail to make adequate room for radical *innovation* by the learner. We do not, after all, feed into the learner's mind all that we hope he will have as an end result of our teaching. Nor can we construe the critical surplus as generated in standard ways out of materials we do supply. We do not, indeed cannot, so construe insight, understanding, new applications of our theories, new theories, new achievements in scholarship, history, poetry, philosophy. There is a fundamental gap which teaching cannot bridge simply by expansion or reorganization of the curriculum input. This gap sets *theoretical* limits to the power and control of the teacher; moreover, it is where his control ends that his fondest hopes for education begin.

3. THE INSIGHT MODEL

The next model I shall consider, the 'insight model', represents a radically different approach. Where the impression model supposes the teacher to be conveying ideas or bits of knowledge into the student's mental treasury, the insight model denies the very possibility of such conveyance. Knowledge, it insists, is a matter of vision, and vision cannot be dissected into elementary sensory or verbal units that can be conveyed from one person to another. It can, at most, be stimulated or prompted by what the teacher does, and if it indeed occurs, it goes beyond what is thus done. Vision defines and organizes particular experiences, and points up their significance. It is vision, or insight into meaning, which makes the crucial difference between simply storing and reproducing learned sentences, on the one hand, and understanding their basis and application, on the other.

The insight model is due to Plato, but I shall here consider the version of St. Augustine, in his dialogue, 'The Teacher',[3] for it bears precisely on the points we have dealt with. Augustine argues roughly as follows: The teacher is commonly thought to convey knowledge by his use of language. But knowledge, or rather *new* knowledge, is not conveyed simply by words sounding in the ear. Words are mere noises unless they signify realities present in some way to the mind. Hence a paradox: If the student already knows the realities to which the teacher's words refer, the teacher teaches him nothing new. Whereas, if the student does not know these realities, the teacher's words can have no meaning for him, and must be mere noises. Augustine concludes that language must have a function wholly distinct from that of the signification of realities; it is used to *prompt* people in certain ways. The teacher's words, in particular, prompt the student to search for realities not already known by him. Finding these realities, which are illuminated for him by internal vision, he acquires new knowledge for himself, though indirectly as a result of the teacher's prompting activity. To *believe* something simply on the basis of authority or hearsay is indeed possible, on Augustine's view; to *know* it is not. Mere beliefs may, in his opinion, of course, be useful; they are not therefore knowledge. For knowledge, in short, requires the individual himself to have a grasp of the realities lying behind the words.

The insight model is strong where the impression model is weakest. While the latter, in its concern with the conservation of knowledge, fails to do justice to innovation, the former addresses itself from the start to the problem of *new* knowledge resulting from teaching. Where the latter stresses atomic manipulable bits at the expense of understanding, the former stresses primarily the acquisition of insight. Where the latter gives inordinate place to the feeding in of materials from the outside, the former stresses the importance of firsthand inspection of realities by the student, the necessity for the student to earn his knowledge by his own efforts.

I should argue, nevertheless, that the case offered by Augustine for the prompting theory is not, as it stands, satisfactory. If the student does not know the realities behind the teacher's words, these words are, presumably, mere noises and can serve only to prompt the student to inquire for himself. Yet if they *are* mere noises, how can they even serve to prompt? If they are not understood in any way by the student, how can they lead him to search for the appropriate realities which underlie them? Augustine, furthermore, allows that a person may believe, though not know, what he accepts on mere authority, without having confronted the relevant realities. Such a person might, presumably, pass from the state of belief to that of knowledge, as a result of prompting, under certain conditions. But what, we may ask, could have been the content of his initial belief if the formulation of it had been literally unintelligible to him? The prompting theory, it seems, will not do as a way of escaping Augustine's original paradox.

There is, however, an easier escape. For the paradox itself rests on a confusion of the meaning of *words* with that of *sentences*. Let me explain. Augustine holds that words acquire intelligibility only through acquaintance with reality. Now it may perhaps be initially objected that understanding a word does not always require acquaintance with its signified reality, for words may also acquire intelligibility through definition, lacking such direct acquaintance. But let us waive this objection and grant, for the sake of argument, that understanding a word *always* does require such acquaintance; it still does not follow that understanding a true sentence similarly requires acquaintance with the state of affairs which it represents. We understand new sentences all the time, on the basis of an understanding of their constituent words and of the grammar by which they are concatenated. Thus, given a sentence signifying some fact, it is simply not true that, unless the student already knows this fact, the sentence must be mere noise to him. For he can understand its meaning indirectly, by a synthesis of its parts, and be led thereafter to inquire whether it is, in reality, true or false.

If my argument is correct, then Augustine's paradox of teaching can be simply rejected, on the ground that we *can* understand statements before becoming acquainted with their signified realities. It follows that the teacher can indeed *inform* the student of new facts by means of language. And it further seems to follow that the basis for Augustine's prompting theory of teaching wholly collapses. We are back to the impression model, with the teacher using language not to prompt the student to inner vision, but simply to inform him of new facts.

The latter conclusion seems to me, however, mistaken. For it does *not* follow that the student will *know* these new facts simply because he has been *informed*; on this point Augustine seems to me perfectly right. It is knowing, after all, that Augustine is interested in, and knowing requires something more than the receipt and acceptance of true information. It requires that the student earn the right to his assurance of the truth of the information in question. New *information*, in short, can be intelligibly conveyed by statements; new *knowledge* cannot. Augustine, I suggest, confuses the two cases, arguing in effect for the impossibility of conveying new knowledge by words, on the basis of an alleged similar impossibility for information. I have been urging the falsity of the latter premise. But if Augustine's premise is indeed false, his conclusion as regards knowledge seems to me perfectly true : To *know* the proposition expressed by a sentence is more than just to have been told it, to have grasped its meaning, and to have accepted it. It is to have earned the right, through one's own effort or position, to an assurance of its truth.

Augustine puts the matter in terms of an insightful searching of reality, an inquiry carried out by oneself, and resting in no way on authority. Indeed, he is perhaps too austerely individualistic in this regard, rejecting even legitimate arguments from authority as a basis for knowledge. But his main thesis seems to me correct : One cannot convey new knowledge by words alone. For knowledge is not simply a storage of information by the learner.

The teacher does, of course, employ *language*, according to the insight model, but its primary function is not to impress his statements on the student's mind for later reproduction. The teacher's statements are, rather, instrumental to the student's own search of reality and vision thereof; teaching is consummated in the student's own insight. The reference to such insight seems to explain, at least partially, how the student can be expected to apply his learning to new situations in the future. For, having acquired this learning not merely by external suggestion but through a personal engagement with reality, the student can appreciate the particular fit which his theories have with real circumstances, and, hence, the proper occasions for them to be brought into play.

There is, furthermore, no reason to construe adoption of the insight model as eliminating the impression model altogether. For the impression model, it may be admitted, does reflect something genuine and important, but mislocates it. It reflects the increase of the culture's written lore, the growth of knowledge as a public and recorded possession. Furthermore, it reflects the primary importance of conserving such knowledge, as a collective heritage. But knowledge in this public sense has nothing to do with the process of learning and the activity of teaching, that is, with the growth of knowledge in the individual learner. The public treasury of knowledge constitutes a basic source of materials for the teacher, but he cannot hope to transfer it bit by bit in growing accumulation within the student's mind. In conducting his teaching, he must rather give up the hope of such simple transfer, and strive instead to encourage individual insight into the meaning and use of public knowledge.

Despite the important emphases of the insight model which we have been considering, there are, however, two respects in which it falls short. One concerns the simplicity of its constituent notion of insight, or vision, as a condition of knowing; the other relates to its specifically cognitive bias, which it shares with the impression model earlier considered. First, the notion that what is crucial in knowledge is a vision of underlying realities, a consulting of what is found within the mind, is far too simple. Certainly, as we have seen, the knower must satisfy *some* condition beyond simply being informed, in order to have the right to his assurance on the matter in question. But to construe this condition in terms of an intellectual inspection of reality is not at all satisfactory. It is plausible only if we restrict ourselves to very simple cases of truths accessible to observation or introspection. As soon as we attempt to characterize the knowing of propositions normally encountered in practical affairs, in the sciences, in politics, history, or the law, we realize that the concept of a *vision of reality* is impossibly simple. Vision is just the wrong metaphor. What seems indubitably more appropriate in all these cases of knowing is an emphasis on the processes of deliberation, argument, judgment, appraisal of reasons *pro* and *con,* weighing of evidence, appeal to principles, and decision-making, none of which fits at all well with the insight model. This model, in short, does not make adequate room for principled deliberation in the characterization of knowing. It is in terms of such principled deliberation, or the potentiality for it, rather than in terms of simple vision, that the distinctiveness of knowing is primarily to be understood.

Secondly, the insight model is specifically cognitive in emphasis, and cannot readily be stretched so as to cover important aspects of teaching. We noted above, for example, that the application of truths to new situations is somewhat better off in the insight than in the impression model, since the appropriateness of a truth for new situations is better judged with awareness of underlying realities than without. But a judgment of appropriateness is not all there is to application; habits of proper execution are also required, and insight itself does not necessitate such habits. Insight also fails to cover the concept of character and the related notions of attitude and disposition. Character, it is clear, goes beyond insight as well as beyond the impression of information. For it involves general principles of conduct logically independent of both insight and the accumulation of information. Moreover, what has been said of character can be applied also to the various institutions of civilization, including those which channel cognition itself. Science, for example, is not just a collection of true insights; it is embodied in a living tradition composed of demanding principles of judgment and conduct. Beyond the cognitive insight, lies the fundamental commitment to principles by which insights are to be criticized and assessed, in the light of publicly available evidence or reasons. In sum, then, the shortcoming of the insight model may be said to lie in the fact that it provides no role for the concept of *principles,* and the associated concept of *reasons.* This omission is very serious indeed, for the concept of principles and the concept of reasons together underlie not only the notions of rational deliberation and critical judgment, but also the notions of rational and moral conduct.

4. THE RULE MODEL

The shortcoming of the insight model just discussed is remedied in the 'rule model', which I associate with Kant. For Kant, the primary philosophical emphasis is on reason, and reason is always a matter of abiding by general rules or principles. Reason stands always in contrast with inconsistency and with expediency, in the judgment of particular issues. In the cognitive realm, reason is a kind of justice to the evidence, a fair treatment of the merits of the case, in the interests of truth. In the moral realm, reason is action on principle, action which therefore does not bend with the wind, nor lean to the side of advantage or power out of weakness or self-interest. Whether in the cognitive or the moral realm, reason is always a matter of treating equal reasons equally, and of judging the issues in the light of general principles to which one has bound oneself.

In thus binding myself to a set of principles, I act freely; this is my dignity as a being with the power of choice. But my own free commitment obligates me to obey the principles I have adopted, when they rule against me. This is what fairness or consistency in conduct means : if I could judge reasons differently when they bear on my interests, or disregard my principles when they conflict with my own advantage, I should have no principles at all. The concepts of *principles, reasons,* and *consistency* thus go together and they apply both in the cognitive judgment of beliefs and the moral assessment of conduct. In fact, they define a general concept of rationality. A rational man is one who is consistent in thought and in action, abiding by impartial and generalizable principles freely chosen as binding upon himself. Rationality is an essential aspect of human dignity and the rational goal of humanity is to construct a society in which such dignity shall flower, a society so ordered as to adjudicate rationally the affairs of free rational agents, an international and democratic republic. The job of education is to develop character in the broadest sense, that is, principled thought and action, in which the dignity of man is manifest.

In contrast to the insight model, the rule model clearly emphasizes the role of principles in the exercise of cognitive judgment. The strong point of the insight model can thus be preserved: The knower must indeed satisfy a further condition beyond the mere receiving and storing of a bit of information. But this condition need not, as in the insight model, be taken to involve simply the vision of an underlying reality; rather, it generally involves the capacity for a principled assessment of reasons bearing on justification of the belief in question. The knower, in short, must typically earn the right to confidence in his belief by acquiring the capacity to make a reasonable case for the belief in question. Nor is it sufficient for this case to have been explicitly taught. What is generally expected of the knower is that his autonomy be evidenced in the ability to construct and evaluate fresh and alternative arguments, the power to innovate, rather than just the capacity to reproduce stale arguments earlier stored. The emphasis on innovation, which we found to be an advantage of the insight model, is thus capable of being preserved by the rule model as well.

Nor does the rule model in any way deny the psychological phenomenon of insight. It merely stresses that insight itself, wherever it is relevant to decision or judgment, is filtered through a network of background principles. It brings out thereby that insight is not an isolated, momentary, or personal matter, that the growth of knowledge is not to be construed as a personal interaction between teacher and student, but rather as mediated by general principles definitive of rationality.

Furthermore, while the previous models, as we have seen, are peculiarly and narrowly *cognitive* in relevance, the rule model embraces *conduct* as well as cognition, itself broadly conceived as including processes of judgment and deliberation. Teaching, it suggests, should be geared not simply to the transfer of information nor even to the development of insight, but to the inculcation of principled judgment and conduct, the building of autonomous and rational character which underlies the enterprises of science, morality and culture. Such inculcation should not, of course, be construed mechanically. Rational character and critical judgment grow only through increased participation in adult experience and criticism, through treatment which respects the dignity of learner as well as teacher. We have here, again, a radical gap which cannot be closed by the teacher's efforts alone. He must rely on the spirit of rational dialogue and critical reflection for the development of character, acknowledging that this implies the freedom to reject as well as to accept what is taught. Kant himself holds, however, that rational principles are somehow embedded in the structure of the human mind, so that education builds on a solid foundation. In any event, the stakes are high, for on such building by education depends the prospect of humanity as an ideal quality of life.

There is much of value in the rule model, as I have sketched it. Certainly, rationality is a fundamental cognitive and moral virtue and as such should, I believe, form a basic objective of teaching. Nor should the many historical connotations of the term 'rationality' here mislead us. There is no intent to suggest a faculty of reason, nor to oppose reason to experience or to the emotions. Nor is rationality being construed as the process of making logical deductions. What is in point here is simply the autonomy of the student's judgment, his right to seek reasons in support of claims upon his credibilities and loyalties, and his correlative obligation to deal with such reasons in a principled manner.

Moreover, adoption of the rule model does not necessarily exclude what is important in the other two models; in fact, it can be construed quite plausibly as supplementing their legitimate emphases. For, intermediate between the public treasury of accumulated lore mirrored by the impression model, and the personal and intuitive grasp of the student mirrored by the insight model, it places general principles of rational judgment capable of linking them.

Yet, there is something too formal and abstract in the rule model, as I have thus far presented it. For the operative principles of rational judgment at any given time are, after all, much more detailed and specific than a mere requirement of formal consistency. Such consistency is certainly fundamental, but the way its demands are concretely interpreted, elaborated, and supplemented in any field of inquiry or practice, varies with the field, the state of knowledge, and the advance of relevant methodological sophistication. The concrete rules governing inference and procedure in the special sciences, for example, are surely not all embedded in the human mind, even if the demands of formal consistency, as such, *are* universally compelling. These concrete rules and standards, techniques and methodological criteria evolve and grow with the advance of knowledge itself; they form a live tradition of rationality in the realm of science.

Indeed, the notion of tradition is a better guide here, it seems to me, than appeal to the innate structure of the human mind. Rationality in natural inquiry is embodied in the relatively young tradition of science, which defines and redefines those principles by means of which evidence is to be interpreted and meshed with theory. Rational judgment in the realm of science is, consequently, judgment which accords with such principles, as crystallized at the time in question. To teach rationality in science is to interiorize these principles in the student, but furthermore, to introduce him to the live and evolving *tradition* of natural science, which forms their significant context of development and purpose.

Scholarship in history is subject to an analogous interpretation, for beyond the formal demands of reason, in the sense of consistency, there is a concrete tradition of technique and methodology defining the historian's procedure and his assessment of reasons for or against particular historical accounts. To teach rationality in history is, in effect, here also to introduce the student to a live tradition of historical scholarship. Similar remarks might be made also with respect to other areas, e.g. law, philosophy and the politics of democratic society. The fundamental point is that rationality cannot be taken simply as an abstract and general ideal. It is embodied in *multiple evolving traditions*, in which the basic condition holds that issues are resolved by reference to *reasons*, themselves defined by *principles* purporting to be impartial and universal. These traditions should, I believe, provide an important focus for teaching.

5. CONCLUSION

I have intimated that I find something important in each of the models we have considered. The impression model reflects, as I have said, the cumulative growth of knowledge in its *public* sense. Our aim in teaching should surely be to preserve and extend this growth. But we cannot do this by storing it piecemeal within the learner. We preserve it, as the insight model stresses, only if we succeed in transmitting the live spark that keeps it growing, the insight which is a product of each learner's efforts to make sense of public knowledge in his own terms, and to confront it with reality. Finally, as the rule model suggests, such confrontation involves deliberation and judgment, and hence presupposes general and impartial principles governing the assessment of reasons bearing on the issues. Without such guiding principles, the very conception of rational deliberation collapses, and the concepts of rational and moral conduct, moreover, lose their meaning. Our teaching needs thus to introduce students to those principles we ourselves acknowledge as fundamental, general, and impartial, in the various departments of thought and action.

We need not pretend that these principles of ours are immutable or innate. It is enough that they are what we ourselves acknowledge, that they are the best we know, and that we are prepared to improve them should the need and occasion arise. Such improvement is possible, however, only if we succeed in passing on, too, the multiple live traditions in which they are embodied, and in which a sense of their history, spirit, and direction may be discerned. Teaching, from this point of view, is clearly not, as the behaviourists would have it, a matter of the teacher's shaping the student's behaviour or of controlling his mind. It is a matter of passing on those traditions of principled thought and action which define the rational life for teacher as well as student.

As Professor Richard Peters has recently written,[4]

The critical procedures by means of which established content is assessed, revised, and adapted to new discoveries have public criteria written into them that stand as impersonal standards to which both teacher and learner must give their allegiance. . . . To liken education to therapy, to conceive of it as imposing a pattern on another person or as fixing the environment so that he 'grows', fails to do justice to the shared impersonality both of the content that is handed on and of the criteria by reference to which it is criticized and revised. The teacher is not a detached operator who is bringing about some kind of result in another person which is external to him. His task is to try to get others on the inside of a public form of life that he shares and considers to be worthwhile.

In teaching, we do not impose our wills on the student, but introduce him to the many mansions of the heritage in which we ourselves strive to live, and to the improvement of which we are ourselves dedicated.

NOTES

1. Dewey, J., *Democracy and Education* (New York, The Macmillan Company, 1916), p. 62.

2. Dewey, J., ibid., 'The supposed original faculties of observation, recollection, willing, thinking, etc. are purely mythological. There are no such ready-made powers waiting to be exercised and thereby trained.'

3. *Ancient Christian Writers*, No. 9, St. Augustine, 'The Teacher', edited by Quasten, J. and Plumpe, J. C., translated and annotated by Colleran, J. M., Newman Press, Westminster, Md.: 1950; relevant passages may also be found in Price, Kingsley, *Education and Philosophical Thought* (Boston, Allyn and Bacon, Inc., 1962), pp. 145–59.

4. *Education as Initiation*, an inaugural lecture delivered at the University of London Institute of Education, 9 December 1963; published for the University of London Institute of Education by Evans Brothers, Ltd, London.

9

INSTRUCTION AND LEARNING BY DISCOVERY
R. F. Dearden

I. INTRODUCTION: 'TEACHING'

The purpose of this article is to examine and compare two conceptions of teaching which have often been set in sharp contrast to each other. The contrast which I have in mind is that between the teacher as an instructor and the teacher as a facilitator of the children's own creations and discoveries. This contrast has been much more prominent in discussions of primary education than of education at any other stage and is representative of two distinct traditions of teaching which are present at that stage. These might be called, as Blyth calls them in his recent book,[1] the elementary school tradition and the developmental tradition, which latter is especially associated with Froebel and those theories often referred to as 'child-centred'. There are, of course, many aspects to the contrast between these two traditions. One could discuss it in terms of personal relationships, pupil motivation, creativity, classroom climate and so on, but the aspect which I want quite specifically to focus attention on is that of knowledge and the passing on of that knowledge. It is for that reason that the title 'Instruction and Learning by Discovery', which has a strong cognitive flavour to it, seemed most apt.

Now it might well seem to some that a misleading twist or bias is already being imported into the discussion at the start by insisting that instruction and learning by discovery pick out two conceptions of *teaching*. For the point about learning by discovery, it might be objected, is precisely that the teacher does not teach: the children find out everything for themselves. The answer to this is immediately to grant the point of the objection, namely that being told something is quite different from finding it out for oneself, but to deny that it is only in the case of instruction that we can properly speak of 'teaching'. This 'finding out for oneself' which is contrasted with being instructed is of a peculiar kind. No sane person really supposes that children are going to rediscover the whole of what they need to know quite apart from the teacher's agency; if that were possible we should not need schools at all. In other words, it is not by chance that these discoveries are made but as a result of the teacher's deliberate contrivance, in 'structuring the environment' for example, or in practising discovery 'methods'. Both in the case of instruction and in the case of learning by discovery, then, the teacher's agency and influence are present, though admittedly they are present in very different ways.

Behind the objection to allowing that learning by discovery involves 'teaching' there lies a confusion over what sort of concept 'teaching' is. It may seem that for a variety of operations all to be called 'teaching' there must be some one nuclear operation common to them all on account of which the concept is applied. In that case instruction might readily suggest itself as the most promising candidate for this nuclear role, and then there would be some justice in denying that learning by discovery involved teaching. But the assumption at work here is mistaken, and the way in which it is mistaken merits attention. It can be brought out by some examples which I have adapted from Ryle's *Concept of Mind*.

If we were to consider 'farming' as an activity, we might note that ploughing was one farming job and tree-spraying another, while applying fertilizer is a third job and milking is a fourth, yet there is no one common nuclear operation by virtue of doing which alone a man is to be called a farmer. Similarly with solicitoring, drafting wills is one job and arranging for the transfer of property another, while defending a client in court is a third and explaining some point of law is a fourth, but again there is no one common nuclear operation present in all. So with teaching, I suggest, there is a whole range of operations any of which may, under suitable conditions, be examples of it, such as writing on a blackboard, correcting exercises, punishing, answering questions, demonstrating a procedure, setting material for reading, supervising practical work and so on. Teaching is what Ryle has called a 'polymorphous' concept: it can take many forms, and instructing is only one of them.

What, then, is characteristic of teaching as an activity, if it is not some nuclear operation such as instructing? This question is not to be answered by a review, even a very extensive review, of the particular things which a teacher might do, but by considering the central *intention* which lies behind his efforts. That intention is to bring it about that someone learns something. Teaching is not just placing things before people for their consideration, or informing, or telling, or conversing, or narrating, but taking such measures as will bring it about that something envisaged by the teacher is learned, by which I mean that it is both understood and remembered. What we teach is intended not just to be registered, but to be kept in mind : teaching involves the deliberate equipping of a person in some way, whether in respect of knowledge, skill or settled habit.

The next question to ask is whether there are any restrictions to be placed on this process vaguely called 'bringing it about'. Since it is necessarily the aim of the teacher to get someone to understand and remember something, such measures as he adopts must be consistent with achieving that aim. But nothing more specific than that is implied. What *method* to adopt in teaching, or what kind of *approach* to use, is not further indicated by the concept, but depends on the specific sorts of thing we wish to teach and the various psychological and other conditions which bear upon being effective in teaching. If we know that a person has been teaching, and we have no other clues supplied by the context as to what in particular he has been teaching, or how, then we know very little indeed of the form which his activities took. Such images as come to mind will reflect the idiosyncrasies, experience or prejudices of the particular individuals whose images they are and will be in no way warranted by the information here given. But what people customarily think of when they hear a word is of no philosophical interest; it is what they are entitled to think that matters, and that is a question of what is implied by a concept. Knowing that a person has been teaching entitles us to think only that he has been active in such ways as are consistent with the intention to bring it about that someone will learn something. That way may have been to instruct, or to have staged the making of discoveries by someone—discoveries relative to the learner and not to the teacher, that is—so that we return once again to the point that it is two conceptions of teaching that are being compared here.

2. INSTRUCTION

If we turn now to consider instruction, we shall have to be on our guard against the very same mistake that was pointed out in connection with the concept of teaching. On hearing the word 'instruction', we may form a picture of a browbeating, hectoring, offensive teacher of a sort admittedly sufficiently common in the past to have formed a public stereotype, and in rejecting this *picture* we may think that we have validly rejected all instruction. But that would be so only if it could first be shown that all instruction must necessarily be of this bullying and insensitive kind. A further feature of this picture which is no necessary accompaniment of instruction is that of baldly telling someone something, for example who followed whom on the throne of England, or what the exports of South Wales are, so that things are learned by rote. Instruction *need* not be confined to such a bald exposition of various items of information, but may include a reasoned explanation of something or an experimental demonstration of it. The principle of 'learning by experience' may be interpreted here as requiring *sense*-experience and be satisfied by a reference to what can be seen in some visual aid, or by an excursion to some instructive museum, gallery or historical site. Again, instruction *need* not be given by word of mouth, but may be given by referring the learner to a lesson in a textbook or to the appropriate programme in a machine. Far from being tied to some particular form which the accident of tradition has given to it, instruction may take many forms and be given in more than one manner. Furthermore, an important distinction often unmade in discussing instruction is that between formal instruction and incidental instruction, the former implying a set time when the teacher or teacher-substitute delivers some planned lesson, while the latter may be present in a much more loosely structured classroom regime. The one may be defensible where the other is not.

If we ask what is distinctive of instruction as a way of passing on knowledge, the answer would seem to be that in instruction this knowledge is directly imparted. Instruction does not hint at, or seek to elicit, or guide one in finding out for oneself, but directly imparts, and hence in this respect stands in sharp contrast as a way of teaching to contriving that children learn by discovery. Instruction stands in contrast also, though this is very often overlooked, to other forms of verbal teaching. The fact that instruction, as the imparting of knowledge, requires the use of language, does not entail the converse that all use of language by the teacher must be instruction. In Plato's dialogue the *Meno*, Socrates teaches a slave that a square double the area of a given square is to be constructed on the diagonal of the given square, and not by doubling the length of its sides, but he does not actually impart this information : he

138

elicits it. At one point he comments to Meno as follows :

> Now notice what, starting from this state of perplexity, he will discover by seeking the truth in company with me . . . . Be ready to catch me if I give him any instruction or explanation instead of simply interrogating him on his own opinions.[2]

Though all instruction may require the use of language, then, not all teaching by the use of language is instruction, and though this may seem obvious enough when once it has been pointed out, it has nevertheless escaped the notice of the more extreme reactionaries against the teacher as instructor who dominates the elementary school tradition. To argue that a teacher ought not to teach by instructing does not mean that he must be silent, which would make him about as effective as a boxer with his hands tied behind his back, or an Alpine guide forbidden to use his feet, but leaves a great range of linguistic uses open to him, such as eliciting by questioning, hinting, commenting and even professing ignorance.

If teaching by instructing implies the imparting of knowledge, or more briefly if it is teaching by telling, what are we to think of it? No doubt there are many things to be said here about pupil motivation and so on, but I shall confine comment to an appraisal of the adequacy of instruction as a way of passing on *knowledge*. From this point of view it would seem sensible enough, if teachers have to pass on in a few years what has taken the labour of centuries and often the insight of genius to arrive at, to set up special institutions called schools and to make them places of instruction, though instruction doubtless enlightened by psychology and less harsh in manner than in the traditional picture. How better than by instruction could you teach French, handwriting, how to read, swimming, technical drawing or metalwork, assuming that you wanted to teach these things? Especially where *skill* is concerned, whether physical skills like swimming, or practical skills like carpentry, intelligent instruction, whether formal or incidental, together with practice, would seem to be quite the best way of teaching, and we may notice that wherever a teaching job is specifically that of passing on such a skill we do talk of 'instructors', such as driving, gunnery and flying instructors, or instructors in the various crafts.

There are, however, kinds of knowledge not normally referred to as 'skills' which require the acquisition and operational mastery of concepts, principles and criteria of critical appraisal, as for example in mathematics, science and history. To teach subjects such as these solely by instruction would be to treat them as collections of information, an error which was in fact conspicuously perpetrated in the elementary school tradition. Learning science or history, for example, was a stocking up with a mass of information imparted by the teacher, a conception of teaching which the Hadow Report of 1931 (Section 75) made famous in the phrase 'knowledge to be acquired and facts to be stored'. What are we to think of instruction, then, not in relation to French, handwriting, swimming, metalwork and so on, but in relation to such subjects as mathematics and science?

From the point of view of knowledge still, and not that of motivation, it might seem that instruction was to be criticized because the knowledge passed on was 'knowledge' only as being based on the authority of the teacher and not as being seen by the learner to be appropriately justified by proofs, evidences, arguments and so on. But this will not do, because there is no reason at all why proofs, evidences and arguments could not be made the content of instruction quite as much as what they are the reasons for. Nor is it the case that instruction must be limited to material of a fairly low level of generality. In primary school mathematics, for example, the laws of arithmetic and the concepts of place-value and of a base *could* all be made the objects of instruction. So long as there is something definite to be imparted, then it can be made the content of instruction. If instruction is to be found inadequate, therefore, it cannot be from the point of view of the instructor, but from the point of view of the learner's mastery of the instruction.

If not just memorization of the content of instruction is desirable, but an intelligent mastery of it, involving judgment in its application, then instruction cannot be wholly adequate. But the implication of this is that instruction needs to be supplemented, not supplanted. It needs to be supplemented by opportunities for trying out for oneself how the knowledge which is being imparted is to be applied. Just as instruction in a skill needs to be supplemented by practice if performance is to be raised to the level of being 'good at' whatever skill it is, so with instruction in the various academic subjects opportunities need to be given for exercising judgment in applying the concepts, principles and criteria in a suitable variety of cases. And when that is done, then instruction would seem to be at its most intelligent, and from the point of view of knowledge and passing on that knowledge, would seem not to be open to any important

objection. We might next consider, then, the much canvassed alternative to it of learning by discovery, in which what is to be learnt
is not imparted and then mastered but is found out by oneself in the
first place.

3. 'DISCOVERY'

In discussing discovery methods, or 'finding out' as opposed to being
told, not a great deal turns on analysis of the meanings of these
words. It is the particular conception of *how* one is supposed to discover, or find out, that is crucial. But there are one or two points
perhaps worth making about discovery in general before proceeding
to a more particularized discussion. In the first place, the frequently
rhapsodic description of making a discovery in terms of thrills and
glows is apt to suggest that discovery is essentially an exciting psychological experience, perhaps the sort of experience that we have
on finding a cherished object we thought we had lost, or on finishing
a difficult piece of work with a sigh of deep satisfaction. But such a
connection between making a discovery and glows of satisfaction is
purely contingent, since one could have all of these feelings in the
false belief that one had discovered something, and on the other
hand one really could have discovered something yet without feeling
anything in particular about it.

'Discovery' and 'finding out' are what Ryle has called 'achievement words' like winning, seeing and hearing, which are to be contrasted with 'task words', such as running, travelling, looking and
listening. In using an achievement word we are asserting there to be
some state of affairs over and above the person's activity or state of
mind, and a biographical account of a person's efforts and feelings
does not by itself tell us whether he has brought about that state of
affairs or not. We may try in vain, or try and rashly claim success,
but whether what we do is to count as an achievement depends on
how things are in the end, not on how we feel or the effort we
exerted. Faced with finding the area of a parallelogram for the first
time, I may have the most thrilling and deeply satisfying experience
you can imagine of seeing how it is to be done, but unless I have got
it *right* this cannot count as a discovery, or a finding out, or an insight, in spite of all the thrills and glows, because 'discovery' carries
an implication of the *truth* of what is put forward. A false or mistaken discovery is a contradiction. The achievement implied by
discovery, then, is that of getting at the truth in some sought for

respect, and this is a matter independent of our pleasures or pains.

The consequence of ignoring this point is that 'discovery methods' of teaching may be made to sound more reliable than they really are, but the illusion of guaranteed success engendered by the proleptic use of 'discovery' here is like talking of 'creative writing' before anyone has yet had a chance to have a look at it. The upshot of a lot of bustling activity might be confusion, muddle, uncritical acceptance of first ideas, or failure to have any ideas at all, as well as possibly having the result of making a discovery. Evidently this teaching method must involve considerable art if the chances of success are in fact to be high. But having noticed that the epithet 'discovery' could easily falsely prejudge the issue, I shall pass on to consider some particular conceptions of *how* success is to be reasonably assured, since it is here that the really important issues are likely to lie. One of the main points of what follows will be to try to show that the blanket term 'discovery methods' conceals and confuses certain crucial distinctions, distinctions of which we ought to be sharply aware if muddled practice is to be avoided.

4. LEARNING BY DISCOVERY

(1) *The pre-school model*

A convenient point at which to begin is with what is frequently held up as the very paradigm of how children should learn, namely the learning of the pre-school child as he trots round the garden, plays with his friends or explores the neighbourhood. He discovers in this way a bird's nest in a hedge, that worms wriggle, that table tops are slippy, where the milkman goes, and so on. School learning, it is said, should be just like that, or as near like it as possible: a discovering for oneself under the pressure of real interest and in the course of a spontaneous activity. Finding out about mathematics and science should be an eager lighting on one fascinating fact after another, just like exploring a wood or seeing what is in a pond; for mathematics and science, it is pointed out, are not confined to the study or laboratory, but are 'all around us'.

Now what needs to be questioned here is not the validity which this conception may have for the learning of various miscellaneous facts about the world. There would seem to be no reason to deny that a child would, in normal circumstances, almost inevitably learn many facts about himself and his situation simply as a condition of forming and carrying out purposes. It is the validity of this as a conception of how we could learn such subjects as mathematics or science which is questionable. To take the case of science first, if all that is meant is a pottering about in which one may or may not notice that reflections in a spoon are distorted, what things look like when seen through coloured glass, that some objects float while others sink and so on, then no doubt this account is unexceptionable. With very young children especially there is an important place for this kind of learning, but such limited and undirected curiosity does not amount to science. All of this could and did and does go on where science has never been heard of. Such finding out does not even begin to resemble science until problems start to present themselves which cannot be solved without putting forward, and then testing experimentally, suggested solutions of a non-obvious kind.[3] Even the perception of a scientific problem requires more than naïve curiosity, and the concept of an experiment implies more than pushing and poking at things. This point tends to be obscured by the belief that scientific discoveries are accidents which could happen to anybody. Certainly a scientific discovery might be made by accident, but the point to notice is that these accidents only happen to people with a certain kind of training and with certain things preoccupying them. 'Discovery, like surprise, favors the well prepared mind.'[4]

If elementary scientific investigation was as natural as this account likes to make out, it would require explaining how it is that this tradition of inquiry is historically so late to get started and geographically still so limited in extent. Even to try to classify what floats and what sinks, quite apart from trying to arrive at the general conditions for flotation, marks a sophistication which would still be strange to many. Far from being like trotting round a garden, learning science and what is characteristic of a scientific inquiry involves initiation into a particular social tradition of inquiry and is therefore something which, one way or another, has to be taught. In case this should now seem so obvious as not to be worth pointing out, it must be added that not only is it thought by some that science somehow just arises out of pottering about with things, but it may also be thought not even necessary that the teacher should know any science for this to happen. According to a recent article in *Educational Research*,[5] 'such is the interest among our young children that even the non-scientist can do a great deal by merely providing opportunities and encouragement'. How it is that a person himself ignorant of science is nevertheless able to 'provide opportunities' and reliably to ascertain that scientific 'discoveries' are in fact being made by his class is left unexplained in this article. But there cannot be many practising teachers who suppose that ignorance of anything is a qualification for teaching it. To teach something in ignorance of it is not just difficult : it is logically impossible.

With mathematics, the pre-school model is even less adequate, since the concepts and truths of mathematics are not even empirical, and hence can even less plausibly be represented as wide open to the curious gaze of tireless young investigators. Indeed, there have been and are societies which have never progressed beyond such primitive forms of counting as the tally-stick, though they probably all noticed that worms wriggle, what floats and a similar mixed assortment of empirical facts. But although a spontaneous generation theory of mathematical knowledge might seem to be implicit in the doctrines of the more extreme reactionaries against instruction, if these theorists were faced with the implications of their view, they would probably disown it, at least verbally. Much more usual, and at least apparently less extreme, is a conception of learning by discovery in terms of 'planned experience'. That is to say, the teacher is to contrive situations or to present materials which are so 'structured' that appropriate experiences must be provided for the children. What we do, on this theory, is to embed a conceptual structure in some materials, or in a 'concept kindergarten', from which it can then be 'abstracted' in the course of play. The child is to 'notice' the common features which certain things have, or the relationships which they have one to another, and 'abstract' them, this 'abstraction' being regarded as a *process*.

(2) *Abstractionism*

A clear example of abstractionism as a theory of concept formation is provided by the writings of Dr. Z. P. Dienes, whose wooden blocks for forming concepts of place-value and of a base are now quite well known. Dienes writes of the child as 'extracting' the requisite features and as 'discarding' irrelevances, almost as if a mental prising off of what the designer had embedded in the blocks were going on. The process, he writes, 'should probably run as follows : an abstraction process, followed by a symbolization process, followed again by the learning of the use of the symbols'.[6] The 'abstraction process', it should be added, is allotted by Dienes to a period of a few weeks of free play with the materials. Again, the recent publication *Mathematics in Primary Schools* similarly speaks of 'abstractive teaching methods',[7] the 'abstraction of an idea'[8] and of what happens 'once a child has abstracted the concept'.[9] And just as Dienes writes of following up the abstraction process with 'symbolization', so here there is a process of 'making explicit' what has already been learned in the 'planned' experience provided.

This theory is, of course, at least quite as old as John Locke, whose *Essay Concerning Human Understanding,* published in the seventeenth century, based a whole theory of knowledge on abstraction. It lies behind the view that science is 'inductive', in the sense that the scientist is supposed to proceed by gathering instances and then moving to cautious generalizations based on them, rather than by boldly setting up hypotheses and then testing them experimentally. It was implicit also in the didactic apparatus of Montessori and the idea of 'sense training', so that it is not some brand new theory that we are here invited to espouse. A convincing refutation of abstractionism as a theory of concept formation, however, was recently given by Geach, so that only a few points specifically tailored to this as a theoretical basis for discovery methods of teaching need to be made here.[10]

To begin with, we may agree that any situation or state of affairs can always be conceived of in a great variety of ways, depending for example on the present interests and past learning of those who come to it. Assuming that a certain moving object in a field has been discriminated, we may conceive of it as an animal, a quadruped, a horned creature, a ruminant, the mother of a calf, a menace to our safe passage, a milk production unit, or indeed just as a cow. In fact, the potential variety of the ways in which something may be conceived is now being exploited in the so-called 'creativity tests' in which the person tested is called on to conceive of some object, such as a brick, in as many different ways as possible. Suppose we take as a further example a child's toy, say a set of bricks. What conceptions of the bricks will he develop in the course of playing with them? Here again we may agree that the potential variety is enormous. He may conceive of a tower, a ship, a train, a pattern of colours, a sorting of the bricks into various kinds, their use as missiles, and so on, depending on the concepts which he has acquired and his present interests.

Now the point I want to make is this. When a teacher presents a child with some apparatus or materials, such as Cuisenaire rods, Dienes blocks or an assortment of objects on an investigation table, he typically has in mind some one particular conception of what he presents in this way. But then the incredible assumption seems to be made that the teacher's conception of the situation somehow confers a special uniqueness upon it such that the children must also quite inevitably conceive of it in this way too, even though they may not even possess the concepts involved. In some mysterious way, a special potency is thought to inhere in teaching apparatus such that if children play with it or manipulate it, significant experiences must be had, and important concepts must be abstracted. For example, if we let children play with Cuisenaire rods, then in building houses with them and so on it is reasonable to suppose that they will find out that two sticks placed end to end give the same length whichever way round the sticks go. But because the *teacher* sees this fact as a concrete illustration of the commutative law that $a + b = b + a$, the *child* is credited with having had an important mathematical experience. Far from having just played with sticks, he is seen as being poised on the brink of, or even as having made, a major mathematical discovery. Again, a child given a block of Plasticine to play with naturally breaks it up for modelling purposes and later puts it together again. But he has not just fingered Plasticine it is thought. The sage onlooking of the hovering teacher has conferred a special significance on his manipulations such that important steps have been taken in this episode towards abstracting the concept of the conservation of volume. To put the point quite generally, an unconscious assumption behind the advocacy of *this* notion of discovery methods is that in spite of the variety of ways in which any situation may be conceived, the teacher's conceiving of it in one particular way is somehow thought to confer a special uniqueness on it such that children must come to conceive of it in that way too.

The explanation of this strange belief seems to be twofold. In the first place it is reasoned, quite correctly, that instead of just *telling* children about various things they ought to know, it would be valuable to provide concrete examples or models of those things. We can provide a set of sticks which supply a model of the natural numbers from 1 to 10, or a set of blocks which model the relative values of different places in number notation. This is correct and important. But then it is falsely assumed that a person who does not possess the knowledge that we possess must still see these materials as *examples* or *models,* and hence will be able to 'get back' to the way in which we conceive them. Yet without possession of our concepts in the first place, it makes no sense to talk of examples or models, because an example, or a model, or an instance, or a feature, is always an example, model, instance or feature *of* something, and unless you know what follows this 'of' you logically cannot perceive the thing *as* an example, model, and so on. This is not to say that there can be no value in a short initial period of play with new materials, for example to satisfy curiosity, but that such value as there may be is quite different from what it is here being claimed to be.

Suppose I wish to teach someone syllogistic logic, and to do this I require to make clear to him the logical powers of expressions such as 'all S is P', 'some S is not P', 'no S is P' and so on, where S and P stand for classes of things. I might do this by drawing various circles, some overlapping and some wholly outside or inside others. This would be a model of the various class relationships involved. But instead I issue compasses to a class and instruct them freely to draw circles. Can I say that important experiences in syllogistic logic are being provided here? Can I say that during four weeks or so of play with circles, important abstractings have been going on and now need merely to be symbolized, or just to be made explicit, as logical relationships? Surely this is no more likely, short of Divine intervention, than that advances have been made in the design of spectacle frames, or that the symbol of the Olympic Games has been arrived at, or that a value for pi has been discovered? While freely drawing circles may look to *me,* with my preconceptions, to be an important logical or pre-logical experience, and I may write books on the abstraction of formal logic from play with circles, the fact remains that from the child's point of view the truest description of what occurred is probably that fun was had just drawing circles. To return to the real case, we may well ask why it is that although children have played with blocks and bricks for years, it is only now, when they are provided in schools, that important mathematical concept-abstractings are supposed to accompany play with them. Perhaps it is the sign of a new state of mathematical grace which has now descended upon children.

A second explanation of the belief in abstractionism may lie in the experiments which psychologists have carried out on concept-formation. Bruner, for example, has done a famous series of experiments[11] in which sets of cards, each set patterned in such a way as to have some one feature which makes it a set, are presented to subjects who are then asked to find the feature which the cards have in common. In this way, Bruner has produced interesting results about the strategies adopted by different people in setting about this task. Now it might be said that in giving children apparatus which illustrates or exemplifies some concept or relationship, we are doing nothing very different from what Bruner did, so why is abstractionism so plainly erroneous? The answer is that there is all the difference in the world between experiments such as Bruner's and free play with concept-forming blocks of wood. In Bruner's case it is a requirement of the experimental set-up that the subjects shall have clear instructions as to what they must try to do. They do not just play, while Bruner hovers in the background weaving stories round their play, but at the very start of the experiment, when they are instructed what to do, they already have a vague concept of what they are looking for; they know the *sort* of thing it is, and their task is to specify that vague concept more precisely. There is no abstractionism here, but the usual guess-and-test of purposeful enquiry. But a child who is presented with apparatus which *we* call structured, and who is then left to 'have experiences', is not in this position at all. He is not searching for anything of which he has been given a rough idea already, but is just playing as he pleases, and only the belief in innate ideas and a natural tendency towards mathematical understanding could lead us to suppose that he will do more than learn a few very obvious empirical facts about the materials with which he is playing.

Even if a child has some mathematical knowledge, however, all sorts of unconscious assumptions on our part may blind us to the possible variety of conceptions open to him. For example, if we take this arrangement of Cuisenaire rods

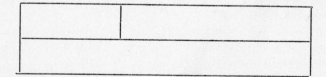

it is by no means obvious that this is a structured representation of anything mathematical. It may be just a pattern of colours, the start of a model wall, a test to see whether the two layers are exactly the same in length, and so on. Even if we give the rods their usual values in the Cuisenaire system of 2, 4 and 6, and say that this arrangement represents $2 + 4 = 6$, all sorts of conventions of representation are being presupposed here. For example, we could as well regard this as a representation of $2 + 4 + 6 = 12$, so bringing out the assumed convention of what represents 'equality'. We could regard it as $\frac{1}{3} + \frac{2}{3} = 1$, or as $40 + 80 = 120$, so bringing out the assumed convention of what represents a unit. In short, the situation is 'structured', not in some sense 'by itself', but only in the eyes of the person who has been specifically taught how to conceive of it, though how he conceives of it may come to seem so natural and obvious to *him* that he may assume anyone must conceive of it in this way too. In just the same way it is often assumed that if we put pictures over the sentences in a reading primer, it must be just *obvious* to the child what the sentence 'says' from looking at the picture, whereas it may be doubted how many adults would respond in the way required if someone presented them with a picture and just said 'What sentence does this depict?'[12]

'Mathematics is all around us' the advocates of this sort of discovery say. And of course mathematics is all around us; so too are atomic physics, gravitation, molecular biology and organic chemistry. They are all, in a sense, though not all in the same sense, 'there': but the point is that you need more than eyes to see them, and if children are to conceive of their environment in mathematical or in scientific ways, they will have to be more than placed in contact with it. They will have to be taught *how* to conceive it, though the fact that other influences besides that of the school are always at work may blur the issue by making it really seem that some child has just spun it all out of his head, or 'abstracted' it from apparatus. Children are not, as seems often to be assumed, like a teacher on a refresher course who enjoys finding all sorts of new and interesting ways of applying his already *existing* knowledge to the latest apparatus, but are more like such a teacher faced with set theory, if he has never met that before. Even this, however, is an unfair analogy, since such a teacher has at least a notion of the sort of thing that a mathematical relation or structure is, whereas in all of this young children are complete beginners.

(3) *Problem solving*
The two conceptions of learning by discovery which have been considered so far, and strongly criticized, do not exhaust the possibilities however. 'Learning by discovery' can be given another, and much

more plausible, interpretation besides the interpretations based on the model of pre-school learning or on abstractionism. What this alternative is we can begin to see by returning to the point, made earlier in discussing instruction, that not all use of language by the teacher need be instruction. For example, in questioning Meno's slave, Socrates drew attention to what the boy was discovering. This alternative conception, in which the teacher much more actively participates, is often present alongside the conceptions that have already been criticized, but is rarely distinguished from them. Yet the resemblance is in fact slight. *Mathematics in Primary Schools,* for example, vacillates throughout between 'providing experience' and something like the Socratic method. In that recent publication of the new Schools Council, the Socratic method is in fact in one place explicitly endorsed,[13] and *discussion* is stressed in several places. For instance, after citing an example of the discovery of the commutative law of addition, that a + b = b + a, the text continues : 'It was quite clear that if the teacher had not discussed the number patterns with the boy, and questioned him, he would not have made the discovery at all.'[14] But the writer seems to be quite unconscious of the fact that this is a very different sort of 'discovery method' from the 'planned experiences' of abstractionism.

In this third conception of discovery methods, the teacher is much more than the hovering provider of materials, or the structurer of an environment from which new concepts are supposed to be abstracted in the course of undirected activity. In this third conception, the teacher questions, discusses, hints, suggests and instructs what to do to find out. But this way of teaching is not, or not predominantly, a way of instruction, because what has actually to be learned is not imparted. The stress is on the individual's mastery of knowledge, so that throughout all this teacher activity what the teacher says is specific enough to focus attention and effort in the desired direction, but at the same time open enough to leave genuine discoveries still to be made, discoveries which the teacher can be reasonably confident will be made on the basis of what he knows has already been learned in the past and the deliberate guidance he is now giving. For example, he may instruct that squares of numbers be drawn and that the answers to some multiplication tables be shaded on them, but leave open the discovery of the patterns so revealed. He may instruct in the conventions governing the representation of cardinal numbers and the four processes of arithmetic with certain materials, but leave open the discovery of a multitude of particular number relationships which can then be made. Posing the problem of how to find the area of an irregular shape, he may alternately prompt, tell, question, encourage and then watch, in a subtle interplay of minds which follows no set pattern. Where elementary science is concerned, he may suggest, orally or on a card, a certain problem and indicate or discuss how the solution might be found, but leave open the finding of the answer. For example, he may suggest an enquiry into how a bean extends itself in growth, and suggest marking it at intervals as a way of finding out; but he does not say what will be found out, whether the bean extends at its tip, emerges from the ground or stretches like elastic, for example. Similarly, it may be suggested in discussion that electric bulbs could be wired in series or in parallel, but without actually saying how this affects brightness, or how the failure of one of the bulbs affects the others : that can be left to be found out. He may give instructions for the use of a hydrometer in fresh and salt water and in paraffin, but leave it to be discovered how flotation is affected in each case. And once the concept of an experiment has been taught, there is no reason to doubt that a few children at least will be able sometimes to devise simple experimental tests for themselves to answer questions that have come up.

This interpretation of 'learning by discovery' has to be set in the strongest possible contrast to the interpretations based on pre-school learning or on abstractionism which have already been discussed. This kind of discovery is not a romantic sailing forth into the unknown on a journey which will bring who-knows-what ecstatic joys and thrills, nor is it the illumination of the soul by an intellectual grace which somehow proceeds from apparatus. The teacher does not 'provide experiences' but *guides* experience, by the subtle use of language, towards learning something that is regarded as educationally valuable. In its recognition of the crucial role of language this conception is more like instruction than it is like abstractionism, though the centre of attention is the individual's mastery of what is to be learned rather than the instructional imparting of it. Again like instruction, this conception of teaching involves the planning of work, both to ensure steady progression and to allow for practice or revision, though the planning is more flexible than with a course of instruction since the sequence of learning is deliberately less closely controlled, and can be adapted to any useful side-interests that may arise. The only resemblance of this conception to abstractionism lies in its recognition of the importance of instances or examples of what is learned.

What are the merits of teaching by this kind of 'discovery method' as against teaching by instruction? Plainly it would be far too time-consuming for *everything* to have to be found out in this way.[15] Before trying to answer this question any further however, it needs to be pointed out that we do not have to make an exclusive choice between these two and presumably the intelligent teacher, as opposed to the doctrinaire who fervently adheres to the dogmas of a particular ideology, will make his own judgment as to what a particular occasion requires in the light of all its special circumstances. To vary what one does according to the situation is part of what it means to be intelligent. But the merits of the alternatives have to be appreciated to do this, so that the virtues of the discovery method have to be known.

Much is often said on the merits of learning by discovery from the point of view of improved motivation and the better retention of what is learned, though to discuss these points would fall outside the restricted scope of the present discussion. We might note, however, that in the midst of the acclaim for a new golden road to knowledge there are cautious and informed voices that doubt the factual basis of some of the claims which are being made.[16] What has to be considered here, however, is the possible merit of learning by discovery from the point of view of the *knowledge* gained by it. Is it superior in any important way to knowledge gained by formal or incidental instruction, for example?

One way in which learning by discovery is often thought to have merit is that in this way children do not just learn, but they 'learn how to learn'. The source of this popular, if somewhat obscure, phrase can be traced back to some experiments performed on monkeys by Harlow.[17] Harlow set a long and varied series of discrimination problems to his monkeys and found that their ability to solve them improved very considerably as the experiment proceeded. They were somehow using past experience to cope more easily with new problems. In short, they had done something, called by Harlow 'forming a learning set', which made the solution of new but similar problems much more efficient. The notion would therefore seem to be a variant on our old friend, transfer of training, the special point of this new experiment having been to refute the reduction of all learning to the formation of stimulus-response bonds by trial and error. Where school learning is concerned, what we would seem to have to suppose is that in learning by discovery children form certain general heuristic principles which enable them to get onto the right track with new problems much more rapidly and efficiently than would have been the case if the knowledge had been imparted by instruction. Two points need to be made about that.

First, whether there could be such general principles is not an empirical matter for psychologists to settle, though contentment with showing a correlation without seeking its explanation may make it seem otherwise. It is not obvious, for example, how discovering the area of a parallelogram would later facilitate discovering which numbers are prime, or how discovering which materials are electrical conductors would later facilitate finding out the conditions governing the period of a pendulum. A person might do better through greater confidence or interest gained from the previous success, but that is not 'learning how to learn' in any conceivable sense. The second point is that in so far as there could be general principles which would facilitate later learning, there does not seem to be any reason why they should not be made part of the content of instruction, as is done by people who lecture and write books on how to study, for example. The fact that instruction has in the past often been uninformed by the psychology of learning, and has been of a narrow and mentally limiting kind, is no argument at all against all possible forms of instruction, as was stressed earlier.

Another alternative, however, is that learning by discovery may have an advantage over instruction in respect of the mastery of what has to be learned, and for the kind of reason that Dewey gave. A pupil being instructed is in a receptive role which requires that the pace at which he goes and the sequence of what he attends to are determined by someone else, whereas a pupil working to find something out for himself can proceed at a pace individually suited to him and by a sequence of acts intelligently ordered in view of the end towards which he sees himself as moving. In short, learning by discovery allows more room for individual differences and permits a more intelligent appreciation of what one is doing. But to offset this gain a little is the greater chanciness which then necessarily enters into learning, since a teaching method which genuinely leaves things open for discovery also necessarily leaves open the opportunity for not discovering them. It would seem, however, that there really is the possibility here of a superiority over instruction in learning by discovery.

What I have tried to distinguish, then, is a conception of teaching by discovery which draws in the active verbal participation of the teacher in framing problems, suggesting, discussing, or instructing what initially to do, but which leaves the result of the learner's activity open in some important respect, so that what is to be learned has indeed to be found out, and is not imparted. The only resemblance between this conception of learning by discovery and the conception based on abstractionism is in the stress on first-hand experience wherever possible, but apart from that it is analogous more to instruction. The possible superiority of this third conception of learning by discovery over learning from intelligent instruction would need to be shown empirically, though one can see that on some occasions at least it might well be superior on account of its greater adaptation to individual differences and greater scope for intelligence. But whether this possibility is in fact realized is something that a philosopher ought to realize is not possible for him to say. In fact, with some idea of what we are looking for in mind, it is precisely the sort of thing that we could usefully set out to discover.

NOTES

1. Blyth, W. A. L., *English Primary Education* (1965), Vol. 2, Ch. 2.
2. Plato, *Meno*, 84 c.d. (W. K. C. Guthrie's translation).
3. Toulmin, S. E., *The Philosophy of Science* (1953), Ch. 2.
4. Bruner, J. S., 'The Act of Discovery' in *Readings in the Psychology of Cognition* (1965), ed. Anderson, R. C. and Ausubel, D. P., p. 607.
5. Barker, D., 'Primary School Science' in *Educational Research*, Vol. VII, No. 2 (Feb. 1965), p. 157.
6. Dienes, Z. P., 'Research in Progress' in *New Approaches to Mathematics Teaching* (1963), ed. Land, F. W.
7. H.M.S.O., *Mathematics in Primary Schools* (Curriculum Bulletin No. 1. of the Schools Council, 1965), p. 8.
8. Op. cit., p. 53.
9. Op. cit., p. 92.
10. Geach, P., *Mental Acts* (1957), sects. 4–11. Geach criticizes abstractionism as giving an impossible account of how we could *learn* new concepts, i.e. by supposedly noticing and abstracting common features of things. For : (i) How could *logical* concepts such as 'not' and 'or' be abstracted in this way? Where are the features of 'nottishness' or 'alternativeness' to abstract from? (ii) With *arithmetical* concepts we must first conceive of things as being of a certain kind, e.g. people or molecules,

before it is even intelligible to talk of their number. Moreover, the concept of number is much wider than just of how many in a visible group. (iii) With *relations* abstractionism fails, for where is that feature, e.g. of bigness, possessed by big fleas and big elephants, but not by little elephants, which we are to abstract? (iv) Even with *colour* concepts the theory fails, for where are the three separable features in an object which might truly be described as its being yellow, lemon and coloured? Geach stresses that such distinctions and classifications as our concepts mark do not just hit us when we open our eyes but are *made* by the mind. Language, of course, is crucially important in leading us to make such distinctions. Far from 'symbolization' being a trivial capping of concepts already formed, it would be truer to say that forming a concept *is* learning the use of a symbol. Cf. also Wittgenstein, L., *Philosophical Investigations* (1953), Pt. I, sects. 1–43.

11. Described in Thomson R., *The Psychology of Thinking* (Pelican, 1959), pp. 67–70.

12. Cf. Daitz, E., 'The Picture Theory of Meaning' in *Essays in Conceptual Analysis* (1956), ed. Flew, A. G. N. Of course, pictures may be a considerable aid to someone already able to read *part* of the sentence, since then the picture particularizes something of which he already has a rough idea.

13. Op. cit., p. 86.

14. Op. cit., p. 12 (see also pp. 7 and 92).

15. Cf. Ausubel, D. F., 'In Defence of Verbal Learning' in *Educational Theory* (1961), p. 15.

16. E.g. Friedlander, B. Z., 'A Psychologist's Second Thoughts on Concepts, Curiosity and Discovery in Teaching and Learning' in *Harvard Ed. Review* (Winter 1965).

17. Harlow, H., 'The Formation of Learning Sets' in *Psychological Review* (1949), p. 51.

10

LEARNING AND TEACHING
Michael Oakeshott

Even an amateur, like myself, when he fishes around in his head for some bright ideas, hopes to catch something. But nowadays fish don't come so easily; and I wish that what I have found to say on this topic did not look to me so shamefully dull. Let me, however, detain you a while with some clumsy thoughts on learning and teaching.

1

Learning is the comprehensive activity in which we come to know ourselves and the world around us. It is a paradoxical activity : it is doing and submitting at the same time. And its achievements range from merely being aware, to what may be called understanding and being able to explain.

In each of us, it begins at birth; it takes place not in some ideal abstract world, but in the local world we inhabit; for the individual it terminates only in death, for a civilization it ends in the collapse of the characteristic manner of life, and for the race it is, in principle, interminable.

The activity of learning may, however, be suspended from time to time while we enjoy what we have learned. The distinction between a driver and a learner-driver is not insignificant; a master-tailor making a suit of clothes is doing something other than learning to make a suit of clothes. But the suspension is, perhaps, never either decisive or complete : learning itself often entails practising what we have in some sense learned already, and there is probably a component of learning in every notable performance. Moreover, some activities, like intellectual enquiries, remain always activities of learning.

By learning I mean an activity possible only to an intelligence capable of choice and self-direction in relation to his own impulses and to the world around him. These, of course, are pre-eminently human characteristics, and, as I understand it, only human beings are capable of learning. A learner is not a passive recipient of impressions, or one whose accomplishments spring from mere reactions to circumstances, or one who attempts nothing he does not know how to accomplish. He is a creature of wants rather than of needs, of recollection as well as memory; he wants to know what to think and what to believe and not merely what to do. Learning concerns conduct, not behaviour. In short, these analogies of clay and wax, of receptacles to be filled and empty rooms to be furnished, have nothing to do with learning and learners.

I do not mean that the attention of a learner is focussed always upon understanding and being able to explain, or that nothing can be learned which is not understood; nor do I mean that human beings are uniquely predestined learners whatever their circumstances. I mean only that an activity which may include understanding and being able to explain within its range is different, not only at this point, but at all points in the scale of its achievements, from one to which this possibility is denied.

Teaching is a practical activity in which a 'learned' person (to use an archaism) 'learns' his pupils. No doubt one may properly be said to learn from books, from gazing at the sky or from listening to the waves (so long as one's disposition is that mixture of activity and submission we call curiosity), but to say that the book, the sky or the sea has taught us anything, or that we have taught ourselves, is to speak in the language of unfortunate metaphor. The counterpart of the teacher is not the learner in general, but the pupil. And I am concerned with the learner as pupil, one who learns from a teacher, one who learns by being taught. This does not mean that I subscribe to the prejudice which attributes all learning to teaching, it means only that I am concerned here with learning when it is the counterpart of teaching.

The activity of the teacher is, then, specified in the first place by the character of his partner. The ruler is partnered by the citizen, the physician by his patient, the master by his servant, the duenna by her charge, the commander by his subordinates, the lawyer by his client, the prophet by his disciple, the clown by his audience, the hypnotist by his subject, and both the tamer and trainer by creatures whose aptitudes are of being tamed or trained. Each of these is engaged in a practical activity, but it is not teaching; each has a partner, but he is not a pupil. Teaching is not taming or ruling or restoring

157

to health, or conditioning, or commanding, because none of these activities is possible in relation to a pupil. Like the ruler, or the hypnotist, the teacher communicates something to his partner; his peculiarity is that what he communicates is appropriate to a partner who is a pupil—it is something which may be received only by being learned. And there can, I think, be no doubt about what this is.

Every human being is born an heir to an inheritance to which he can succeed only in a process of learning. If this inheritance were an estate composed of woods and meadows, a villa in Venice, a portion of Pimlico and a chain of village stores, the heir would expect to succeed to it automatically, on the death of his father or on coming of age. It would be conveyed to him by lawyers, and the most that would be expected of him would be legal acknowledgement.

But the inheritance I speak of is not exactly like this; and, indeed, this is not exactly like what I have made it out to be. What every man is born an heir to is an inheritance of human achievements; an inheritance of feelings, emotions, images, visions, thoughts, beliefs, ideas, understandings, intellectual and practical enterprises, languages, relationships, organizations, canons and maxims of conduct, procedures, rituals, skills, works of art, books, musical compositions, tools, artefacts and utensils—in short, what Dilthey called a *geistige Welt*.

The components of this world are not abstractions ('physical objects') but beliefs. It is a world of facts, not 'things'; of 'expressions' which have meanings and require to be understood because they are the 'expressions' of human minds. The landed estate itself belongs to this world; indeed, this is the only world known to human beings. The starry heavens above us and the moral law within, are alike human achievements. And it is a world, not because it has itself any meaning (it has none), but because it is a whole of interlocking meanings which establish and interpret one another.

Now, this world can be entered, possessed and enjoyed only in a process of learning. A 'picture' may be purchased, but one cannot purchase an understanding of it. And I have called this world our common inheritance because to enter it is the only way of becoming a human being, and to inhabit it is to be a human being. It is into this *geistige Welt* that the child, even in its earliest adventures in awareness, initiates itself; and to initiate his pupils into it is the business of the teacher. Not only may it be entered only by learning, but there is nothing else for a pupil to learn. If, from one point of view, the analogies of wax and clay are inappropriate to learning, from another point of view the analogies of sagacious apes and accomplished horses are no less inappropriate. These admirable creatures have no such inheritance; they may only be trained to react to a stimulus and to perform tricks.[1]

There is an ancient oriental image of human life which recognizes this account of our circumstances. In it the child is understood to owe its physical life to its father, a debt to be acknowledged with appropriate respect. But initiation into the *geistige Welt* of human achievement is owed to the Sage, the teacher : and this debt is to be acknowledged with the profoundest reverence—for to whom can a man be more deeply indebted than to the one to whom he owes, not his mere existence, but his participation in human life? It is the Sage, the teacher, who is the agent of civilization. And, as Dr. Johnson said, not to name the school and the masters of illustrious men is a kind of historical fraud.

2

Now, most of what I have to say about learning and teaching relates to the character of what is taught and learned, and to the bearing of this upon the activities concerned; but there are two general considerations, one about the teacher and the other about the pupil, which I must notice first.

It is difficult to think of any circumstances where learning may be said to be impossible. Of course, in some conditions it will take place more rapidly and more successfully than in others; but, in principle, it does not depend upon any specifiable degree of attention, and it is not uncommon to find oneself to have learned without knowing how or when it happened. Thus, the random utterances of anyone, however foolish or ignorant, may serve to enlighten a learner, who receives from them as much or as little as he happens to be ready to receive, and receives often what the speaker did not himself know or did not know he was conveying.

But such casual utterances are not teaching; and he who scatters them is not, properly speaking, a teacher. Teaching is the deliberate and intentional initiation of a pupil into the world of human achievement, or into some part of it. The teacher is one whose utterances (or silences) are designed to promote this initiation in respect of a pupil—that is, in respect of a learner whom he recognizes to be ready to receive what he has resolved to communicate. In short, a pupil is a learner known to a teacher; and teaching, properly speaking, is impossible in his absence.

This, of course, does not mean that 'readiness to receive' is an easily discernible condition, or that it should be identified as the condition in which reception will come most easily. Jean Paul Richter's maxim that in teaching a two-year-old one should speak to him as if he were six, may be a profound observation. Nor does it mean that the relationship of teacher and pupil is emancipated from the latitudes and imprecisions common to all human relationships. Indeed, it is probably more subject to these imprecisions than any other relationship. What it means is that a teacher is one who studies his pupil, that the initiation *he* undertakes is one which has a deliberated order and arrangement, and that, as well as knowing what he designs to transmit, he has considered the manner of transmission. I once knew a wise man who, wishing to learn the art of the farrier, looked, not only for a man practised in the art, but for one accustomed to teaching, and he was gratified when he found a farrier who was also a teacher of boxing.

With regard to the pupil, there is a famous dilemma which has haunted reflection on education for long enough. Is learning to be understood as acquiring knowledge, or is it to be regarded as the development of the personality of the learner? Is teaching concerned with initiating a pupil into an inheritance of human achievement, or is it enabling the pupil to make the most or the best of himself? Like many such cruxes, this one points to what I believe to be a genuine discrepancy, but misinterprets it.

To escape from it we may recognize learning, not merely as the acquisition of knowledge, but also as the extension of the ability to learn, as the education and not merely the furnishing of a mind, as an inheritance coming to be possessed in such a manner that it loses its second-hand or antique character; and we may recognize teaching, not as passing on something to be received, nor as merely planting a seed, but as setting on foot the cultivation of a mind so that what is planted may grow. But the escape from the dilemma this affords us is imperfect; and, in any case, it is not an escape but a resolution we should be seeking.

What, I think, we must understand is that there is no discrepancy between a pupil succeeding to his inheritance of human achievement and his making the most of himself. 'Self-realization' for human beings is not, of course, the realization of an exactly predetermined end which requires only circumstances favourable to this end in order that it should be achieved; but nor is this self an infinite, unknown potentiality which an inheritance of human achievement is as likely to thwart as to promote. Selves are not rational abstractions, they are historic personalities, they are among the components of this world of human achievements; and there is no other way for a human being to make the most of himself than by learning to recognize himself in the mirror of this inheritance.

A discrepancy, however, remains; but it is a discrepancy, not between the self and its world, but between learning and teaching. It is a divergence of point of view. For the pupil, to learn is not to endeavour to make the most of himself, it is to acquire knowledge, to distinguish between truth and error, to understand and become possessor of what he was born heir to. But to the teacher things must appear differently. Obliquely and upon a consequence he is an agent of civilization. But his direct relationship is with his pupil. His engagement is, specifically, to get his pupil to make the most of himself by teaching him to recognize himself in the mirror of the human achievements which compose his inheritance. This is the somewhat complicated manner in which he performs his work of initiation, and this is what distinguishes him from others who hand on the fruits of civilization; namely, that he has a pupil.

Now, to make a 'civilization' available to a pupil is not to put him in touch with the dead, nor is it to rehearse before him the social history of mankind. Death belongs to nature, not *geist*; and it is only in nature that generation involves a process of recapitulating all earlier forms of life. To initiate a pupil into the world of human achievement is to make available to him much that does not lie upon the surface of his present world. An inheritance will contain much that may not be in current use, much that has come to be neglected and something even that for the time being is forgotten. And to know only the dominant is to become acquainted with only an attenuated version of this inheritance. To see oneself reflected in the mirror of the present modish world is to see a sadly distorted image of a human being; for there is nothing to encourage us to believe that what has captured current fancy is the most valuable part of our inheritance, or that the better survives more readily than the worse. And nothing survives in this world which is not cared for by human beings. The business of the teacher (indeed, this may be said to be his peculiar quality as an agent of civilization) is to release his pupils from servitude to the current dominant feelings, emotions, images, ideas, beliefs and even skills, not by inventing alternatives to them which seem to him more desirable, but by making available to him something which approximates more closely to the whole of his inheritance.

But this inheritance is an historic achievement; it is 'positive', not 'necessary'; it is contingent upon circumstances, it is miscellaneous and incoherent; it is what human beings have achieved, not by the impulsion of a final cause, but by exploiting the opportunities of fortune and by means of their own efforts. It comprises the standards of conduct to which from time to time they have given their preferences, the pro- and con- feelings to which they have given their approval and disapproval, the intellectual enterprises they have happened upon and pursued, the duties they have imposed upon themselves, the activities they have delighted in, the hopes they have entertained and the disappointments they have suffered. The notions of 'finished' and 'unfinished' are equally inapplicable to it. It does deliver to us a clear and unambiguous message; it speaks often in riddles; it offers us advice and suggestion, recommendations, aids to reflection, rather than directives. It has been put together, not by designers but by men who knew only dimly what they did. It has no meaning as a whole; it cannot be learnt or taught in principle, only in detail.

A teacher, then, engaged in initiating his pupils into so contingent an inheritance, might be excused for thinking that he needed some assurance of its worth. For, like many of us, he may be expected to have a superstitious prejudice against the human race and to be satisfied only when he can feel himself anchored to something for which human beings are not responsible. But he must be urged to have the courage of his circumstances. This man-made inheritance contains everything to which value may be attributed; it is the ground and context of every judgment of better and worse. If there were a mirror of perfection which he could hold up to his pupils, he might be expected to prefer it to this home-made article. But there is no such mirror. He may be excused if he finds the present dominant image of civilized life too disagreeable to impart with any enthusiasm to his pupils. But if he has no confidence in any of the standards of worth written into this inheritance of human achievement, he had better not be a teacher; he would have nothing to teach.

But teachers are modest people, and we are likely to disclaim so large an engagement as initiating our pupils into the civilized inherit-ance of mankind. We do not pretend to hand on anything but scraps of that inheritance; and it does not escape us that the civilization we are directly concerned with is not alone in the world and that this is a further limitation of our activities. And all this constitutes a renewed recognition of the contingency of what we have to teach. But the important point here is that whether we are concerned with a relatively simple or (like ours) an exceedingly complex civilization, whether we are concerned with a small or a large part of it, and whether we are concerned with practical skills, with moral conduct or with large intellectual enterprises (like philosophy or science), teaching and learning always relate to an historic inheritance of human achievement and that what is to be handed on and learned, known and understood, are thoughts and various 'expressions' of thoughts.

3

Now, from one important point of view, all we can be said to know constitutes a manifold of different 'abilities', different amounts of knowledge being represented in different degress of ability, and every complex ability being a manifold of simpler abilities.

When an ability is recognized as an ability to do or to make something, and it is recognized to be significantly composed of phy-sical movements, we usually call it a skill. Playing billiards and ploughing a field are skills; each may be enjoyed in different degrees and each may be seen to be a manifold of simpler skills. Thus the ability to plough entails the ability to manage the horse as well as the plough; and the ability to manage the horse entails the ability to manage the leads and the ability to make the appropriate noises.

Further, we are apt to extend this notion of skill to abilities not so significantly composed of physical movements. A navigator, a chair-man or a painter may be said to be 'skilful'. But when we say this we usually mean that the abilities concerned in these activities are large and complex and that in this case they are enjoyed to only a limited extent : we mean that his ability runs to a *merely* skilful perform-ance. And this draws attention to abilities which we do not normally call skills.

These are usually more complicated, less obviously concerned with doing and making and more obviously concerned with the performance of mental operations—like speaking, diagnosing, understanding, describing, explaining, etc. And the complex 'abilities' denoted in the expressions engineer, latin scholar, explorer, actor, surgeon, lawyer, army commander, physicist, teacher, painter, farmer, etc. are each manifolds in which simpler abilities are grouped and given a specific focus.

This conjunction, in a concept of 'abilities', of what we know and the use we make of it, is not designed to prove anything, but merely to indicate the way in which we carry about with us what we may be said to know. What we are aware of is not a number of items of knowledge available for use, but having powers of specific kinds—the power of being able to solve a legal problem, or to understand a Latin inscription or to perform a surgical operation. What we know constitutes an equipment which we possess in terms of what it enables us to do or to understand. And the 'pragmatism' which this way of thinking might seem to commit us to may be avoided if it is recognized that abilities are of different kinds and cannot be assimilated to one another—that (for example) the ability to understand and to explain cannot be assimilated to the ability to do or to make.

Now, these abilities of various kinds and dimensions which constitute what we may be said to know will be found to be conjunctions of what is called 'information' and what I shall call 'judgment'.

The component of 'information' is easily recognized. It is the explicit ingredient of knowledge, where what we know may be itemized. Information consists of facts, specific intellectual artefacts (often arranged in sets or bunches). It is impersonal (not a matter of opinion). Most of it is accepted on authority, and it is to be found in dictionaries, manuals, textbooks and encyclopaedias. It is the appropriate answer to questions which ask : who? what? where? which? how long? how much? etc. Typical pieces of information are : the date of Shakespeare's death or St. Paul's conversion; the average annual rainfall in Bournemouth, the ingredients of welsh rarebit; the specific gravity of alcohol; the age of consent; the atomic structure of nitrogen; the reasons given by Milton for favouring polygamy; the seating capacity of the Albert Hall.

Except in quizzes, where it is notoriously inert, information is a component of knowledge, and (unlike knowledge itself) it may be useful or useless. Useful information is composed of facts related to a particular skill or ability. There is no inherently useless information; there are only facts irrelevant to the matter in hand.

164

Some facts seem to convey detached pieces of information—
'Mummy, Mrs. Smith wears a wig', 'we cook on gas', 'that is a
bicycle', 'this is a bassoon'—and they lose their inertness merely by
reason of their place in a conversation. But the importance of
information lies in its provision of rules or rule-like propositions
relating to abilities. Every ability has its rules, and they are contained
in that component of knowledge we call information. This is clearly
the case with mathematical or chemical formulae, or with information like, 'glass is brittle', or 'hemlock is poisonous'; but it is also
the case with other items of information. A recipe tells me what
ingredients I should use in making a dish, and one of the uses of
knowing the seating capacity of the Albert Hall is that it tells me
how many tickets I may sell.

But rules or rule-like propositions such as are supplied in pieces
of information may be related to knowledge (that is, to a specific
ability or skill) in either of two different ways. They may be items
of information which must be known as a condition of being able to
perform; or they may constitute the criterion by means of which a
performance may be known to be incorrect, though here they are
never the only means by which mistakes may be detected.

First, nobody could read or receive a message in morse unless he
were correctly informed about the morse-code equivalents of the
letters of the alphabet. This is information in the exact sense. It is a
set of facts (specific intellectual artefacts), not opinions; it is stated
in propositions; it is received on authority; it is capable of being
forgotten and it needs to be recollected; and it appears in rules to be
followed—rules which must be known and recollected as a condition
of being able to perform.

Secondly, the grammar of a language may be said to constitute
the criterion by which a performance may be known to be incorrect.
It consists of facts, stated in propositions, and it appears as rules.
But, while this information may obliquely promote a laudable performance, it is not necessary to it. A laudable performance is possible
to somebody who never possessed this information, or to somebody
who once had it but has now forgotten it. There are a number of
things directly related to a performance which a person ignorant of
these facts could not do; but among them is neither the ability of
speak intelligently and to understand what is said in the language,
nor the ability to detect mistakes. The rules, here, are observed in
the performance and they are capable of being known. They are the

criterion for determining an incorrect performance, but a knowledge of them is not a condition of a laudable performance.

There is, indeed, a third sort of rule-like proposition which, in order to distinguish it from other sorts, is often called a 'principle'. These are propositions which are advanced in order to explain what is going on in any performance; they supply what may be called its 'underlying *rationale*'. And, consequently, as I understand them, they are never components of the knowledge which constitutes the performance. They belong to a separate performance of their own—the performance of explaining a performance. Let me offer two examples of what I mean.

First, riding a bicycle is a skill which consists wholly of making the appropriate physical movements. In order to enjoy this skill certain information must have been acquired, and there may also be what could be called the 'grammar' of the skill. But beyond all this, the skill may be said to be an exemplification of certain principles of mechanics. But these principles are utterly unknown to even the most successful cyclist, and being able to recite them would not help him to be more proficient. They do not constitute a criterion. Their sole value is the contribution they may make to our understanding of what is going on. In short, they are unrelated either to learning or to practising the skill. They belong to a separate performance, the performance of explaining.

Secondly, moral conduct may be said to be the ability to behave well. Here, again, certain information must be known; and there may also be what could be called the 'grammar' of moral conduct—the rules and rule-like propositions which constitute the criterion by means of which a performance may be known to be 'incorrect'. But, again, beyond all this there are, or may be, 'principles' in terms of which what is going on in moral conduct may be understood and explained. Aristotle, for example, in the 'principle of the Mean', formulated what he believed to be the 'underlying *rationale*' of all good conduct. But a knowledge of this, or of any other such 'principle', is not a condition of being able to behave well, nor does this principle constitute a criterion by means of which a performance may be known to be 'incorrect'. It is unrelated either to learning good conduct or to a good performance.

There is, then, as I understand it, a sort of information which is designed to explain a performance (and also to explain the rules of a performance), but which is never a component of the knowledge which constitutes the performance. And this, of course, is so even when the performance is itself a performance of understanding and explanation, as, for example, in history or in science.

But, to return from this not unnecessary digression; there is in all knowledge an ingredient of information. It consists of facts which may range from the recognitions and identifications in which knowledge of any sort emerges from indeterminate awareness, to rules or rule-like propositions which inform the skills and abilities in which we carry about what we may be said to know, and which are sometimes, but not always, expressly known and followed. This ingredient of information, however, never constitutes the whole of what we know. Before any concrete skill or ability can appear, information must be partnered by 'judgment', 'knowing *how*' must be added to the 'knowing *what*' of information.

By 'judgment' I mean the tacit or implicit component of knowledge, the ingredient which is not merely unspecified in propositions but is unspecifiable in propositions. It is the component of knowledge which does not appear in the form of rules and which, therefore, cannot be resolved into information or itemized in the manner characteristic of information.

That we enjoy such knowledge has seemed to some writers undeniable. They direct our attention, in the first place, to skills—that is, to abilities which are significantly composed of physical movements. We may know how to do something without being able to state explicitly the manner of acting involved. This, for example, appears to be the case in swimming, riding a horse, playing a fish, using a chisel and in turning a bowl on a potter's wheel. And these writers point out, further, that we may recognize an action as being of a known kind without being able to specify how we recognized it; that we are able to discover similarities in things without being able to say what they consist of, or patterns without being aware of the elements they are composed of or the rules they exemplify; and that we may speak a language without knowing the rules we are following and even without those rules ever having been formulated.

All this, I think, is true. But what it suggests to me is that there are skills and abilities where what is known may lack certain sorts of informatory content (particularly the sort of information we call 'the rules'), rather than that there is a 'knowing *how*' which can be divorced from any 'knowing *what*'. And I have used 'judgment' to distinguish 'knowing *how*' from information because I think 'knowing *how*' is an ingredient of all genuine knowledge, and not a separate kind of knowing specified by an ignorance of rules.

Facts, rules, all that may come to us as information, itemized and explicit, never themselves endow us with an ability to do, or to make, or to understand and explain anything. Information has to be used, and it does not itself indicate how, on any occasion, it should be used. What is required in addition to information is knowledge which enables us to interpret it, to decide upon its relevance, to recognize what rule to apply and to discover what action permitted by the rule should, in the circumstances, be performed, knowledge (in short) capable of carrying us across those wide open spaces, to be found in every ability, where no rule runs. For rules are always disjunctive. They specify only an act or a conclusion of a certain general kind and they never relieve us of the necessity of choice. And they never yield more than partial explanations : to understand anything as an example of the operation of a rule is to understand it very imperfectly.

'Judgment', then, is not to be recognized as merely information of another sort; its deliverances cannot be itemized, they cannot be specified in propositions, and they are neither remembered not forgotten. It is, for example, all that is contained in what has been called 'the unspecifiable art of scientific enquiry' without which 'the articulate contents of scientific knowledge' remains unintelligible.

And if we are obliged to retreat a little from the notion of an entirely independent 'knowing *how*' (because every ability has an ingredient of fact, recognized as fact and specifiable in propositions), I do not think we can avoid recognizing what I have called 'judgment' as a partner, not only in those abilities we call skills, but in all abilities whatever, and, indeed, more particularly in those abilities which are almost exclusively concerned with mental operations.

The connoisseurship we recognize to belong to the knowledge entailed in riding a horse, for example, or in transmitting or receiving a message in the morse code, has its counterpart elsewhere. Indeed, the further we go from manual and sensual skills the larger becomes the place occupied by this component of knowledge. Whatever its place in tea-tasting and in the diagnosis of disease, its place in art and literature, in historical, philosophical or scientific understanding is almost immeasurably greater.

It is represented, for example, in the so-called *divinatio* of the textual critic in which a corrupt reading is detected and an emendation suggested. It is what comes into play where the information to be got from the collation of MSS and recension stops. It is all that goes beyond the point where critical rules and methods leave off, and all that is required to drag appropriate precepts from these rules. It is what escapes even the most meticulous list of the qualities required for practising the craft of the textual critic.

A similar ingredient appears in the practical relationships of human beings. The moral and legal rules which set out in propositional form the recognized rights and duties, and the prudential maxims which give some flexibility to those rules, constitute only a small part of the knowledge comprised in the ability to live a civilized life. The precepts themselves require interpretation in respect of persons and circumstances; where there is a conflict between precepts, it cannot be resolved by the application of other rules. 'Casuistry', as it has been said, 'is the grave of moral judgment.'

In short, in every 'ability' there is an ingredient of knowledge which cannot be resolved into information, and in some skills this may be the greater part of the knowledge required for their practice. Moreover, 'abilities' do not exist in the abstract but in individual examples: the norms by which they are recognized are afterthoughts, not categorical imperatives. And each individual example has what may be called a style or idiom of its own which cannot be specified in propositions. Not to detect a man's style is to have missed three-quarters of the meaning of his actions and utterances; and not to have acquired a style is to have shut oneself off from the ability to convey any but the crudest meanings.

What, then, is significant is not the observation that one may know how to speak a language without knowing the rules one is following, but the observation that until one can speak the language in a manner not expressly provided for in the rules, one can make no significant utterance in it. And, of course, by a 'language' I do not mean merely Latin and Spanish, I mean also the languages of history, philosophy, science and practical life. The rules of art are there, but they do not determine the practice of the art; the rules of understanding are there, but they do not themselves endow us with understanding. They set limits—often telling us only what *not* to do if we wish to speak any of the languages of our civilization; but they provide no prescription for all that must go on in the interval between these limits.

4

The inheritance of human achievements into which the teacher is to initiate his pupil is knowledge; and (on this reading of it) knowledge is to be recognized as manifolds of abilities, in each of which there is a synthesis of 'information' and 'judgment'. What bearing has this view of things upon the activities of learning and teaching—learning which is succeeding to the inheritance, and teaching which is deliberately initiating a pupil into it? I doubt very much whether there are any practical conclusions to be drawn from it for either learners or teachers; but I think it may have some virtue as part of an attempt to understand what is going on in learning and teaching.

It suggests, first, that what I have called the two components of knowledge ('information' and 'judgment') can both be communicated and acquired, but cannot be communicated or acquired separately—at least, not on separate occasions or in separate 'lessons'. This, I think, is certainly true in respect of all the more important abilities and passages in the inheritance, and it is not seriously qualified by the observations that it is possible to communicate and acquire inert information, and that there are some skills in which the component of information is minimal.

But, secondly, it suggests that these two components of knowledge cannot be communicated in the same manner. Indeed, as I understand it, the distinction between 'information' and 'judgment' is a distinction between different manners of communication rather than a dichotomy in what is known; and for me it springs from reflecting upon teaching and learning rather than from reflecting upon the nature of knowledge. Thus teaching may be said to be a twofold activity of communicating 'information' (which I shall call 'instructing') and communicating 'judgment' (which I shall call 'imparting'); and learning may be said to be a twofold activity of acquiring 'information' and coming to possess 'judgment'.

And the rest of what I have to say concerns this distinction and the understanding it may give of what is going on in learning and teaching.

All teaching has a component of instruction, because all knowledge has a component of information. The teacher as instructor is the deliberate conveyor of information to his pupil.

The facts which compose information are specific, impersonal and mostly to be taken on trust; they are also apt to be hard, isolated, arbitrary and inert. They may be stored in encyclopaedias and dictionaries. Their immediate appeal is not to the pupil's desire to understand, but to his curiosity, his desire not to be ignorant—that is, perhaps, to his vanity. And this desire not to be ignorant is, for the most part, satisfied by knowing things in terms of their names and by knowing the signification of words and expressions. From his earliest years the pupil has been used to making such discoveries for himself; he has become accustomed to distinguishing in an elementary way between fact and not-fact—without, of course, knowing the rules he is observing in doing so. And, for the most part, he is used to doing all this as part of the process of coming to be at home in the world he inhabits. Thus, when he falls into the hands of an instructor, he is already familiar with the activity of acquiring information, particularly information of immediate use.

Now the task of the teacher as instructor is to introduce his pupil to facts which have no immediate practical significance. (If there were no such facts, or if they composed an unimportant part of our inheritance, he would be a luxury rather than a necessity.) And, therefore, his first business is to consider and decide what information to convey to his pupil. This may be decided by circumstances : the Sergeant-Instructor does not have to consider whether or not he shall inform his class about the names and uses of the parts of the Bren-gun. But, if it is not decided by such circumstances as these, it is something which falls to the teacher as instructor to consider. What part or parts of our inheritance of information shall be transmitted to his pupil?

His second task is to make the information he has to convey more readily learnable by giving it an organisation in which the inertness of its component facts is modified.

The organization provided by an immediate application to the practical life of his pupil is spurious; much of the information he has to convey has no such application and would be corrupted by being turned in this direction. The organization provided by a dictionary or an encyclopaedia is not designed for learning but for the rapid discovery of items of information in reponse to a recognition of specific ignorance. And the organization of information in terms of the modes of thought, or languages, which are the greatest achievements of civilization, is much too sophisticated for the beginner. In these circumstances, what we have settled for, and what the instructor may be expected to settle for, is the organization of information in terms of the more or less arbitrarily distinguished 'subjects' of a school or university curriculum: geography, Latin, chemistry, arithmetic, 'current affairs' or what-not. Each of these is an organization of information and not a mode of thought; but each permits facts to begin to reveal their rule-like character (that is, their character as tools to be used in doing, making or understanding) and thus to throw off some of their inertness. Moreover, there is, I think, some positive advantage in devising, for pedagogical purposes, special organizations of information which differ from the significant modes of thought of our civilization. For these modes of thought are not themselves organizations of information; and when one of them appears as a school 'subject'—as, for example, 'philosophy' in the curriculum of a *lycée*—its character is apt to be misrepresented. No great harm may be thought to come from representing 'geography' or even 'Latin' as information to be acquired, but there is something odd about 'philosophy' when it appears as the ability (for example) to remember and rehearse the second proof for the existence of God or what Descartes said about dreams.

There are, I think, two other tasks which obviously fall to the teacher as instructor. First, he has to consider the order in which the information contained in each of these somewhat arbitrary organizations of facts shall be transmitted to his pupil. It is this sort of consideration which goes into devising a syllabus, writing a textbook, or composing the programme of an instructing machine. And second, he has to exercise his pupil in this information so that what has been acquired may be recognized in forms other than those in which it was first acquired, and may be recollected on all the occasions when it is relevant. That is, the instructor has not only to hear his pupils recite the Catechism, the Highway Code, the Capes and Bays, the eight-times multiplication table and the Kings of England, but he has also to see that they can answer questions in which this information is properly used. For the importance of information is the accuracy with which it is learned and the readiness with which it can be recollected and used.

Nevertheless, our inheritance of information is so great that, whatever devices the instructor may use to modify its inertness, much of it must be acquired with only the dimmest notion of how it might be used. No doubt it would be a good thing (as Lichtenberg said) if we could be educated in such a way that everything unclear to us was totally incomprehensible; but this is not possible. Learning begins not in ignorance, but in error. Besides, in acquiring information we may learn something else, other and more valuable than either the information itself or perceiving that it is something to be used. And to understand what this is we must turn from 'information' to 'judgment', from the activity of 'instructing' to the activity of 'imparting'.

Now, something of what I mean by 'judgment' has begun to appear whenever the pupil perceives that information must be used, and perceives the possibility of irrelevance. And something of this is imparted in the organization of information itself; although these organizations are apt to give a restrictive impression of relevance. It is clear that this is not itself information; it cannot be taught in the way in which information may be conveyed, and it cannot be learned, recollected or forgotten in the way in which information may be learned, recollected and forgotten. But it is clear, also, that this is only an intimation of 'judgment', for there is much more to be noticed which no mere organization of information can impart. To perceive that facts are rules or tools, to perceive that rules are always disjunctive and never categorical, is one thing, to have acquired the ability to use them is another.

'Judgment', then, is that which, when united with information, generates knowledge or 'ability' to do, to make, or to understand and explain. It is being able to think—not to think in no manner in particular, but to think with an appreciation of the considerations which belong to different modes of thought. This, of course, is something which must be *learned*; it does not belong to the pupil by the light of nature, and it is as much a part of our civilized inheritance as the information which is its counterpart. But since learning to think is not acquiring additional information it cannot be pursued in the same way as we add to our stock of information.

Further, 'judgment' may be *taught*; and it belongs to the deliberate enterprise of the teacher to teach it. But, although a pupil cannot be explicitly instructed in how to think (there being, here, no rules), 'judgment' can be taught only in conjunction with the transmission of information. That is to say, it cannot be taught in a separate lesson which is not (for example) a geography, a Latin or an algebra lesson. Thus, from the pupil's point of view, the ability to think is something learned as a by-product of acquiring information; and, from the teacher's point of view, it is something which, if it is taught, must be imparted obliquely in the course of instruction. How this is done is to be understood from considering the character of what has to be imparted.

'Judgment', the ability to think, appears first, not in merely being aware that information is to be used, that it is a capital and not a stock, but in the ability to use it—the ability to invest it in answering questions. The rules may have been mastered, the maxims may be familiar, the facts may be available to recollection; but what do they look like in a concrete situation, and how may a concrete situation (an artefact or an understanding) be generated from this information? How does Latin grammar appear in a page from Cicero (whence, indeed, it was abstracted) and how can it be made to generate a page of genuine Latin prose? What do the copybook maxims look like in moral conduct observed, and how can they be made to generate conduct? These are the facts, but what conclusions do they authorize or forbid? This is the literature—the articulate contents, for example, of current knowledge about magnetic effects—but how does a pupil learn to speak the language in which it is written down : the language of science? How does he acquire the connoisseurship which enables him to determine relevance, which allows him to distinguish between different sorts of questions and the different sorts of answers they call for, which emancipates him from crude absolutes and suffers him to give his assent or dissent in graduate terms?

But learning to think is not merely learning how to judge, to interpret and to use information, it is learning to recognize and enjoy the intellectual virtues. How does a pupil learn disinterested curiosity, patience, intellectual honesty, exactness, industry, concentration and doubt? How does he acquire a sensibility to small differences and the ability to recognize intellectual elegance? How does he come to inherit the disposition to submit to refutation? How does he, not merely learn the love of truth and justice, but learn it in such a way as to escape the reproach of fanaticism?

And beyond all this there is something more difficult to acquire, but more important than any of it; namely, the ability to detect the individual intelligence which is at work in every utterance, even in those which convey impersonal information. For every significant act or utterance has a style of its own, a personal idiom, an individual manner of thinking of which it is a reflection. This, what I have called style, is the choice made, not according to the rules, but within the area of freedom left by the negative operation of rules. We may listen to what a man has to say, but unless we overhear in it a mind at work and can detect the idiom of thought, we have understood nothing. Art and conduct, science, philosophy and history, these are not modes of thought *defined* by rules; they exist only in personal explorations of territories only the boundaries of which are subject to definition. To have command over the languages of our civilization is, not to know the rules of their grammar, but to have the opportunity of a syntax and a vocabulary, rich in fine distinctions, in which to think for oneself. Learning, then, is acquiring the ability to feel and to think, and the pupil will never acquire these abilities unless he has learned to listen for them and to recognize them in the conduct and utterances of others.

Besides information, then, this is what has to be learned; for this (and not the dead weight of its products) is the real substance of our inheritance—and nothing can be inherited without learning. And this is what the teacher has to 'impart' to his pupil, together with whatever information he chooses to convey.

It cannot be *learned* separately; it is never explicitly learned and it is known only in practice; but it may be learned in everything that is learned, in the carpentry shop as well as in the Latin or chemistry lesson. If it is learned, it can never be forgotten, and it does not need to be recollected in order to be enjoyed. It is, indeed, often enough, the residue which remains when all else is forgotten; the shadow of lost knowledge.

It cannot be *taught* separately; it can have no place of its own in a timetable of a curriculum. It cannot be taught overtly, by precept, because it comprises what is required to animate precept; but it may be taught in everything that is taught. It is implanted unobstrusively in the manner in which information is conveyed, in a tone of voice, in the gesture which accompanies instruction, in asides and oblique utterances, and by example. For 'teaching by example', which is sometimes dismissed as an inferior sort of teaching, generating inflexible knowledge because the rules of what is known remain concealed, is emancipating the pupil from the half-utterances of rules by making him aware of a concrete situation. And in imitating the example he acquires, not merely a model for the particular occasion, but the disposition to recognize everything as an occasion. It is a habit of listening for an individual intelligence at work in every utterance that may be acquired by imitating a teacher who has this habit. And the intellectual virtues may be imparted only by a teacher who really cares about them for their own sake and never stoops to the priggishness of mentioning them. Not the cry, but the rising of the wild duck impels the flock to follow him in flight.

When I consider, as in private duty bound, how I first became dimly aware that there was something else in learning than the acquisition of information, that the way a man thought was more important than what he said, it was, I think, on the occasion when we had before us concrete situations. It was when we had, not an array of historical 'facts', but (for a moment) the facts suspended in an historian's argument. It was on those occasions when we were made to learn by heart, not the declension of *bonus* (which, of course, had to be learned), but a passage of literature, the reflection of a mind at work in a language. It was on those occasions when one was not being talked to but had the opportunity of overhearing an intelligent conversation.

And if you were to ask me the circumstances in which patience, accuracy, economy, elegance and style first dawned upon me, I would have to say that I did not come to recognize them in literature, in argument or in geometrical proof until I had first recognized them elsewhere; and that I owed this recognition to a Sergeant gymnastics instructor who lived long before the days of 'physical education' and for whom gymnastics was an intellectual art—and I owed it to him, not on account of anything he ever said, but because he was a man of patience, accuracy, economy, elegance and style.

NOTES

1. The horses I refer to are, of course, those of Elberfield. But it is, perhaps, worth recalling that the ancient Athenians delighted in the horse above all other animals because they recognized in it an affinity to man, and an animal uniquely capable of education. The horse had no *geistige* inheritance of its own, but (while other animals might be set to work) the horse was capable of sharing an inheritance imparted to it by man. And, in partnership with a rider (so Xenophon observed), it could acquire talents, accomplishments and even a grace of movement unknown to it in its 'natural' condition.

INDOCTRINATION
J. P. White

I. INTRODUCTION

When I used to teach 'Liberal Studies' to Technical College students, I used to find myself in a dilemma. I had given up history teaching in a Grammar School because I did not want to teach about May Day in Shakespeare's England to the younger boys or the causes of the Hundred Years' War to sixth-formers. I began to teach, among other things, about the rise of the Labour Party and the origin of the Welfare State. But, at the same time, I felt that I was treading on dangerous ground. How far was I getting my students consciously or unconsciously to share my own political beliefs, however carefully I stuck to the 'facts'? And if they did come to share them was I not indoctrinating them, not educating them? In my very selection of topics to include these political issues was I not doing with different content what a planner of a history syllabus in Soviet Russia does— and wasn't this indoctrination? I thought back to what my head master had told me after a disastrous lesson on sex I had given to a class of fourteen-year-old boys in a Secondary Modern School when I first taught: 'I've always said so, and I'll say it again, lad: you can teach anything you like in school, as long as you keep off just three things : religion, sex and politics.'

History teaching in schools is one area where the question 'Is this indoctrination?' is notoriously apt to arise; another is religious education. But there are two further contexts in which it appears, in one of which the question is likely to be aired by certain moral philosophers, and in the other by certain educational theorists. The first of these is the moral education of the very young child. Children are brought up to obey moral rules. They cannot be given reasons for following these rules, for any reason that might be provided would be incomprehensible to them. So they have to be made to follow the rules by non-rational means, e.g. by fear of the withdrawal of their mother's love if they are disobedient. The question is : is this non-rationally based moral 'education' indoctrination? Green[1] argues that it is. Indoctrination is marked, for Green, by a person coming to hold a belief unintelligently, that is, without evidence. 'Indoctrination', he says, 'may be useful as the prelude to teaching (i.e. teaching which is rationally based)[2] . . . we need not offer reasons for every belief we think important for children and adults to hold.' Atkinson,[3] on the other hand, holds that one must distinguish between two sorts of 'non-rational teaching procedures that we may be obliged to use . . . . because of the immaturity and/or incapacity of the taught'. We are instructing, not indoctrinating, if the non-rational beliefs which the child learns, *can* be justified, and if they are inculcated in such a way as not to impair, or impair as little as possible the recipient's capacity for subsequent instruction and training. But if the beliefs are unjustifiable we must be indoctrinating. So, for Atkinson, the crucial issue in early moral education is the objectivity or otherwise of moral judgments. 'There can be moral teaching, instruction in, as opposed to instruction about morality, only if there are criteria of truth, cogency, correctness, in the field. Are there such criteria?' Hare[4] differs, yet again, in giving a negative answer to the last question (there are no objective moral judgments; the latter depends on 'decisions of principle' which each must freely make for himself) while claiming that early moral education is not indoctrination, as long as the teacher's aim is not to 'stop the growth in our children of the capacity to think for themselves about moral questions' (p. 52). Briefly, then, Green holds all early moral education to be indoctrination, independently of the question whether moral judgments can be known to be true or false; Atkinson holds that it is indoctrination only if they cannot be known to be true or false; and Hare holds that it is not necessarily indoctrination even though they cannot be known to be true or false. I do not want to examine these positions here, although I shall do so later; I merely want to indicate the philosophical controversy that can arise over questions of indoctrination in the moral sphere.

The other area of interest in indoctrination comes from the controversy between 'child centred' and 'traditional' theories of education. One of the charges of the former way of thinking against the latter is that the traditional teacher merely tries to implant items of information into some pupils' minds, without letting them discover this information for themselves. For some child-centred theorists, any attempt the teacher makes to get children to learn things, is labelled 'indoctrination', and one is indoctrinating when one is getting children to learn up geographical facts for rote reproduction, or when one is teaching algebra by 'chalk and talk'.

The above examples are enough to show that there is considerable room for clarification on what is meant when one talks of 'indoctrination'. The confusion surrounding the word is further increased by reports from Russia and China about indoctrination programmes based on 'brainwashing' techniques. Is not indoctrination, after all, some sort of tampering with and restructuring of the brain as Sargant presents it in 'Battle of the Mind'? If so, what is the connexion between brainwashing of this sort and the forms of so-called indoctrination which we have just examined? Are the other examples of indoctrination not examples at all, because they do not rely on brainwashing techniques? Or do they, in some subtle way, involve brainwashing? What, after all, is brainwashing?

2. THE AMBIGUITY OF 'INDOCTRINATION'

Questions about indoctrination tend to arise in the sorts of contexts which I have mentioned, but it is not clear that in every case when people talk about indoctrination, they mean the same thing. It will be helpful to distinguish here a number of different intentions which a parent or schoolteacher might have in getting children to learn things. We can distinguish the intentions that :

(i) the child should learn words or phrases that he is able to repeat by rote.

(ii) the child should believe that a proposition 'p' is true. This is different from (i) in that in (ii) the child must *understand* what 'p' means. The child in (i) may learn to repeat the words 'I ought not to steal' without understanding what stealing is. (This is not, of course, to deny that rote learning *excludes* understanding, but merely to affirm that it does not *require* it). But the child in (ii) cannot believe 'p' if he does not know what it means.

(iii) the child should believe that 'p' is true, in such a way that nothing will shake this belief.

(iv) the child should believe that 'p' is true, if and only if he has come to see that there are good grounds for believing it. This implies the intention that the child reject 'p' if he comes to see that there are no good grounds for believing it.

Both (ii) and (iv) are compatible with (ii); but they are incompatible with each other; for the teacher with intention (iii) intends so to fix 'p' in the child's mind that the later production of good grounds for rejecting 'p' will not lead the child to give up 'p'.

Some, but not all, of the controversies about indoctrination have arisen because all three intentions (i), (ii), and (iii) have been used as defining attributes of indoctrination—and some uses of the term cover (iv) as well.

(i) Those who claim that a teacher is indoctrinating because he is merely getting his pupils to learn things by rote, are defining 'indoctrination' in terms of intention (i).

(ii) Those who argue, like Green (above, p. 178), that early moral education must be indoctrination because the teacher is getting the child to believe that he ought to behave in such and such a way without giving reasons, define 'indoctrination' as a non-rational way of trying to achieve intention (ii).

(iii) Those who deny that early moral education is indoctrination as long as the teacher has no intention of getting the child to believe unshakably that he ought to behave in such and such a way, are not really at issue with those of Green's persuasion, because they define 'indoctrination' in terms of intention (iii).

(iv) For those child-centred theorists who hold that all attempts to get a child to learn anything (as distinct from letting him 'discover' things) are forms of indoctrination, the term is broad enough to cover all four intentions.

The word 'indoctrination' was often used in the past to refer to teaching generally : to indoctrinate a person was merely to get him to learn something. In this century the word has taken on more precise meanings. It now usually refers to particular *types* of teaching, distinguished by different intentions that some teachers have in mind, e.g. to get children to learn by rote, or without reasons, or in an unshakable way—intentions that were not clearly distinguished in the past when the word was used more widely. As different educationists tend for different reasons to disapprove of one or more of these intentions, the word has come to be used pejoratively in most cases. (But not in all : the American Army clearly approves of the Indoctrination Courses it arranges for its troops, although it is not clear in what sense 'indoctrination' is to be taken here.)

3. INTENTION, METHOD AND CONTENT
AS CRITERIA OF INDOCTRINATION

Teachers who are worried about indoctrination in schools today are not on the whole worried because they are teaching children to learn by rote; neither do they mean by 'indoctrination' any sort of 'formal' teaching. Like myself, in my history teaching days, they have in mind, as paradigm cases of indoctrination, communist systems of 'political education' or, perhaps, the teaching of religion in Roman Catholic schools. I want to argue that 'indoctrination' in this sense is definable solely in terms of intention (iii). Indoctrinating someone is trying to get him to believe that a proposition 'p' is true, in such a way that nothing will shake that belief.[5] Definitions in terms of the sort of proposition which is taught (content) or in terms of the methods of teaching 'p', will not do. To show this, I would like now to consider in detail some attempts which have been made to define 'indoctrination' otherwise than in terms of intention (iii) alone.

(a) John Wilson[6] implicitly denies that the indoctrinator need have *any* intention of getting a person to believe anything. (For him indoctrination is distinguished by the *content* of what the pupil comes to believe: the beliefs are uncertain, not in the sense that they cannot be 100 per cent proved, but in the sense that there is no publicly acceptable evidence for them. Religious, political and moral beliefs provide, for Wilson, paradigm cases of beliefs that can be indoctrinated. He argues that if a child kicks up a row when there are adults in the room who want a quiet conversation and we don't make the child shut up, this 'is as much indoctrination as to stop it making a noise in its own playroom, because it presents the child with a false picture—a picture of lunatic adults who are willing to stop talking just because some kid is screaming'. Here, notice, we need not have the intention of presenting the child with a false belief —we may just intend to make it stop screaming. The false belief that the child gets may be an unintentional result of our behaviour.

But *is* this 'indoctrination'? If so, the term becomes so wide as to be meaningless. For if whenever a person comes to have a false belief 'y' as a result of my acting on intention 'x', I am indoctrinating him, then I may be indoctrinating someone whenever I act on *any* intention. Wilson's case is one of neglect, rather than of indoctrination. To say that it is one of neglect is to say that the adults responsible for the child *did not do* what they ought to have done (i.e. shut him up). At least a minimal necessary condition of something's being indoctrination is that it is an activity: the indoctrinator must be *doing* something. Now, we normally distinguish one activity from another in terms of the agent's intention.[7] We can say that a person raising his arm is engaged in one activity rather than another, say signalling rather than doing P.T., not from observing his bodily movements (which may be the same in both cases), or from looking at the results of what he is doing (in both cases a taxi may draw up), but only when we know what intention he has in mind. Since indoctrination is an activity, it can only be distinguished from other activities in terms of the particular intention the indoctrinator has in mind.

(b) A second argument that intention (iii) is not a necessary condition runs as follows. *Some* indoctrinators may have the intention of fixing their pupils' beliefs so that they are unshakable, but not all. For many indoctrinators—e.g. of Marxism or of Roman Catholicism —have themselves been indoctrinated. They believe that the doctrines that they hold cannot but be true. Therefore many of them are fully prepared to accept rational discussion of these doctrines in their teaching, for they do not believe that such discussion could ever undermine them. If asked to describe what their intentions are in teaching, they say that they are trying to get their charges to think for themselves and deny that they are trying to rivet unquestionable beliefs into the mind. That is, they claim that they are motivated by intention (iv), not intention (iii). Yet however what they are doing might be described from within the religious or political system in which they are working, if viewed from outside the system, they would rightly be called indoctrinators. We would call them this not because they have intention (iii), but because of the particular subject matter which they are teaching: it is because they are teaching religious and political *doctrines*, that we call them 'indoctrinators'.

Not all arguments that the content of what is taught is important in deciding whether or not this is a case of indoctrination deny the importance of a particular intention as an additional criterion. We shall examine just such an argument in a moment. But what of arguments like the present one, which claim that the indoctrinator need not have any particular intention? One criticism of it, as it stands, is that it assumes that the teacher's avowed intention is necessarily his real intention. But is it conceivable, that his avowed intention is also his real intention? If so, then if any of his pupils questions a fundamental proposition of the doctrine, like 'There is a God' or 'The course of history is predetermined', he will not fob him off with specious argument or use non-rational techniques of persuasion to get him to believe the proposition, but will try to explore with the pupil whether there are any good grounds for it. But if he is as open-minded as this, would we, seeing him from outside the system, say that he is indoctrinating? If so, then there seems no reason why the philosopher of religion or of politics, who is also concerned to explore whether or not there are good grounds for the propositions mentioned, should not also be called an indoctrinator, a conclusion which the original proponent of argument (b) would surely wish to deny. If the teacher inside the system *is* an indoctrinator, it is therefore inconceivable that his avowed intention is also his real intention.

(c) Let us now look at the argument, that while intention (iii) to implant unshakable beliefs, is a necessary feature of indoctrination, it is not sufficient, for the beliefs to be thus implanted must be of a certain sort, i.e. doctrinal beliefs. What is meant by 'doctrinal beliefs' are beliefs in e.g. the two propositions discussed in the previous section, which form part of a religious, scientific or political system of beliefs, or ideology.

But what grounds are there for restricting the content of indoctrination to such beliefs as these? One might argue that the very word 'indoctrination' indicates that one is concerned with doctrines. But what turns on this? It is true that one meaning of 'doctrine' is 'a belief forming a part of a religious, scientific or political system'. But another meaning of the word, given in the O.E.D., is simply 'What is taught': and we have already seen that once all teaching could be referred to as 'indoctrination'. So appealing to linguistic usage is not helpful.

One problem with this analysis is that it does not seem to cover all cases of what people have in mind when they worry about indoctrination. What of those schools where in a hundred and one different ways some teachers try to get their pupils to see themselves as future hewers of wood and drawers of water? Such indoctrination may use an ideology, as Plato's guardians used the Myth of the Earthborn for a similar purpose; but this is not always present. What, too, of teachers who try to fix in some of their pupils' minds the ineradicable belief that they are of limited intelligence? I see no reason why this should not be called 'indoctrination'. One reply might be that in both these cases the teachers in question have themselves been indoctrinated into, say, political ideologies, of which the beliefs they are inculcating form a part. But it is equally likely that the teachers' beliefs rest on widespread untested assumptions about human nature which are not tied together into a close-knit system, like the religious and political beliefs we have been discussing.

I may, of course, be open to defeat on empirical grounds here, so I shall introduce what I hope is a stronger argument. It is not logically impossible to conceive of a teacher who tries to get a pupil to have an unshakable belief, which is not connected to a doctrine, in the 'system' sense. A teacher may want to get a child to believe that Melbourne is the capital of Australia. He may try to fix this belief unshakably by associating it with his charismatic influence on the boy : for the boy, whatever the teacher says *must* be right. The teacher may, further, try to prevent the boy from revising his belief in the face of contrary evidence by, for instance, not allowing any atlases in his school, getting the boy to believe that it is wrong to look up things in atlases at home, persuading him to enter a Trappist monastery on leaving school, etc. If a teacher did this, would it not be indoctrination? The fact that we *generally use* the word 'indoctrination' only in connexion with the teaching of ideological beliefs cannot be used to prove that the *concept* of indoctrination covers only such cases.

There are two ways at least in which one may attempt to deny that this is a case of indoctrination. First, one might argue that the example *is* inconceivable unless the teacher has some ulterior purpose in mind—for why else would he teach as he does? The only conceivable ulterior purpose is that he wants the belief to be held as a part of some wider ideology. One might object to this that the teacher might be crazy; but this objection could be blocked by the argument that there must be some reason why he is trying to get the boy to hold *this* belief, and that this is unintelligible unless one assumes that it forms part of some private, crazy ideology that the teacher has himself. But what of the teacher who is not crazy, but wants to get the boy to hold the belief unshakably, just to show that it can be done? He has no reason for selecting this belief rather than another, beyond the convenience of this one for his purposes; it would be harder, for instance, to get him to believe that Melton

Mowbray was the capital of England. In this case, the belief need not form part of an ideology.

The second argument is that in his attempts to prevent the boy from finding out the truth about the capital of Australia, the teacher has to get him to believe all sorts of other things, e.g. (in our own example) that it is wrong to look up things in atlases. If his intention is to be realized, he will also have to teach him that it is wrong to speak to Australians, to be interested in Test Matches, radio quiz games, etc. He may have to teach other beliefs to back up these demands if the child wants to know why listening to quiz programmes, for instance, is wrong. In this way a whole network of beliefs will be created, all clustering round and supporting the original belief. Together they form a self-contained ideology of their own. So, if this is to be called 'indoctrination', this is because of the way the belief is enmeshed in an ideological system, not only because of the teacher's intention.

There are two points to be made about this argument. First, if 'ideology' is to be taken to cover not only political and religious systems, as originally proposed, but to cover also such cases as these, then indoctrination has nothing to do with the *content* of beliefs, if one means by 'content' that they be political rather than religious, or scientific rather than metaphysical. If indoctrination has to do with content, then on the above argument, 'content' must refer to the fact that the beliefs to be indoctrinated must form part of an ideological system, in the broader sense. But, secondly, it is not necessary to indoctrination that the belief be associated with an ideology. This is only important when a pupil is likely to question a belief: he has to be taught that he should avoid certain people and certain books, etc. which might start him thinking. But a case could be imagined where the pupil is not likely to find counter evidence. Beliefs about what is happening on distant planets are less likely to be contraverted than false beliefs about Australia. A teacher on a tiny, remote island might want to see if he can get a pupil to believe unshakably that Uranus has seven moons. The boy trusts him utterly: he has no access to books on astronomy; he is never going to leave the island; and no one ever visits the island. Given such conditions, the teacher would be indoctrinating, but without an ideology.

If this argument is correct, then the claim that all indoctrination is ideological throws no light on the concept of 'indoctrination' but only on one instance of it. It is, of course, always possible to make indoctrination require an ideology *by definition*, as this is how the term is generally used. One might deny that the imaginary case described above was really a case of indoctrination, for this reason. But in this case, there is nothing to argue about. The supporter of a 'content' criterion wins his case by making it trivially true. It may be true that we usually use the word 'indoctrination' only in ideological cases, but that is no reason to let the matter rest there. The problem is to find what concepts are necessarily connected to 'indoctrination' and what are only contingently so. The hypothetical example given above gives grounds for saying that while intention (iii) is necessarily connected, 'doctrine' or 'ideology' are not. If one asked the teacher on the island what he was doing, and he replied, 'I am indoctrinating the boy', why should we disbelieve him? The case is sufficiently like the more usual cases of ideological indoctrination to justify him in so calling it.

The contingency of 'ideology' is even more apparent if 'ideology' is used to refer not to the *content* of one's beliefs—e.g. a religious or political system—but to the various beliefs which might be taught in order to prevent a person questioning the particular belief or beliefs to be indoctrinated, like the beliefs used above to prevent the child from questioning whether or not Melbourne was the capital of Australia. For to say that in *this* sense indoctrination is connected with ideologies is to make a point, not as much about the content of what is taught, but about the *method* of teaching it. Ideological indoctrination in this sense of 'ideology' attempts to get certain beliefs drummed home, by enmeshing them in other beliefs, not only beliefs that one should not look at certain books, etc. but also, especially if the pupil is of an enquiring nature, beliefs which apparently provide grounds for the original beliefs (e.g. 'There must be an afterlife, because otherwise life would have no purpose'). Here ideologies are useful methods of indoctrinating people. But they are not the only method. Threats and torture might be effective in some cases. So may critical discussion, to a point. A skilful religious indoctrinator may get his class intelligently to discuss the validity of some religious argument. But the subject chosen may be such (e.g. Is God one person or three?) that merely to have agreed to enter into the discussion commits one to a belief in God, a belief which is reinforced by taking part in the discussion itself. (A discussion about whether the invention of the radio telescope will increase our astrological knowledge can only go on when the participants all accept that the stars influence our destinies.) The indoctrinator may encourage people, therefore, to air their views in such a discussion, because this commits them to accepting another (presupposed) belief. The only belief that cannot be subjected to critical examination is the belief presupposed.

The conclusion of this section is, therefore, that to say that indoctrination requires an ideology in this wider sense of 'ideology' is to confuse the concept of indoctrination with a particular method in which instances of indoctrination may be carried out. Threats, tortures, critical discussion are other methods, on a par with ideologies.

(d) This brings us to 'brainwashing'. It is sometimes said and often believed that indoctrination is a sort of process. It is a matter of breaking down established patterns of neural activity in a man's brain and building up fresh patterns, so that the man's beliefs become fixed in a new mould. What marks out the indoctrinator, therefore, is the *method* he uses to reach his end, i.e. the 'brainwashing' method.

This view is put forward in William Sargant's 'Battle for the Mind'. Religious and political conversions are said to be based on the same techniques which Pavlov used to produce 'experimental neuroses' in dogs; and these 'neuroses' are said to have involved the deliberate creation of structural changes in the brain. There are all sorts of difficulties in this thesis, and I cannot go into them all here. But what is clear is that while the structure of the brain *may* change when a person comes to hold a new belief, the indoctrinator does not do anything directly to the brain to bring about a change in belief. The term 'brainwashing', as Schein points out in his study of the Chinese Indoctrination Program for Prisoners of War in Korea (Maccoby, Newcomb and Hartley: *Readings in Social Psychology,* Third Edition), does not refer to a new and awe-inspiring process of social control, but to a whole battery of techniques, many used since antiquity, to enforce belief: punishment, reward, group discussion, lectures, social isolation, interrogations, forced confessions, self-criticisms. As he says, 'the only novelty in the Chinese methods was the attempt *to use a combination of all these techniques and to apply them simultaneously . . . .* ' (His italics). It is wrong, therefore, to identify indoctrination with a process; a polymorphous concept, like 'education' or 'gardening', the concept of 'indoctrination' may be used to describe all sorts of processes, as long as they are seen by the indoctrinator as effective ways of enforcing belief. But it is also wrong to identify indoctrination with brainwashing, taking this to mean the all-out assault on one's beliefs which has been described. This may be a particular form of indoctrination—and not apparently a very successful one— thought necessary in an age when, for one reason and another, *adults'* beliefs have sometimes to be remoulded; but this battering ram is not necessary for indoctrinating *children,* whose conceptual schemes are not yet formed, and therefore more susceptible to subtler methods. Once again, we might *choose* to define 'indoctrination' as brainwashing, but, as before, nothing turns on this.

4. SOME EDUCATIONAL IMPLICATIONS OF THIS ANALYSIS

I would like to conclude by touching on the problems of indoctrination in particular areas—political history, religion and morality— which were adumbrated at the beginning of this paper.

(a) *Political history* The question I was here concerned with was : given that one has a free hand in choosing one's syllabus, how far can one teach recent political history without indoctrinating if one sympathizes with the views of a particular party? At first sight, it looks as if the answer depends on whether or not one intends to implant one's own political beliefs unshakably : if one is not doing this, one is not indoctrinating. But a difficulty arises. If several students of a particular political history teacher emerge with unshakable political beliefs similar to his own, we may well say, 'They have been indoctrinated.' Their teacher denies that he had any intention of indoctrinating. It is also clear that he is not deceiving us about this : independent observers report that he goes out of his way to show the many-sidedness of political issues and get the children to think critically about them. The difficulty is that even knowing all this, we might *still* want to say that students emerge from Mr. Jones' class indoctrinated with the belief that Tory freedom works. If it is legitimate to talk in this way, this would seem to imply that one can talk of unintentional indoctrination. Just as one can offend people without meaning to, so too, perhaps, one can indoctrinate them without meaning to. But it does seem rather odd to say this, for if indoctrinating is a matter of getting people to believe things unshakably, does it make sense to talk of *getting* someone to do something without meaning to? 'Indoctrinating' goes perhaps with 'marrying', 'sending for', 'signing' as a member of a whole class of activities that, as Anscombe points out,[8] can *only* be intentional or voluntary. If so, then do we merely mean, when we say the students have been indoctrinated, that they have come to hold unshakable beliefs? It cannot be *merely* this. For a man may come to believe unshakably that he had once seen a flying saucer, but we would not say he was indoctrinated. We would deny this, because no one was getting him to learn anything. It is because the students have come to hold fixed beliefs as a result of being in a learning situation, that we would call them—if indeed we would call them—'indoctrinated'. Whether or not we accept this extended use of the term does not affect the practical issue that a teacher of political history who is committed to a particular political viewpoint does run the risk that his pupils may adopt his attitudes unshakably if they identify with him in other respects. If the teacher's main aim is to get his pupils to think about current political issues, he might be better advised not to do this through history but more directly, by openly discussing them with his pupils.

(b) *Religion* In religious education, as in history, there is also a danger that a pupil who identifies with a teacher who is himself a believer will be indoctrinated—or, if the term is inapplicable, will come to have fixed beliefs—even though the teacher is not intending to fix these. For taking part in a religious discussion, or in hymn-singing, or saying 'Amen' at the end of a prayer have no point unless the participants accept certain implicit propositions, e.g. that God exists, or that there is a life hereafter; and participating in these ways may reinforce acceptance of these propositions, so that they become entrenched in one's view of the world.

There is also reason to be concerned about the possibility of indoctrination in religion, not only in the sense described, but also in the full-blooded intentional sense. For many religious teachers openly avow that they want their pupils to have faith, to believe in God etc. This faith must moreover be held with intensity, with passion : the belief must be rock-like.

> 'Only believe and thou shalt see
> Thy joy and crown eternally.'

It looks as if such teachers are trying to get their pupils to hold unshakable beliefs. That this is indoctrination is only thinly disguised by the aura of mystery and positive emotion with which the notion of 'faith' is surrounded—an aura which effectively prevents one from analysing what it involves. The difficulty with religious education is that if the teacher denies having this intention, it is hard to see what other intention he might have which is compatible with there being such a subject as religious education. He might say that his intention is to get his pupils to think historically about the life of Jesus or the Prophets. But—apart from the difficulties about how far he could prevent his pupils getting fixed beliefs if he is a believer, which we examined just now—there is also the doubt whether, while he is certainly teaching history, he is still teaching religion. An alternative intention he might have might be to get his pupils to think for themselves about *all* religious questions, including the fundamental ones about the existence of God and immortality. But the only problem here would be—assuming that he can prevent his own beliefs from affecting his handling of the discussion—that he could never proceed beyond discussing the fundamental questions into more substantive issues unless everyone in the class was rationally convinced of the truth of the basic presuppositions. If rational conviction is here impossible, it is difficult to see how one could teach religion (*qua* religion) without indoctrinating.

(c) *Morality* Whether teaching moral rules without rational backing to a young child who is incapable of understanding such reasons is indoctrination depends on one's definition of indoctrination. If this merely means teaching without giving reasons, as it does for Green, (above, p. 178) then obviously early moral education involves indoctrination in this sense. What of Atkinson's claim (loc. cit.) that such teaching is only indoctrination if the moral rules which are taught cannot be known to be true? But this definition of indoctrination in terms of the content of what is believed will not do. For suppose moral rules were rationally justifiable and a parent tries to fix in his child's mind the unshakable beliefs that he ought not to lie, to steal etc.—is this man not an indoctrinator? The notion of indoctrination is independent of the notion of the justifiability or otherwise of the beliefs indoctrinated.

Hare's article (op. cit.) argues for a similar position. But it is important to notice that on the non-propositional account of moral judgments that Hare gives in 'The Language of Morals', his position could not be the *same* as this, because, on Hare's view to indoctrinate a child in the rule that he ought to do x cannot mean to get the child to *believe* unshakably that he ought to do x. If moral rules are not propositional, they are not the sort of thing that can be believed. Indeed, in his article on indoctrination, Hare never describes indoctrination in terms of belief. He says (p. 52), 'indoctrination only begins when we are trying to stop the growth in our children of the capacity to think for themselves about moral questions'. To decide whether Hare is justified in talking of indoctrination in terms of preventing thinking, but not in terms of getting people to believe things, would require an analysis of his non-propositional moral theory, which is here out of place. But it does seem, prima facie, odd to say that one could indoctrinate and not be interested in what one's pupils believed.

For the rest, the problems about indoctrination in morality concern the same issue as was raised when we discussed indoctrination in history. The moral educator has to be careful that his pupils do not grow up indoctrinated, in the sense that they have introjected his moral attitudes unshakably without his having intended this. The danger is more acute in moral education than in later learning, because here our attitudes are implanted so early and are so constantly reinforced in our behaviour that they may easily be held unreflectingly for the rest of our lives.

NOTES

1. Green, T. F., 'The Topology of the Teaching Concept' in *Studies in Philosophy and Education*, Vol. III, No. 4 (Winter 1964–65), p. 312.

2. My bracket.

3. Atkinson, R.F., 'Instruction and Indoctrination' in *Philosophical Analysis and Education*, ed. Archambault, R. D.

4. Hare, R. M., 'Adolescents into Adults' in *Aims in Education*, ed. Hollins, T. H. B.

5. 'X indoctrinated Y' is ambiguous. X might have attempted to get Y to hold a belief unshakably, but not succeeded in doing so. In this case, we might say that 'X indoctrinated Y' is false because he did not succeed, or true because he attempted to do so. What we say depends on whether we take 'indoctrination' in the 'task' ('attempt' sense of the word, or in the 'achievement' ('success') sense. On the 'task-achievement' distinction as applied to education, see R. S. Peters' article in this volume.

6. Wilson, J., 'Education and Indoctrination' in Hollins, op. cit.

7. Not, of course, in the case of unintentional activities. But the criteria for identifying unintentional activities are parasitic on those for identifying intentional activities.

8. Anscombe, G. E. M., *Intention*, p. 84.

ON TEACHING TO BE CRITICAL

John Passmore

What is it to teach a child to be critical, and how can we tell whether we have been successful in doing so? Is it a matter of imparting facts, of inculcating habits, of training in skills, of developing capacities, of forming the character, or something different from any of these?

Pretty clearly, it is not a matter of imparting facts. Of course a teacher can impart to his pupils a variety of facts about the practice of criticism—that it is vital to democracy, that it is essential to the development of science, and so on. He can tell them stories about Socrates or about Galileo. Perhaps, even, imparting facts about criticism, or telling stories about famous representatives of the critical spirit, is a useful method of encouraging children to be critical. But at least this much is clear : imparting facts of this sort to children is not *sufficient* to make them critical, any more than talking to them about the importance of honesty in commercial relations or telling them stories about honest men is sufficient to make them honest. Being critical is not only logically but empirically dissociated from being in possession of certain facts about criticism.

Then is being critical a habit? This question does not admit of so straightforward an answer. For the word 'habit' is sometimes used in a very broad sense to refer to any type of regular behaviour acquired in the course of experience, whether it takes the form of regularly scratching one's head in moments of stress, or using a tool intelligently, or making good decisions. Thus, for example, in his chapter on 'habit' in *The Principles of Psychology* William James seems to count even what he calls 'the power of judging' as a habit.[1]

James also says, however, that 'habit diminishes the conscious attention with which our acts are performed', and that 'in an habitual action, mere sensation is a sufficient guide'.[2] We can all cite examples of habits, thus defined. To take a simple instance of a habit learned at school, the child acquires the habit of translating 'merci' by 'thank you'. Although at first he has to think about what he is doing, eventually the appearance of the word 'merci' in a book—the 'mere sensation'—provokes the translation 'thank you'.

Consider now the case of the skilful translator, as distinct from the well-drilled schoolboy. The skilful translator will not automatically translate 'merci' by 'thank you'. Sometimes he will translate it by 'thanks' or by 'ta'. He retains a level of vigilance, of conscious attention, which is quite lacking in the person who acts merely out of habit. It is characteristic of a skilful person, a well-trained person, as distinct from somebody who has merely been drilled, that for him 'mere sensation' is *not* a sufficient guide to action.

Of course, there are habitual ingredients in any skill. The translator does not, for example, think about how to read : he responds automatically to 'merci' as a word, he does not pause to consider the possibility that it is simply a set of squiggles on paper. But what makes him a skilful translator is precisely that he does not respond automatically, without thought, to the 'mere sensation' of a French word. So acquiring a skill is not the same thing as acquiring a habit, although it is generally necessary first to acquire certain habits before we can acquire a skill.

James tells the story of an old soldier who was carrying his dinner home when a practical joker called out 'Attention!' The soldier at once stood to attention, at the cost of dropping his dinner. We can imagine someone who was so drilled that to any assertion he responded with 'I question that!', however inappropriate the response in relation to its association. Such a person might be said to have formed a habit of questioning, but he would certainly not have learnt to be critical. This case is, of course, an imaginary one, but there are real instances not so very dissimilar. A person can be drilled into uttering stock criticisms. He can be taught to say, whenever he sees a non-representational painting or hears jazz, 'That's decadent.' Or whenever he hears a certain type of philosophical view put forward: 'That's nineteenth-century materialism,' or 'That's old-fashioned rationalism.' Such a person has not been taught to be critical.

The process of drilling pupils in such stock-responses can properly be described as *indoctrination*. It is quite preposterous to say, although it has been said, that 'children are indoctrinated with the multiplication table',[3] for exactly the same reason that it would be preposterous to say of anyone that 'his *doctrine* is that $2 \times 2 = 4$'. The old soldier in James' example had not been indoctrinated. He had simply been drilled. Indoctrination is a special form of drilling in which the pupil is drilled—e.g. by way of a catechism—in doctrines and in stock replies to stock objections to doctrine. But if indoctrination is a special kind of drill, it is nevertheless a kind of drill.

By drill a child can be taught the multiplication table, irregular French verbs, a religious or political catechism, the order in which to test a motor-car for faults, the order in which to analyse the salts in a chemical solution. But a person cannot be drilled into appreciating a poem, making a good translation, detecting defects in a new type of car, or suggesting a modification in accepted chemical routines. Nor can he be drilled into being critical.

Should we say, then, that being critical is a skill to be taught, as skills are, by training as distinct from simple drill? There are certainly books which profess to teach critical thinking, just as there are books which profess to teach us how to drive.

But suppose an undergraduate has read and mastered, let us say, Max Black's *Critical Thinking*. Suppose, that is, he can work out all the problems Black sets for his readers, and can answer any questions we care to ask him about the content of Black's book. He never for a moment doubts, however, that everything Black says is correct; he is content to learn by heart what Black says and to follow in every detail Black's advice on doing exercises. His reverential attitude to whatever he reads, that is, remains unchanged; it never even occurs to him to apply the skills he has learned to anything except Black's exercises. Has such a person learnt to be critical? The answer, I should say, must clearly be in the negative.

It is, of course, obvious that a person could answer any question we cared to ask him about a book called *Better Driving*, without being, after reading it, a better driver than he was before. We should have no hesitation, under these circumstances, in denying that he had learnt to improve his driving. Skill in driving is quite different from skill in reading books about driving. Is the situation, then, simply this: that although my imaginary—or not so imaginary—student of Black's *Critical Thinking* has learned how to read Black and to do Black's exercises, what he still lacks is skill in critical thinking, just as the man who has learned how to answer the questions set as exercises in a book on *Better Driving* may still lack skill in driving?

The two examples, however, are not analogous. For in so far as critical thinking is a skill, it consists in being able to solve problems of the sort Black sets his readers, in a sense in which skill in driving does not consist in being able to ask the question about driving which the author of *Better Driving* might ask his readers. One can answer the question 'What should you do when you are about to descend a steep hill?' with the answer : 'Change to a lower gear' without being in the slightest degree a skilful driver. But one cannot be in a position to answer such questions as 'In what does the fallacy of the following argument consist?' without being in some measure skilled in criticism. If being critical simply consisted in possessing a skill, then it ought to be the case that to master Black's *Critical Thinking* would be to master, or gain some degree of mastery over, that skill. Our line of reasoning suggests, however, that one can master Black's book without having learnt to be critical, even in a slight degree.

'Being critical' is, indeed, more like the sort of thing we call a 'character-trait' than it is like a skill. To call a person 'critical' is to characterize him, to describe his nature, in a sense in which to describe him, simply, as 'capable of analysing certain kinds of fallacy' is not to describe his nature. It is a natural answer to the question 'What kind of person is he?' to reply 'Very critical', when it would not be a natural answer that the person in question is a skilful driver.

Skills, as Plato pointed out, are 'capabilities for opposites'. A driver can use his skill to put himself into, as well as to extricate himself from, dangerous positions. Similarly, an expert in the detection of fallacies can use his skill in order to conceal the fallacies in his own case, by drawing attention away from them, rather than in a disinterested attempt to arrive at the truth. It is one of Socrates' reasons for objecting to the Sophists that they taught their pupils precisely this sort of skill.

In contrast, the critical spirit, in the sense in which an educator is interested in encouraging it, cannot be misused. No doubt those who possess it may sometimes be led, as a result of their exercise of criticism, to abandon views which are actually correct, as a just man can make a wrong decision, in virtue of being just, in a case where he would have made the right decision had he allowed partiality to sway him. (There are examples of this in Mr. Allworthy's treatment of Tom Jones.) But this is quite different from the case where a judge uses the sort of skill he has acquired as a judge in order to pervert the course of justice. The skills of a judge, or the skills of a critic, can be used or misused; justice or the critical spirit can be neither used nor misused. And this is because neither being just nor being critical is a skill.

If it is true that to be critical is a character trait, we can easily understand why it is in practice difficult for teachers to teach their pupils to be critical. That sort of teaching which sets out to develop character-traits relies to a considerable degree upon example and upon what is often called 'the atmosphere of the school'. Admittedly, whatever the character of school and teacher, an exceptional student —exceptional in any respect, with no implication in this description of moral superiority—may react against it. But, for example, a school in which teachers never deviate from a fixed syllabus, in which masters and students alike frown on every deviation from the conventional norm, is unlikely to encourage originality in its pupils, although its products may be well-drilled and, within limits, highly skilled.

It is hard enough, the conditions of school-life being what they are, for a teacher to set an example to his pupils in respect to such qualities as courtesy, justice, consideration. But to set an example of the critical spirit is still more difficult. In this instance difficulties arise not only from personal defects of the teacher—out of his fear, for example, that he may be unable to cope with a class in which the critical spirit has been aroused—but even from the very conditions of his employment.

Of course, the teacher himself will, inevitably, in the everyday course of his work, be critical—critical of his pupils, of the answers they give to his questions, of the work they present for his attention, of their behaviour, of the principles by which they govern their conduct. If by a 'critical person' we mean nothing more than a person who regularly draws attention to defects in what confronts him, a teacher cannot help being critical. And no doubt many of his pupils will in some degree imitate him. They will take over his critical standards and apply them to their own behaviour and to the behaviour of their fellow pupils.

The teacher, however, is ordinarily content to draw attention to the deviations of his pupils from fixed norms : their failure to work out their sums by an approved method, to conform to the school rules, to say the right things about Shakespeare, to adopt the accepted techniques of folding a filter-paper. He may be in all these respects highly critical of his pupils, he may devote himself zealously, even fanatically, to criticizing them at every point at which they deviate from accepted norms and he may arouse a similar zeal, a similar fanaticism, in his pupils without being in the slightest degree a critical person, in that sense of the word which now concerns us. Authoritarian systems of education very commonly produce pupils who are extremely critical, but only of those who do not fully adhere to the accepted beliefs, the accepted rules, the accepted modes of action.

Critical ability of this sort is a skill: the sort of skill possessed by an expert tennis-coach as compared with an expert tennis-player. Every expert possesses in some degree, as part of his expertness, the capacity to criticize his own performance and the performances of others, but in teachers this capacity is raised to the level of a skill. When we call a person 'highly critical' we are not infrequently suggesting that he is the kind of person—his enemies may call him 'querulous' or 'arrogant' or 'pedantic' or 'priggish'—who demands of everybody around him that they conform to what he likes to call 'high standards'. To a considerable degree that, in every society, is the stereotype of the teacher—although ideas about what constitutes 'high standards' vary, of course, from society to society. Nor is the stereotype unjustified. The competent teacher will rightly demand from his pupils a high standard of performance in the skills he is teaching: he will be hostile to shoddiness, laziness, contented mediocrity. But in teaching his pupils skills at a high standard, or in encouraging them to examine critically their own performances and the performances of their fellow-pupils, the teacher is not, I have suggested, automatically engendering in them a critical spirit, as distinct from the capacity to be critical of certain types of specialized performance. For to exhibit a critical spirit one must be alert to the possibility that the established norms themselves ought to be rejected, that the rules ought to be changed, the criteria used in judging performances modified. Or perhaps even that the mode of performance ought not to take place at all.

Fagin, for example, taught his young thieves to be critical of their own performances and those of their fellow pickpockets; an authoritarian society may, through its teachers, teach its young to recognize and to be expert at criticizing heresy. But neither Fagin nor the authoritarian society is at all anxious to encourage in the young a critical attitude towards their own procedures—quite the contrary.

On Teaching to be Critical

Teaching a child to be critical does, in contrast, involve encouraging him to look critically at the value of the performances in which he is taught to engage, as distinct from the level of achievement arrived at within such a performance. It is characteristic of societies in which criticism flourishes and develops that they abandon, under criticism, types of performance; they abandon, let us say, executions as distinct from seeking a higher level of skill in their executioners. A critical person, in this sense, must possess initiative, independence, courage, imagination, of a kind which may be completely absent in, let us say, the skilful critic of the performance of a laboratory technician.

To encourage the critical spirit, as distinct from professional competence as a critic of techniques, a teacher has to develop in his pupils an enthusiasm for the give-and-take of critical discussion. Sometimes he tries to do this by setting aside special occasions for formal debate. But debates are more likely to develop forensic skills than to encourage a genuinely critical spirit. A child will be encouraged to be critical only if he finds that both he and his teacher can be at any time called upon to defend what they say—to produce, in relation to it, the relevant kind of ground. This is very different from being called upon, on a set occasion, to produce a case in favour of one side in a debate.

The difficulty with encouraging critical discussion is that the teacher will almost certainly have many beliefs which he is not prepared to submit to criticism, and he will be enforcing many rules of which the same is true. These beliefs and these rules may be closely related to subjects which the pupils are particularly eager to discuss in critical terms—sex, for example, or religion and politics. If the teacher refuses to allow critical discussion on these questions, if he reacts to dissent with anger or shocked disapproval, he is unlikely to encourage a critical spirit in his pupils. If being critical consisted simply in the application of a skill then it could in principle be taught by teachers who never engaged in it except as a game or a defensive device, somewhat as a crack rifle shot who happened to be a pacifist might nevertheless be able to teach rifle-shooting to soldiers. But in fact being critical can be taught only by men who can themselves freely partake in critical discussion.

Secondly, even if the teacher is himself critical, there may be social pressure upon him not to admit that certain beliefs, certain practices, certain authorities, can properly be examined in a critical spirit. 'The values of rational critical inquiry', A. C. MacIntyre has suggested, 'stand in the sharpest contrast to the prevailing social values.'[4] The word 'prevailing' may conceal an exaggeration. In no society, certainly, is rational critical inquiry the dominant social force; in every society, it meets with opposition. But there are differences between societies: our own society not only pays a certain lip-service to critical inquiry but in some measure values it. So the teacher who tries to encourage the critical spirit is not wholly isolated. But he will certainly find life less troublesome if he permits criticism only of what is generally admitted to be a proper subject for criticism—astrology but not Christianity, promiscuity but not monogamy.

A third difficulty arises from the fact that the teacher's training is very often not of a kind to encourage in him a willingness to participate in critical discussion. In some cases this is quite obvious. A Roman Catholic critic of the *collèges* of Quebec has written of the teachers in them in the following terms : 'In the ecclesiastical world, statements concerning learning and dogma from a higher authority are unquestioningly accepted as the most potent of arguments. Priests are not really trained to discuss. . . . They try to make their pupils reflections of themselves. They find it difficult not to put a brake on independence or initiative.'[5]

In many systems of public instruction, indeed, it is a principal object of teacher-training to turn out teachers who will firmly discourage free critical discussion. For in all authoritarian schools, secular or ecclesiastical, the teacher counts himself successful when his pupils leave their school holding certain beliefs so powerful that no future experience could shake them; so committed to certain habits of behaviour that any modification of them will induce overwhelming feelings of guilt; so habitually deferential to authority that their unquestioning obedience can be counted upon. But even in democratic societies the emphasis in teacher-training may be such that the teacher is encouraged to think of his main tasks as consisting in the maintenance of silence in the classroom, 'getting through' the lesson laid down for the day, adherence to a syllabus, the preparation of his pupils for routinized examinations. The ideal teacher as turned out by such systems has been described thus :

'They concentrate their efforts on preparing their pupils for examinations . . . ; they teach precisely the subjects named in the curriculum, guiding themselves by the textbooks in use and attempting to smooth the path for the children; they obey cheerfully the instructions issued by superintendent and principal, in so far as they can understand them.'[6] Such teachers are unlikely to encourage critical discussion amongst their pupils.

John Dewey's early educational writings were in large part directed against this conception of the teacher's task. The 'progressive schools', designed to give institutional expression to Dewey's educational ideas, took as their leading principle that neither teacher nor subject should be allowed to dominate the pupil. But Dewey himself was alarmed at the consequences : 'I am sure that you will appreciate what is meant,' he wrote, 'when I say that many of the newer schools tend to make little or nothing of organized subject-matter of study; to proceed as if any form of direction and guidance by adults were an invasion of individual freedom, and as if the idea that education should be concerned with the present and future meant that acquaintance with the past has little or no role to play in education.'[7]

He went on to describe the effects of such an education thus : 'Energy is dissipated, and a person becomes scatter-brained. Each [school] experience may be lively, vivid and "interesting" and yet their disconnectedness may artificially generate dispersive, disintegrated, centrifugal habits.'[7] Other critics have drawn attention to the fact that in such schools concealed manipulation by the teacher often replaces direct authority; the children end up by thinking that they always wanted to do what the teacher has got them to want to do—the ideal of the demagogue.[8] Explicit instructions are open to criticism, even in the most authoritarian of societies, by the more bold and adventurous spirits; secret manipulation is much harder to cope with.

But there is not the slightest reason why, rebelling against authoritarian schools which are wholly devoted to formal instruction and which inhibit the critical spirit, we should advocate the setting up of schools in which instruction has no place. An educated man—as distinct from a merely 'cultivated' man—must be, let us agree, independent, critical, capable of facing problems. But these qualities, while necessary, are not sufficient; many uneducated nineteenth-century radical workmen possessed them in abundance. To be educated one must be able to participate in the great human traditions of critico-creative thought: science, history, literature, philosophy, technology, and to participate in these traditions one must first be instructed, to learn a discipline. One has to be 'initiated', to use Richard Peters' language.[9]

I have introduced the phrase 'critico-creative' thinking, not through any fondness for it, but because 'critical thinking' may suggest nothing more than the capacity to think up objections. Critical thinking as it is exhibited in the great traditions conjoins imagination and criticism in a single form of thinking; in literature, science, history, philosophy, or technology the free flow of the imagination is controlled by criticism and criticisms are transformed into a new way of looking at things. Not that either the free exercise of the imagination or the raising of objections is in itself to be despised; the first can be suggestive of new ideas, the second can show the need for them. But certainly education tries to develop the two in combination.[10] The educator is interested in encouraging critical discussion, as distinct from the mere raising of objections; and discussion is an exercise of the imagination.

How does instruction come into the story? Consider a relatively simple instance of critico-creative thinking, playing a game of chess. In order to play we must first be taught how the pieces are placed on the board; what move each piece can make; under what circumstances our opponent's pieces can be moved from the board; that the king cannot be taken; that it is allowable to castle and so on. These rules we can be taught by an instructor or we can read them for ourselves in a book, but in either case they have simply to be learnt. No matter how clever we are we could never work them out for ourselves; presented with a chessboard and a set of pieces and told that they are used to play a game we could not possibly deduce how chess is played.

As well as rules, there are in any game useful routines, methods of coping with recurrent situations. Thus in chess there are certain routine ways of playing the end-game. At a certain point, a player who knows these routines cannot lose, provided only that he is not careless. To distinguish these routines from rules, let us call them 'dodges'. They are not arbitrary; we can demonstrate that a player is certain to lose if he disregards them, or certain to win if he pays attention to them.[11] But we can be trained, instructed, in their use; we can make ourselves as good as the best player in the world at coping with certain end-game situations, in a sense in which we cannot be trained to be as good as the best player in the world at the middle-game. At some time, indeed, these 'dodges' had to be worked out by the exercise of critico-creative thinking, but they have now been reduced to routines. It would be the height of foolishness not to learn and to adopt them.

The great traditions are not games. But they are like games in a number of respects; they contain ingredients which are arbitrary, and they have generated dodges. On the first point, they depend, for example, on a capacity to read and write. Now it is a wholly arbitrary rule that the spoken word 'cat' should be represented in English by a particular series of squiggles, and in Chinese by a quite different arrangement of squiggles. No one, however clever, could, on listening to spoken Chinese, work out for himself how it was written down. In order to read and write Chinese we have simply to learn these quite arbitrary connections between the spoken and the written language.[12] Languages differ : knowing how to spell a few Italian words we can work out how to spell any Italian word; knowing how to spell a few English words, we can work out how to spell a great many, but not all, other English words; in the case of Chinese there are very many ideograms which have to be separately learnt. But in every case the starting-point is arbitrary.

The student of chemistry, similarly, must learn a new language—what is signified by suffixes such as 'ic' and 'ous' and 'ate' in words like 'nitric' and 'nitrous' and 'nitrate'; how to read a symbol like 'H_2O' or a molecular diagram. Furthermore, as a result of the enormous success of previous scientists, students are in a position to employ a great many dodges—dodges for collecting gases, for determining what substances a solution contains, for calculating in what percentages it contains these substances. A reasonably intelligent student can be trained to use these dodges as well as the greatest of scientists. Scientists, as well, have made a great many discoveries on a grander scale—laws. It would be wholly absurd not to take steps to ensure that students are acquainted, anyhow, with some of these laws and can apply them to particular cases.

Indeed, although science is the most striking example of critico-creative thinking, it is often taught in such a way as scarcely at all to exercise either the imaginative or the critical powers of the student. Depressingly enough, it might almost be regarded as an educational law that all subjects tend towards an instructional state. No subject, when introduced into a curriculum ever fulfils the hopes that were held out for it as an educational instrument. And this is not an unfortunate accident, nor the result of a conspiracy. It arises out of the large instructional ingredient inherent in developed subjects and the conditions of the schoolroom, which favour the use of instructional methods.

The problem which confronts us can be put thus : inevitably, instruction plays a large part in our school systems. In no other way can students be helped to participate in the great traditions. They have to learn to accommodate themselves to, and to work with, arbitrary rules. They have to learn a variety of dodges. They have to bring themselves abreast of the knowledge that has already been acquired. Only thus can they put themselves into a position fruitfully to criticize, usefully to suggest alternatives. To try to make of one's whole schooling a training in problem-solving, as the 'progressivists' hoped to do, is to produce students who will be quite unprepared to cope with the principal problems within the great traditions. At what point, then, is there room for teaching the child to be critical?

One possible answer is that there is room for it only at a late stage in the schooling process and for a select group of pupils. This, so far as he permitted criticism at all, was Plato's answer. The majority of the citizens in an ideal state are to be instructed, taught to understand how to conform to rules, to apply broad principles to routine cases, but are not to be allowed to realize, even, that there are possible alternatives to those rules, that they can be subjected to criticism and replaced by different rules. Only a small élite is to come to a rational understanding of the rules, an understanding which would proceed by way of a criticism of established principles. For Socrates, in contrast, if we are to believe Plato's *Apology*, the 'unexamined life in not worth living'; instruction should be left to the Sophists, the educator is by his very nature a disturber of the peace.[10]

Something like the Platonic assumption is not uncommonly accepted in our own communities. Only at universities, it is presumed, can students be taught to be critical. It is, indeed, by no means universally admitted that even at the University level students ought to be encouraged to think critically about the accepted beliefs and the accepted institutions of their communities; such critical reflections, it is sometimes suggested, should be restricted to 'mature minds'.[14] Furthermore, as the mass of instructible rules increases in volume, there is a growing tendency to postpone critical discussion, the confronting of genuine problems, to post-graduate levels. University teachers, especially in scientific and professional subjects, will sometimes tell you that they 'haven't time' to encourage independent thinking, or even independent reading, in their students.[15] But many people would, however reluctantly, admit that independent, critical thinking is permissible in universities; at lower levels, they would nevertheless argue, it has no place.

For one thing, it is sometimes suggested, the majority of people *cannot* be educated, cannot participate in the work of facing, and solving, problems. Whether this suggestion is correct there is no way of deciding *a priori*. Very likely, indeed, there is no way of deciding it at all. Most of us could mention some field of activity in which we have learnt more or less effective procedures, without ever having advanced beyond that point.[16] But whether, given better teaching, we could have done so is a matter in which we can speak with much less confidence.

In fact, our views on this matter tend to be determined by our social attitudes. Those who believe that it is right and proper for all but a small minority to accept uncritically the dictates of established authorities are very willing to believe that most human beings are incapable of doing anything else. The democrat is, in contrast, committed to believing that the majority of people are capable of participating at some level in discussions which lead to a change of rules, i.e. that they are capable of thinking critically about, as distinct from simply obeying, a rule. But he is not, of course, committed to believing that all men are equally capable of participating in every discussion which involves the criticism of existing rules or of accepted hypotheses.

This point is fundamental. It is related to the fact that critico-creative thinking is not a subject, in the sense in which chemistry or technical drawing or history are subjects. It can be fostered, or it can be discouraged, as part of the teaching of any subject—even if some subjects provide more opportunities for doing so, at least at an early stage, than others.[17] A student may exhibit it as a translator, but not as a mathematician; as a landscape gardener but not as a historian. There is always the possibility that in a new subject, or a new area of an old subject, a child will develop previously unsuspected critical capacities. It may be the case, too—although I do not know of any decisive evidence on this point—that an attitude of mind thus engendered toward, say, accepted techniques in carpentry will in some degree carry over to other modes of activity.

Plato certainly thought so; if men are allowed in any respect to innovate—in even so harmless-seeming an activity as music—the whole structure of the State, on Plato's view, is in danger. Totalitarian states, operating on this same principle, are rigidly conservative in art, pure science, moral habits; there is good reason to believe that the Soviet attempt to license technical, but no other, innovations has broken down. It would be absurd to suggest that a man must either think critically about everything or about nothing. But it is not absurd to suggest that the critical attitude, once aroused, may extend beyond the particular group of problems which first provoked it. The educator's problem is to break down the tendency to suppose that what is established by authority must be either accepted *in toto* or else merely evaded—a tendency to which, very probably, the child's early training will have inclined him. Once the teacher has done that, once he has aroused a critical attitude to *any* authority, he has made a major step forward.

In any case, even if the teacher wholly fails in his attempt to encourage this or that child to be critical, it is a fatal policy to restrict the attempt to do so to the university level. If from early childhood a child is taught to do whatever he is told to do, if he is discouraged from asking questions, except in order to elicit information or receive instruction, he will completely flounder when he is suddenly called upon to make up his own mind, to face a situation where 'authorities' disagree. Observations made in Australia confirm what we would have expected : children from schools where the emphasis is on formal instruction find it extremely difficult to adjust to the more 'open' university conditions.[18]

How then reconcile the two requirements : the need for building up a body of knowledge, a set of habits, from which criticism can take its departure, and the need for introducing children from an early stage to the practice of critical discussion? The contrast, thus expressed, sounds absolute. But in fact the teacher has failed even as an instructor if he has done no more than inculcate a rigid habit or instil a fixed body of beliefs : his main object—if he knows his business at all—is to help the child to acquire a skill. By means of sheer drill a driving instructor can teach a pupil to sit in a stationary car and change gear but this inculcation of mechanical habits is not itself instruction in driving; nor is it of the slightest use except as a preliminary stage in such instruction. Similarly, there is no point in a child's learning by heart the French equivalents of English names for parts of the body, or the eccentric behaviour of irregular verbs, except as part of the process of learning to speak, read or write the French language; no point in his learning the properties of the halogens unless this helps him to be, or—a more relevant consideration in the case of most children—to understand what it is like to be a scientist.

The exercise of a skill, unlike the capacity to recite a list of all the irregular verbs ending in '-oir', involves thinking—if not the criticism of rules, at least the application of them to circumstances which cannot be wholly predicted in advance. (This sort of thinking we might call 'intelligence' without too much disrespect to ordinary usage.) A French speaker never knows quite what French sentence he might be called upon to utter, whereas the child can know that the teacher will ask him to repeat words from a predetermined list. Furthermore, it is often in the course of exercising their skills that men discover the defects of accepted procedures. If the skill has been properly taught, in an atmosphere in which criticism is welcomed and the possibility of improving procedures emphasized, this discovery will not give rise to a sense of helplessness, or of anger against the teacher and a simple rejection of his authority; rather, it will stimulate the attempt to find an alternative procedure.

So far, then, as a school emphasizes, within the great traditions, the practice of skills rather than rote learning—the use of intelligence rather than the development of habits—it in some measure prepares the way for critico-creative thinking. A great deal depends on how a skill is taught. The crucial principle seems to be : wherever possible and as soon as possible, substitute problems for exercises. By a problem I mean a situation where the student cannot at once decide what rule to apply or how it applies, by an exercise a situation in which this is at once obvious. Thus, for example, a piece of English prose to translate into French is a set of problems involving that imaginative insight checked by facts characteristic of critico-creative thinking; a set of sentences for translation into French at the head of which the child is told that he is to use in each case the imperfect subjunctive—assuming the sentences otherwise contain no novelties—is an exercise. When a child has to ask himself whether a given set of relationships constitute a permutation or a combination, he is faced with a problem; when he is asked to determine the number of possible permutations of a given set, with an exercise. Whether for a particular child a question is an exercise or a problem may, of course, be dependent on what he has learnt.

Questions which look as if they present problems—e.g. 'Why does Hamlet attack Ophelia so fiercely?'—may turn out to be nothing more than an exercise designed to test whether the student can remember what he learnt in class; questions which would be exercises to the mathematics teacher, knowing what he knows, can be problems to the student.

Confronted by a problem, i.e. a situation in which we do not immediately see which way to turn, we can sometimes solve it by taking advice, by looking up a book. It would be absurd so to emphasize the independent tackling of problems as not to recognize this fact. Indeed, no other skill the pupil is called upon to master at school is of such permanent value to him as learning when, and where, and how, to look things up. But it certainly cannot be said of most schools that they concentrate their attention on this skill rather than on encouraging pupils to work problems out for themselves; on the contrary, very few students leave our schools, or even our universities, with any real skill in 'information retrieval'.[19]

However, important though this skill is, we cannot settle all our problems by looking up the answer in a book. Problems fall into two broad classes; those to which the answer is known to the teacher but not to the pupil, and those to which the answer is known neither to teacher nor pupil. (One should add that the very existence of the problem is not, normally, known to the student. One of the educator's tasks is to make his students puzzled.) Most of the time the teacher will be putting before his pupils a problem to which in fact the answer is already known. His pupils come to be practised in the regular methods of tackling this class of problem, in the intelligent application of accepted procedures. But the teacher should certainly place special emphasis, so far as he can, on problems to which the answer is not known, or is a matter of controversy—only in that way can he prepare his pupils for the future.

In practice, of course, a great many teachers deliberately avoid all controversial issues. This is partly because they feel that they are not teaching if they make their pupils puzzled and then do not resolve their puzzlement for them; partly because so many of them, as representatives of authority, think it bad for their pupils to be unsettled—greatly underestimating the degree to which their experiences outside the school are in any case unsettling them. It is certainly *safer* and more comfortable to all concerned not to raise controversial issues. (It is surprising what a range of such issues there are, in any ordinary classroom.) The fact remains that unless his pupils leave school puzzled his teachers have failed as educators, however successful they may have been as instructors.

But at the same time a teacher will not want his pupils to be *merely* bewildered although he will teach them that to be bewildered can be itself a virtue; he will hope to teach them in what way the questions which puzzle them ought to be discussed, what sort of evidence is relevant to their solution. Literature and history classes can be particularly valuable for the discussion of controversial issues. R. S. Peters has recently argued that 'disciplines like history and literature are debased and distorted if they are used consciously to inculcate 'critical thinking'.[20] What he has in mind, I think, is that the study of history and literature must not be thought of as a means to something else, e.g. to the acquisition of certain critical skills. But the fact remains that history and literature classes provide the teacher with opportunities for encouraging critical discussion of a wide variety of human activities, as well as of literature and history themselves. No one would wish to see all literature and history lessons turned into such discussions. But it is equally a mistake to divorce the study of history and literature from the understanding of human relationships.[21]

Quite ordinary children will be aware, for example, that the plays of Shakespeare are in certain respects imperfect. Hearing from all quarters, and most conspicuously from their teachers, that Shakespeare was an overwhelming genius, they are likely to conclude either that genius is not for them, or that education is merely a racket, or merely shrugging their shoulders, that this is one more thing to be learnt as a lesson and repeated in an examination.[22] But there is not the slightest reason why pupils should not be allowed, or indeed encouraged, to do their worst in criticizing Shakespeare, why they should not be allowed to defend the view that his plays are inferior to any well-made television play. Only through critical discussion of this sort can the pupil be brought to understand why Shakespeare is in fact a dramatic genius, as distinct from parroting the view that he is. If he ends up unconvinced, no harm has been done—he was not, anyhow, convinced in the beginning, he merely acquiesced—and he should have learnt a great deal on the way, not only about Shakespeare, but also about the critical discussion of literature in general. It can properly be demanded of him, of course, that at all points he supports his opinions with evidence from the plays.

But what about the earlier stages in schooling, the less intelligent child? From a very early stage he—or anyhow most children—can be taught what it is like to discuss a question critically. Most of us can recall two types of teachers : for the one any criticism of his own views, his own decisions, a school rule or a textbook principle was a moral misdemeanour, to be greeted with wrath and disciplinary measures; for the second teacher such criticisms, unless circumstances were unusually unfavourable, were made the occasion for a rational explanation, with the frank admission, whenever this was the case, that a particular rule was purely arbitrary, not defensible in itself, although perhaps defensible as a rule in the game.[23] (Compare : 'Why should I wear a tie?' with 'Why shouldn't I be allowed to come in late to class?') Any teacher has to instruct, has to teach rules which are arbitrary, at least in the context in which he teaches them. The fundamental difference between the educator and the indoctrinator is that the indoctrinator treats all rules as 'inherent in the nature of things'—as not even *conceivably* bad rules. What he takes to be fact, a principle, or presents as a person or work to be admired is deified as beyond the reach of rational criticism. The educator, on the contrary, welcomes criticisms, and is prepared to admit that he does not always know the answers to them.

Critical discussion, at this level, of accepted rules can begin at a very early stage in the child's life; what happens later, as he begins to enter into the great traditions is that the area of discussion widens and the difference between types of discussion more clearly emerges. Such critical discussion can be embarrassing to a teacher; he may himself not be convinced that a rule is a reasonable one or may never have asked himself how it can be justified. Anybody who sets out to teach his pupils to be critical must expect constantly to be embarrassed. He can also expect to be harassed, by his class, by his headmaster, by parents. If he gives up the idea of teaching his pupils to be critical and salves his conscience by training them in skills, this is not at all surprising. But he should at least be clear about what he is doing, and even more important, what he is *not* doing.

NOTES

1. *The Principles of Psychology* (New York, 1890), Vol. 1, p. 127.
2. Ibid., pp. 114–15.
3. See the passage quoted in Atkinson, R. F., 'Instruction and Indoctri-

nation' in Archambault, R. D., *Philosophical Analysis and Education* (Routledge & Kegan Paul, London, 1965), p. 174, from Brubacher, J. S., *Eclectic Philosophy of Education* (Prentice Hall, New Jersey, 1951), p. 326 : 'Children are indoctrinated with the multiplication table; they are indoctrinated with love of country; they are indoctrinated with the principles of chemistry and physics and mathematics and biology.'

4. 'Against Utilitarianism' in *Aims in Education*, ed. Hollins, T. H. B., (Manchester, 1964), p. 21.

5. Duval, Roch, 'The Roman Catholic *Collèges* of Quebec' in *Year Book of Education* (London, 1957), p. 274.

6. Bereday, G. Z. F., and Lauwerys, J. A., 'Philosophy and Education' in *The Year Book of Education,* London, 1957. I should explain that in the text this is intended as a description of a conformist, not of an ideal, teacher. But in many quarters in Australia, at least, it would serve as a description of the ideal teacher.

7. *Experience and Education* (Ohio, 1938), quoted in Park, Joe, *Selected Readings in the Philosophy of Education* (Macmillan, London and New York, 1962), 2nd edition, pp. 138–9.

8. Kerlinger, Fred N., 'The Implications of the Permissiveness Doctrine in American Education' in *Educational Theory* (April 1960), pp. 120–7, reprinted in Burns, H. W. and Brauner, C. J., *Philosophy of Education* (New York, 1962), esp. pp. 384–5.

9. *Education as Initiation* (Evans Bros., London, 1963).

10. On the problems set for the educator by the attempt to train the child to be critical without killing his imagination see Getzels, J. W., 'Creative thinking, Problem-solving, and Instruction' in the *Sixty-third Yearbook of the National Society for the Study of Education* (Chicago, 1964), pp. 251–4. Does the Oxford tutorial system, for example, over-emphasize the need to be self-critical?

11. The chess-example was suggested to me by P. H. Nowell-Smith's 'Purpose and Intelligent Action' (*Proceedings of the Aristotelian Society,* Supplementary Volume XXXIV, pp. 103–4).

12. It is sometimes suggested that the resultant emphasis on rote learning in the early education of Chinese children helps to explain why China never developed a tradition of critical thinking.

13. See Anderson, John, 'Socrates as an Educator' in *Studies in Empirical Philosophy* (Sydney, Angus and Robertson, 1962).

14. See for example Wild, John, 'Education and Human Society : a Realistic View' in *Modern Philosophies and Education, Fiftyfourth Yearbook of the National Society for the Study of Education*, p. 44.

15. See Section 4.1, 'Teaching for Independence' in Cohen, S. W., Roe, E., Short, L. N., Passmore, J. A., *Teaching in the Australian Universities* (Melbourne University Press, 1965). To say that one 'hasn't time' for an activity implies that what one is now doing is more valuable than that activity. But what could be more valuable than to teach students to think for themselves? Professional men who leave the Universities 'abreast of the latest knowledge' but not knowing how to keep in touch with later developments are certainly not 'well-trained'.

16. For example, in mathematics. For a useful study of the problems confronting the educating of mathematicians see Beatley, Ralph, 'Reason and rule in arithmetic and algebra', *The Mathematics Teacher*, XLVII, No. 4 (1954), pp. 234–44, reprinted in Scheffler, *Philosophy and Education* (Boston, 1958).

17. This is an important consideration in constructing a curriculum. 'Although I will admit', writes R. M. Hutchins, 'that in the hands of Socrates any subject can be made important . . . because any subject can lead to important questions, there was only one Socrates, and I know of none in any educational system today. We have to frame the course of study of American schools, colleges, and universities in the light of the capacity of ordinary teachers.' (*The Conflict in Education in a Democratic Society* (Harper, New York, 1953), p. 13). This has as much application outside as inside America. We have to ask ourselves, too, what a subject is *actually like* at the level at which an ordinary student encounters it, as distinct from what it is like at the level of postgraduate research.

18. See for example Schonell, F. J., Roe, E., Meddleton, I. G., *Promise and Performance* (Brisbane and London, 1962), pp. 218–21.

19. See the Report on *Science, Government and Information,* by the President's Science Advisory Committee (Washington, D. C., 10th January 1963).

20. ' "Mental Health" as an Educational Aim' in *Aims in Education* (Manchester, 1964), p. 88.

21. 'It had never occurred to Sophia, nor to any of the other girls in the Latin class, to connect the words on the printed page with anything that ever really happened. Men marched, camps were struck, winter quarters were gone into; but to Sophia the Latin language did not concern men, camps, winter quarters and cavalry. It existed to provide Subjunctives and Past Participles and (Oh golly!) Gerunds.' (Quoted in Wilkinson, Rupert, *The Prefects* (Oxford, 1964), p. 66, from Lionel Hale, *A Fleece of Lambs*, p. 38).

22. On the child's reaction to the fraudulent picture of life around him commonly presented in courses on 'social studies' see *Design for Learning*, ed. N. Frye (University of Toronto Press, Toronto, 1962). Compare Locke, John, *The Conduct of the Understanding*, § 12.

23. Compare Hare, R. M., 'Adolescents into Adults' in *Aims in Education* (Manchester, 1964). The difference between the two types of teacher is obvious in practice, although not easy to describe in words.

INDEX

ability, 37, 64, 65, 66, 70, 71, 109, 110, 112, 123, 163, 164, 165, 166, 167, 168
and novel response, 61
critical, 197
to feel and think, 175
to learn, 160
unlearnt, 63
see also skill(s)
abstract mental powers, 122
abstract
and concrete, 27, 32, 40, 41, 42
and general, 40, 41
abstraction, 147
process, 144, 145
abstractionism, 144–9, 150, 151, 154, 155n
abstractive teaching methods, 145
abstractness as criterion of difficulty, 30, 31, 32, 35, 40–1
accommodation, 38, 79
achievement, 9, 13, 21, 22, 124
and task, 1–3
aspects of education, 4, 6–9
human, 158, 159, 160, 161, 162, 163, 169, 170, 171, 172, 173, 176n
words, 141
acquisition
of knowledge, 38, 160
of linguistic tools, 34
action, 10, 66, 68, 69, 70, 168, 169
and rules, 92, 93, 94, 95, 97, 98, 99, 100, 101, 104n
causes of, 69
free, 67
on principle, 129, 130
reasons for, 97
'Action/Happening' argument, 67–71
activity, 80, 86, 92, 120, 156
children's, 76–77
intentional, 6
neural, 187
non-serious, 82, 87, 88
play, 83
routine, 76
serious, 81

spontaneous, 75, 142
adults, 79, 149, 181
beliefs of, 188
agent, rule-invoking, 97
aids to education, extrinsic, 10–11
aims, 68, 69
of education, 5, 22n
see also intention
analysis, logical, 47, 51, 60
Anscombe, G. E. M., 189
appreciation, 153
of general principles, 27
of instances, 40
a priori
concepts, 43n
truth, 30
Aristotle, 2, 17, 28, 38, 40, 75, 109, 110
articulation, verbal, 100, 101, 104n
assimilation, 38, 79, 100
assumptions, 18, 20, 184
unconscious, 148
Atkinson, R. F., 178, 190
attention, 10, 159, 104n
attitude(s), 128, 189
critical, 19, 205
social, 204
Augustine, 124, 125, 126, 127
paradox of, 125, 126
prompting theory of, 125, 126
authority, 95, 96, 127, 140, 164, 165, 205
of rules, 96

Bacon, F., 19
behaviour, 61, 70, 102
and conduct, 157
and rules, 98, 99, 100, 101, 102, 103n, 104n
goal-directed, 70
habits of, 199
interpretation of, 68
purposive, 70
behaviourism, 123
behaviourists, 133
'being critical', 195, 196
'being educated', 2, 6, 7, 8, 14, 19

Index

Index

Index

PHILOSOPHICAL ANALYSIS AND EDUCATION

Edited by R. D. Archambault

Contributors: L. Arnaud Reid, R. F. Atkinson, E. Best, J. P. Corbett, P. H. Hirst, L. R. Perry, R. S. Peters, A. Phillips Griffiths, J. Wilson.

'This is an impressive list of contributors, and they live up to their reputations. Their essays, while clearly expressed, make no concessions to the reader who likes his literature pre-digested. Nor do they present one single point of view: far from it. They do not discuss these views *in vacuo,* but in the context of 'relatively concrete and tangible' situations. And, best of all, real situations, not the traditional stereotypes which afflict so much educational writing and discussion.'

—*The Teacher*

'It is timely to have this book. Many of the essays are of great individual interest. Professor Hirst's proposals for a new concept of liberal education are subtle and practical. Professor Perry's descriptive treatment of the assumptions implicit in the traditional and the child-centred novels is, in the clarity of its language, a good tribute to analytical philosophy as a discipline.'

—A. D. C. PETERSON, *New Society*

'The book is comprehensible as well as being related to concepts which should be in the forefront of our thinking. One would wish this book would become part of every student's booklist and on the shelves of many teachers who last considered the philosophy of education thirty years ago—and then restricted their horizon to Emile and the like. It is clearly written, structured well and in the mainstream of philosophical analysis.'

—*Teachers World*

ROUTLEDGE & KEGAN PAUL